Hegemony

Why is hegemony an essential feature of society?

Hegemony: A Realist Analysis is a new and original approach to this important concept. It presents a theoretical history of the use of hegemony in a range of work starting with a discussion of Gramsci and Russian Marxism and going on to look at more recent applications. It examines the current debates and discusses the recent work on Marx by Jacques Derrida, before outlining a critical realist/Marxist alternative.

This book presents a new understanding of hegemony based on a distinction between actual hegemonic projects and a deeper, underlying, structural hegemony. The move away from purely intersubjective and culturalist readings of the concept is reinforced with studies of its objectivity, its relation to ideology and concepts of time and space, and most importantly, its role in the process of social reproduction and transformation. The book also contains a detailed discussion of recent political/economic developments and the debates around post-Fordism, globalisation and international relations. This analysis shifts from the surface level operation of hegemony to the underlying social conditions under which this operation takes place. It suggests that as well as being represented by hegemonic projects, hegemony also exists at a deeper, more structural level, concerned with the unity of the social formation.

Hegemony employs critical realist philosophy in an explanatory way to help clarify the concept of hegemony and its relation to societal processes. This work contributes to recent debates in social science and political philosophy, developing both the concept of hegemony itself, and the work of critical realism.

Jonathan Joseph teaches social science and philosophy at Goldsmiths College, London, and at The Open University. He has written articles on Marxism, critical realism, hegemony and deconstruction and is on the editorial board of *Capital & Class*.

Routledge studies in critical realism
Edited by Margaret Archer, Roy Bhaskar, Andrew Collier, Tony Lawson and Alan Norrie

Critical realism is one of the most influential new developments in the philosophy of science and in the social sciences, providing a powerful alternative to positivism and post modernism. This series will explore the critical realist position in philosophy and across the social sciences.

Also published by Routledge:
Critical realism: interventions
Edited by Margaret Archer, Roy Bhaskar, Andrew Collier, Tony Lawson and Alan Norrie

Critical Realism
Essential readings
Edited by Margaret Archer, Roy Bhaskar, Andrew Collier, Tony Lawson and Alan Norrie

The Possibility of Naturalism
A philosophical critique of the contemporary human sciences
Roy Bhaskar

Being and Worth
Andrew Collier

Quantum Theory and the Flight from Realism
Philosophical responses to quantum mechanics
Christopher Norris

From East to West
Odyssey of a soul
Roy Bhaskar

Realism and Racism
Concepts of race in sociological research
Bob Carter

Rational Choice Theory
Resisting Colonisation
Edited by Margaret Archer and Jonathan Q Tritter

Explaining Society
Critical realism in the social sciences
Berth Danermark, Mats Ekström, Jan Ch Karlsson and Liselotte Jakobsen

Critical Realism and Marxism
Edited by Andrew Brown, Steve Fleetwood and John Michael Roberts

Critical Realism in Economics
Edited by Steve Fleetwood

Realist Perspectives on Management and Organisations
Edited by Stephen Ackroyd and Steve Fleetwood

After International Relations
Critical realism and the (re)construction of world politics
Heikki Patomaki

Hegemony

A realist analysis

Jonathan Joseph

London and New York

First published 2002 by Routledge
11 New Fetter Lane, London EC4P 4EE

Simultaneously published in the USA and Canada
by Routledge
29 West 35th Street, New York, NY 10001

Routledge is an imprint of the Taylor & Francis Group

© 2002 Jonathan Joseph

Typeset in Baskerville by Exe Valley Dataset Ltd, Exeter
Printed and bound in Great Britain by
Antony Rowe Ltd, Chippenham, Wiltshire

British Library Cataloging in Publication Data
A catalogue record for this book is available
from the British Library

Library of Congress Cataloging in Publication Data
A catalog record for this book has been requested

ISBN 0–415–26836–2

In memory of my father, Martin Joseph, 1932–1998

Contents

Tables

Acknowledgements

I would like to thank a number of people for varying degrees of influence, encouragement and friendship. In particular I would like to thank Liam O'Sullivan, William Outhwaite, Abbas Vali, Simon Kennedy, Sarah Honeychurch, Ray Monk, Nick Davies, John Roberts, Bob Jessop and the late Paul Wozny (a great loss to the labour movement). I would like to thank my friends from the Kings College Realism Group – Alan Norrie, Nick Hostettler, Mervyn Hartwig, Rachel Sharp and Kathryn Dean. And I would particularly like to thank Andrew Collier for our many discussions and Phil Walden who, ten years after introducing me to Marxism introduced me to critical realism – he has either given me a great deal or led me seriously astray. I would like to thank Maureen, Simon and Sarah and I dedicate this book to my father, Martin Joseph, wishing, perhaps, that I had not so readily spurned his dinnertime sociology for the pleasures of the table.

1 Realism and hegemony

Introduction

The concept of hegemony is normally understood as emphasising consent in contrast to reliance on the use of force. It describes the way in which dominant social groups achieve rulership or leadership on the basis of attaining social cohesion and consensus. It argues that the position of the ruling group is not automatically given, but rather that it requires the ruling group to attain consent to its leadership through the complex construction of political projects and social alliances. These allow for the unity of the ruling group and for the domination of this group over the rest of society.¶In its simplistic form hegemony concerns the construction of consent and the exercise of leadership by the dominant group over subordinate groups; in its more complex form, this deals with issues such as the elaboration of political projects, the articulation of interests, the construction of social alliances, the development of historical blocs, the deployment of state strategies and the initiating of passive revolutions.

However, this view is still one-sided. In its extreme, this view of hegemony defines it as a purely agential process, that is to say, that hegemony is exclusively concerned with the plans and actions of social agents, groups and individuals. This leads to a Machiavellian view of politics as if hegemony were simply the conscious project or cunning plan of different social groups. The construction of hegemony becomes an intersubjective affair to be worked out by or between different sets of people. If the concept of hegemony is restricted to this agential approach, then a mistaken view of history and politics emerges that sees important social processes as simply the products of significant social actors or groups. By contrast, this book seeks to move away from a purely agential conception of hegemony, although an emphasis on the importance of agency will be maintained. In keeping with the advice of Marx and Engels, it will be argued that although human beings create hegemony through their actions, they do so under conditions not of their own choosing. Two crucial questions immediately arise. First, what are the conditions under which hegemony operates? Second, what makes hegemony a necessary social feature?

These questions push the study of hegemony away from a simplistic examination of agency towards more material, objective factors. This book concentrates on how the agential aspect of hegemony coincides with its basic structurality. The following chapters will trace the understanding of hegemony from Gramsci through classical Marxism to historical, structuralist and post-structuralist analysis. In attempting to draw out the strengths and weaknesses of these approaches, a conception of hegemony will emerge that will hopefully be able to combine both structural and agential aspects of this important social process. This analysis will take a broadly Marxist approach and a number of basic Marxist concepts are taken for granted. Other aspects of Marxism, the more simplistic and deterministic models of the classical tradition, will be challenged. This is in keeping with the idea of hegemony which attempts to replace economic determinism with a more complex view of the social totality. However, this book will also be adopting a critical realist approach based on the ideas recently advocated by Roy Bhaskar, Andrew Collier, Margaret Archer and others. As well as analysing the concept of hegemony this work will also be attempting to assess the relationship between critical realist philosophy and Marxist analysis of society. The arguments of critical realism, although now starting to gain a foothold, are still relatively new, not to mention complex, and are continuing to evolve and develop. The rest of this chapter will therefore be concerned with briefly outlining the basics of critical realism, while some tentative comments on the relationship between realism, Marxism and hegemony will be made. The book will then divide into two parts, with the first section examining how the concept of hegemony develops in the work of such theorists as Gramsci, Lenin, Trotsky, Anderson, Thompson, Williams, Derrida, Laclau and Mouffe. Following this theoretical history, the book will go on to draw out a realist conception of hegemony by posing such theoretical questions as objectivity and intersubjectivity, the economic and the social, and the way that hegemony is articulated in space and time. The main aim of this analysis is to develop a distinction between a structural aspect of hegemony concerned with social reproduction and an agential aspect that depends upon this, but which represents conscious hegemonic projects and strategies. A Marxist under-standing of hegemony will be developed through the use of critical realist arguments. So, first, to the arguments of critical realism.

Method: critical naturalism

The concept of hegemony extends beyond simple political, cultural, humanist or hermeneutic interpretations. Since it is part of an under-standing of the conditions of society it should be treated as a *social scientific* concept. To say that the study of hegemony is part of a scientific study of society is in keeping with a position of *critical naturalism*, which is to argue that the social sciences can and should be treated along similar lines to the natural sciences, using similar methods of analysis, albeit ones that recognise the specificity of the social domain. Thus it is necessary to reject the idea, as is found in the positivist tradition, that there is an identical correspondence between the methods of social and natural science, but it is important to resist the hermeneutic view that there is an absolute separation between the two realms. The term critical implies that it is necessary to make important qualifications to the naturalist approach and these will be outlined below. However, the critical naturalist position also entails a number of common perspectives that link the social and natural sciences together and it is they that provide the starting point for a critical realist approach.

Above all, realism stresses the separation of thought and being and the primacy of being over thought or the ontological over the epistemological (theory of being over theory of knowledge). This distinction can then be used to make a transcendental argument along the lines that given that knowledge is possible and is meaningful, this presupposes that the world itself is a certain way, while the practice of science shows that the world is intelligible and open to investigation. Unlike Kantian transcendental idealism, which moves from the status of knowledge to the necessary structure of the mind, critical or transcendental realism looks at what knowledge and human practice presupposes about the world itself. Given that certain things are intelligible to us, this presupposes that the world is ordered or structured in a particular way. The possibility of knowledge and the forms that it takes (as practices and disciplines) reflects the fact that the world has an ordered, intelligible and relatively enduring structure that is open to scientific investigation. That knowledge is possible presupposes that the world is a certain way.

However, the fact that the world has this structuring makes it necessary for us to distinguish ontologically between the knowledge we have of the world and the independently existing objects that this knowledge is about. The scientificity of a theory depends upon its ability to explain these social or natural objects. This knowledge may develop or change and one theory may replace another, but the objects of this knowledge will remain as they are; in other words, the objects of the real world exist independently of the knowledge we may have of them. Indeed, these objects must exist independently of the knowledge we have of them if changes in our understanding are to have any meaningful significance. The existence of competing theories presupposes an independent reality over which they vary or differ.

This separation of thought and object can be extended to a distinction between practice and structure. The process of knowledge is, after all, just one form of social practice. Indeed, knowledge itself can be divided into a number of sub-practices and these various practices intersect one another in various ways. Scientific practice may be divided into a number of different disciplines such as physics and biology. Knowledge may also be divided into different practices, some of which are scientific, while others, such as common sense, practical knowledge, religion, political ideology and the aesthetic, may be categorised in a different way. Meanwhile, there are other practices – like fishing, shopping and drinking – which are not primarily knowledge-based. But a study of society cannot be reduced to a study of such human activities. As well as studying practices (ordered or established activity), it is also necessary to examine deeper social structures which have a more abstract nature, comprised of a set of elements that are internally related. These are necessary relationships that endure over time. The social world, it will be argued, is made up of a variety of structures and relations – social, economic, political, communicative, etc. – that have a relatively enduring nature. These social structures are not reducible to the activities that they govern or the practices they support; rather, it is these social structures that make human activity and social practices possible and it is within this structural context that a theory of hegemony must be developed.

The transitive and intransitive

To develop the distinction between epistemology and ontology, Roy Bhaskar employs the terms transitive and intransitive. Our knowledge of the world is described as *transitive* and is actively embodied in a set of theories which form a kind of raw material for scientific practice. Transitive knowledge corresponds to an Aristotelian material cause or antecedently established knowledge which is used to generate new knowledge. This includes established theories, models, methods, facts and so on (Bhaskar 1978: 21). The practice of science, although it studies the intransitive world, produces a transitive object.

By contrast the *intransitive* is that which science seeks to study. Intransitive objects of knowledge are those structures, relations, processes and generative mechanisms which exist independently of us in a relatively enduring state. Therefore, while science is a transitive process with antecedent knowledge that is dependent on human activity, its objects are intransitive objects which do not depend on either. As Bhaskar says:

> The intransitive objects of knowledge are in general invariant to our knowledge of them; they are the real things and structures, mechanisms and processes, events and possibilities of the world; and for the most part they are quite independent of us ... They are the intransitive, science-independent, objects of scientific discovery and investigation.
>
> (Bhaskar 1978: 22)

The intransitive, whether natural or social, is largely a transfactual world comprised of structures and mechanisms that are relatively enduring. It is this relatively enduring, independent, intransitive nature of the social and natural worlds that makes scientific practice possible. The identification of scientific laws and relations is dependent upon the relatively enduring, transfactuality of the intransitive realm. This returns us to the ontological argument that, given that scientific investigation is intelligible, this presupposes that the world is structured in a certain way and that these transfactual structures, processes and mechanisms are possible objects of knowledge that are open to scientific investigation. It is the fact that the world is structured and ordered that makes science possible and gives this scientific knowledge, in turn, a structured and intelligible character.

This position has radical consequences for any theory of science. A distinction must be made between the transitive identification of causal laws and the intransitive causal mechanisms themselves. For example, it is necessary to distinguish between the theory of the law of gravity and the existence of this 'law' in nature itself. There is also a distinction in the social world between our transitive social explanation and the real or intransitive mechanism, so, for example, we must distinguish between the Marxist theory that isolates the tendency of the rate of profit to fall and the actual economic mechanisms that may or may not confirm this theory. Science should study these mechanisms and structures and aim to produce a plausible explanation of them. This is in contrast to those theories that rely on identifying a pattern of events or empirical invariances and which consequently fail to adequately identify the deeper causal structures and mechanisms that generate these events. In these cases the theorist undermines the independent existence of causal structures and mechanisms by conflating them with his/her own observations and empirical theories In order to explain the realist approach Bhaskar therefore identifies three differing levels of scientific enquiry and their philosophical underpinnings.

Empirical, actual and real

The crudest form of empiricism defines the world according to human experiences. But while the ontology of empiricism is based on human experience, the sociology of empiricism is based on the passive individual who exists in a world of objective facts which the individual, in turn, observes, but does not create. The observation aspect of such crude empiricism can be dismissed rather easily in that there are many events that are not experienced, yet nevertheless occur. An explanation of the world cannot therefore be reduced to our experience of it. However, this sort of empiricism provides the base for another set of philosophical positions which Bhaskar calls actualism.

Actualism recognises that events occur whether we experience them or not. It therefore moves beyond the crudeness of the former position. However, this version of explanation, like crude empiricism, is still tied to the conception of causality derived from the work of David Hume. According to the Humean conception of causality, scientific laws depend upon constant conjunctions or regularities. The status of scientific theories is then decided according to whether or not these constant conjunctions can be confirmed or falsified by various instances. But to simply posit that A causes B fails to adequately analyse the underlying mechanisms that produce such events. Indeed, Humean accounts effectively deny that such mechanisms exist. Actualism may move beyond the empirical level of perceptions, impressions and sensations, but it does not go beyond the level of events and states of affairs in order to examine deeper structures and mechanisms that may generate these events and regularities.

Another problem with actualism is the tendency to view the world through the closed conditions by which such regularities are produced. Actualism refuses to take account of the fact that the world itself has an open character that contains many more mechanisms than those present under the closed conditions of scientific experimentation that produces such regularities. Reality is thus treated or defined as if it were simply an extension of the closed conditions of experimentation. Actualist theories operate by seeking constant conjunctions of events which are then used to explain causal occurrences and, *ceteris paribus*, reality is produced. However, by tying its explanation to constant conjunctions, actualism fails to go beyond the occurrences of these events. As a consequence, actualist accounts end up denying the existence of underlying structures and mechanisms. In particular, actualism sees everything in terms of the exercise of powers, yet the openness of the world means that there are a whole number of powers and liabilities which may not be realised. We know, for example, that while water is said to boil at 100 degrees centigrade, this is affected by other factors such as air pressure. The real world, rather than being a series of constant conjunctions, is comprised of various interacting and counter-acting structures and causal mechanisms.

Indeed, to reduce the complexity of the world to a series of constant conjunctions, as actualism does, is to remove the need for scientific experimentation at all. Scientific closure is necessary precisely because constant conjunctions are not readily produced in the open and complex social and natural domains. The critical realist approach therefore insists on the need to move beyond regularities, experiences and events and to study the underlying causal structures and generative mechanisms that produce these In open systems a whole number of these structures and mechanisms operate together and determine things in various combinations, giving the world a multi-layered character. Critical realism recognises this in its notion of *ontological depth*. It attempts to move from one level of explanation to an underlying one. When a stratum of reality has been described, the next step is to examine what mechanisms underlie or intersect with this level. This is a radical approach focusing on processes of emergence and change.

The world is seen as *stratified* in the sense that these structures and mechanisms are ordered in a certain way. Science itself reflects this stratification; for example, biology is rooted in and emergent from physics.

We can also see this sort of layering or stratification in society. However, the temptation for reductionism must be avoided. It is not possible to explain a biological process simply in terms of physical ones. Nor is it possible to explain political events by reducing them to economic conditions. An emergence-based theory argues that reality has different layers or strata and that higher layers (e.g. the mind) presuppose lower, more fundamental levels (e.g. matter) but that higher layers cannot be reduced to lower ones. To say that the mind is emergent out of matter is to say that it depends on it in a fundamental way, but that the complexities of the mind and its workings cannot be reduced to a study of grey matter. The mind clearly has its own irreducible emergent properties (e.g. thoughts) which cannot simply be explained in material terms, although they do clearly operate within the framework of material laws which cannot be broken (not least the fact that a brain must exist if a mind is to work).

Traditionally, Marxist explanation has been based on a rather crude and reductionist base-superstructure relationship (where the economic base is said to determine the political–ideological superstructure). An alternative to this model is to see society as comprised of a multitude of strata with structures that interrelate and codetermine one another. Within this, economic structures may still be regarded as the most important or dominant ones, but they are not exclusively determinant and the different strata of the social formation have their own emergent (irreducible) properties, laws and powers. Such a view of society will be important when it comes to assessing how a process such as hegemony relates to a variety of social, economic, political and cultural domains while developing its own character and dynamics.

Critical naturalism and social science

Critical naturalism argues that the social world can be studied along similar lines to the natural world and that therefore social science is as valid a practice as natural science. However, Bhaskar outlines three important differences (Bhaskar 1989b: 185–9). Founded on social relations, social structures are *ontologically* different from natural ones in the sense that they are praxis and concept dependent. Social structures, unlike natural structures, depend both on human activity and on some kind of human conception of that activity. Such a position embraces a kind of critical hermeneutics. The fact that social structures are praxis and concept dependent means that the objects of social science are thus of a social and historical nature, far more specific and context dependent than are the objects of natural science. The objects of social science may be law-like but they are also historical.

Epistemologically social science differs in that, unlike natural science, it is not possible to create the kind of closed conditions under which experimentation takes place. This means that social science should not primarily be predictive – as the positivist and Humean approaches would maintain – but should instead attempt to be explanatory. The explanatory method of critical realism proceeds as (1) the causal analysis of an event, (2) a theoretical re-description of the component causes, (3) a processes of retroduction from the re-described component events or states to the antecedent processes that might have produced them and (4) an elimination of alternative causes. The theory must then be checked or tested empirically.

There is also an important *relational* difference in that social science is part of its own field of enquiry – it is a product of the very social formation it seeks to analyse. This makes it necessary to adopt a critical attitude towards the claims of realism itself, recognising their own social and historical nature. It also means that when the weaknesses of other social theories and ideologies are examined, a realist account must also try to account for the production of these ideas and hence analyse those social conditions which give rise to their inadequacy. Consequently, the explanatory nature of social science must develop as an *explanatory critique*. Critical realism is given a radical edge in its debunking of certain false theories or ideologies and their relation to the social structures and material practices that produce them. It is possible, for example, to develop a critique of classical economics by examining its closeness and subservience to the very economic structures it seeks to explain. In this way, critical realist explanatory critique moves beyond the assessment of ideas themselves, seeking to explain them through examining the social and structural context that gives rise to them.

The idea that social science is part of its own field of enquiry pushes critical naturalism towards the hermeneutic view of society, and the hermeneutic tradition is certainly correct to see that social science deals with a pre-interpreted reality that has been conceptualised by social agents. It is wrong, however, to reduce social science to a study of these meanings and conceptions. Such a position reduces social science to a study of human understanding and behaviour rather than examining the intransitive structures through which these take place. Bhaskar directs his attack at the Witgensteinian social theorist Peter Winch and argues that while Winch concentrates on concepts, meanings, reasons and rules, he cannot explain:

a.   What explains the rules themselves?
b.   What explains the agent's rule observance on any particular occasion?
c.   What explains the acquisition of the rules by the individual in the first place?
d.   What distinguishes where a rule is broken and where it is changed?

(Bhaskar 1989a: 144–5)

The hermeneutic tradition is therefore wrong to see social science as reducible to a study of rules, meanings and understandings. Social science is concerned not just with actions, but with the material conditions for such actions, the structural context within which such actions and meanings develop. Beliefs cannot be studied separately from the material practices in which they are inscribed. Critical realism therefore goes beyond hermeneutics in looking at the social structures which lie behind human action and understanding and which make them possible. No human activity can exist outside the medium of social structures. Social causality is not reducible to the question of rules or understanding, but is the material product of real social structures and practices.

The transformational model of social activity

Social structures do not exist independently of the activities they govern. Nevertheless, the conditions for social activity exist intransitively. Societies pre-exist the human agents who live in them and are a pre-existing condition for human activity. However, the ensemble of structures, practices and conventions require human agency for their reproduction or transformation. As Bhaskar argues:

> Society is both the ever-present *condition* (material cause) and the continually reproduced *outcome* of human agency. And praxis is both work, that is conscious *production*, and (normally unconscious) *reproduction* of the conditions of production, that is society.
>
> (Bhaskar 1989a: 34–5)

To develop this position Bhaskar sets out the *transformational model of social activity* (TMSA). In trying to grapple with the relation between structure and agent while avoiding both voluntarist (e.g. Weberian) and reified (e.g. Durkheimian) conceptions of society, the TMSA argues that social structures exist by virtue of human activity, but they also determine that activity. Human action is necessarily dependent on the existence of these social structures however, the structures themselves depend upon being reproduced through such activity. Agents have some conception of this activity, but they reproduce or transform structures rather than create them.

The transformational model of social activity attempts to locate praxis within the nexus of social structures without, however, turning agents into simple bearers of these structures. Structures definitely have causal primacy over agents so that people, although engaging in conscious activity, mostly unconsciously reproduce these structures. Structures pre-exist social agents while their functioning and effects are beyond the full comprehension or control of agents in their day-to-day activity. However, this does not mean that agents passively occupy structural locations. In fact it is because of their structural location that agents have the *potential* to engage in transformative practice, albeit within definite limits. For example, a worker may consciously act to make a product. However, the unintended consequence of such action is to produce profit and to contribute to the reproduction of the capital–wage-labour relation. A mild transformation of this situation would involve struggling for higher wages. A more radical transformation would affect the structural relationship itself, questioning the whole basis of capital–labour relations. More radical transformational activity would seek to transcend this situation altogether, questioning not just the level of wages, but the production process itself.

If the transformational model of social activity is correct in arguing that social structures need to be reproduced through human activity, then this provides the basis for any potentially transformatory activity as well. The nature of this transformative activity provides a key point at which critical realism and theories of hegemony coincide. Although social structures are often reproduced automatically, smoothly (or at least unconsciously), this is not always guaranteed, particularly because different social structures interact with each other in complex structural ensembles. The fact that the reproduction of social structures or structural ensembles is not always guaranteed means that strategic interventions are both possible and often necessary. This is the point at which the dialectics of reproduction/transformation and enablement/constraint are made concrete. For hegemony, it will be argued, is concerned with the process by which social structures are reproduced and transformed, and it is precisely this location in the process of social reproduction/transformation which places constraints but also allows for the possibility of different agents to construct and elaborate their own hegemonic blocs, projects and alliances.

Critical realism and socialism

It has been mentioned that this book will take a broadly Marxist approach. From the above it should be clear that critical realism is of interest to socialists in that it conceptualises the relation between social structures and human activity in a radical sense based on reproductive activity and transformative capacity. It avoids both the demoralising structuralist position that structures reproduce themselves and are all powerful, and the voluntarist humanism that believes that everything can be explained in terms of human activity. It is also capable of incorporating Marxist conceptions of class and class struggle into the processes of social reproduction, transformation and conservation. However, here a concept of hegemony is essential. Whereas the process of social reproduction is largely automatic, acts of transformation or conservation involve conscious interventions. The process of transformation/conservation assumes a strategic character and thus poses the question of hegemonic projects. However, these activities still occur within definite structural limits and critical realism locates these strategies within the potentialities allowed by the social conditions. Indeed, we will go on to define hegemony in a structuralist sense. A hegemonic strategy must take account of this particular structural context. Critical realism points to how a socialist strategy should be based on the transformation of a specific set of social structures.

Having passed through the stages of transcendental realism and critical naturalism the third stage of the critical realist journey is concerned with the idea of explanatory critique. Critical realist theory emerges not just as an analysis of structures but as a critique of these structures and their effects. It argues that a critique of inadequate theories and ideologies necessarily entails an analysis of the nature of the social structures that produce them, so that, for example, a critique of positivist social science requires an analysis of the atomised and commodified social conditions that these theories 'reflect'. The same might be said for the relation between classical or neo-liberal economic theory and the structure of the capitalist economy, or between bourgeois theories of government and the state and the actual bodies themselves. Once the origins of the inadequacies of these ideas are sought in the inadequacies of social structures and institutions, the question is immediately posed as to whether alternative structures or bodies might be envisaged. Just as Marx urged us to change the world, so the answer to many false ideas is to change the social relations behind them.

The radical nature of this approach lies in critical realism's focus on structures and underlying causes and not just on ideas, events and states of affairs. This affects socialist strategy in that an approach that focuses on social structures and generative mechanisms points to the inter-connectedness of different social processes and relations and to the decisive areas of social struggle and conflict. By looking to underlying structural causes, a critical realist approach questions those socialist theories that place primary emphasis on such things as class consciousness and world-views. Critical realism rejects not only the 'flat ontologies' provided by various ideologies like positivism or classical economics, but also the kind of 'praxis-ontology' provided by many versions of Marxism that effectively defines the world according to the social actions and ideas that it contains. The praxis approach to Marxism is wrong if, as Gramsci is sometimes prone to do, it reduces the social world to the ideas and beliefs of social groups, or if it commits the 'historicist' error of reducing Marxist theory to the philosophical viewpoint or world-outlook of a subject group. Consequently, a hegemonic struggle is more than just a clash of world-views or group consciousnesses, it must challenge not just the dominant ideas within society, but the very social structures that produce them.

Critical realism as a philosophy

The above suggests that critical realism and Marxism are closely related, although there is no necessary correspondence and it is quite possible that critical realism can be related to other social theories. The critical realist position emerges, after all, in relation to the methodology of the sciences more generally, acting as a philosophical 'underlabourer' that comments upon and clarifies scientific methodology. It is the job of the philosophical underlabourer to clear away the weeds of confusion, clarify theoretical claims and understandings and provide the necessary conceptual nourishment for scientific theories to develop. Philosophy, like science, does produce knowledge, but it is knowledge of the second order, or knowledge of the necessary conditions for the production of knowledge (Bhaskar 1989a: 8). This second order or conceptual knowledge can, however, be used to great effect. One of the main roles of realist underlabouring is to render explicit what is already implicit in theories and their claims. It has been mentioned already how this is useful in criticising the (often denied) philosophical basis of other theories such as the Humean conception of atomistic events (implicit in empiricism and positivism) or the Kantian construction of ideal models. Critical realism instead argues for the importance of ontology and for a conception of the world as structured, stratified and enduring. So although it does not make first-order scientific claims, critical realism is able to establish a priori transcendental arguments as to the existence of these underlying structures and mechanisms (as necessary conditions) and the status of our knowledge of them.

Critical realism also unmasks what Bhaskar has termed the *epistemic fallacy* or the conflation of the state of the world with the knowledge we have of it. The epistemic fallacy confuses ontology and epistemology, reducing the question of being (or claims about the world) to statements about what we know, or the knowledge we have. As an example, Bhaskar points to how Kant sees the problems of philosophy as the conditions, limits and forms of knowledge, while Wittgenstein, committing a *linguistic fallacy*, reduces the problems of philosophy to the conditions, limits and forms of language. Both cases involve the denial of ontology and the collapse of the intransitive dimension. We will go on to see how post-structuralist theories of hegemony also commit this error, either by avoiding questions of ontology (Derrida) or by reducing the world to its discursive articulation though hegemonic projects (Laclau and Mouffe).

In *Dialectic* (1993), Bhaskar develops these points and relates them to questions of structure, intransitivity, absence, totality and praxis. The epistemic fallacy is connected to other forms of *irrealism* such as actualism's reduction of powers to their exercise, flat ontologising (denial of depth and stratification), atomisation (denial of structural complexity), detotalisation (such as analytical approaches that bracket off the totality) and ontological monovalence (an undialectical privileging of the positive or present at the expense of the negative or absent). On all these questions philosophy has a crucial role to play.

While Bhaskar insists on the irreducibility of the intransitive, his transitive is necessarily flexible. Philosophy must recognise knowledge to be transient and influenced by social, historical and ideological factors. Consequently, critical realism advocates *epistemic relativity*. This is to be relativistic about the transitive but not about the intransitive object. It is to recognise that we have no guaranteed access to truth, that knowledge is socially constructed, and that there is no direct correspondence between knowledge and its object. However, critical realism is opposed to judgmental relativism or the view, as is advocated by postmodernist forms of relativism, that there are no rational grounds for preferring one belief to another and that essentially all beliefs are equally valid. Although it is correct to assert that there is no direct correspondence between knowledge and the independently existing objects of knowledge (epistemic relativism), it is necessary to assert that all theories are not equal, and that we should make judgements as to which theories and explanations are better than others on the grounds of explanatory adequacy (judgemental rationality).

Critical critical realism?

This is not the place to go into a lengthy critique of recent develops in critical realism, now redefined by Bhaskar as dialectical critical realism. It needs to be said, however, that a distinction has to be drawn between Bhaskar's earlier work and his more recent project. While critical realism was always going to grow in scope and make new claims, the nature of these claims goes well beyond the initial 'underlabouring' project. In keeping with this underlabouring conception, it is important to distinguish between a realist philosophical approach to science and a Marxist approach to the social world. By maintaining this distinction, critical realism can act as a useful critical tool in analysing the theories and claims of Marxism without actually becoming, or worse, replacing Marxism. In its role as a philosophical underlabourer, critical realism should make no specifically Marxist claims. But while the early critical realism seems to keep this careful balance with Marxist social science, the later work seems to be getting more involved in providing a social explanation itself. Indeed, the development of dialectical critical realism seems to be an attempt to *replace* Marxism or at least to transcend it.

Bhaskar's book *Dialectic* marks out four areas or dialectical categories: structures and non-identity (1M), absence and negation (2E), open totality (3L) and transformative praxis (4D). Some of these are already familiar issues and their development is very important. However, Bhaskar's 'second edge' is key to the transformation of critical realism. It makes all-powerful the category of absence and is aimed against 'ontological monovalence' or a purely positive conception of the world. This stress on the importance of absence and non-being is correct. But Bhaskar goes beyond a balanced 'ontological bivalence' (between positive and negative) to insist on the primacy of the negative. This is speculative at the very least and constitutes a threat to detailed causal analysis. The dialectic of absence makes dialectical critical realism even more abstract and moves the analysis away from a focus on concrete social relations. Yet at the same time, fundamental claims are being made about the nature of human behaviour.

The emphasis on the primacy of non-being is an attempt to use absence as the objective basis for a dialectic of freedom where freedom is seen as the absenting of constraints. This dialectic of freedom represents Bhaskar's shift from underlabouring philosophy to political expression. He attempts to turn critical realism into a philosophy of emancipation.

The strength of the early critical realism lies in its focus on the particular and its rejection of universalistic theories. Unfortunately, Bhaskar's new dialectic of freedom has precisely this universalistic character. It fails to uphold the specificity of social structures and actions and thus fails to define the particularity of freedom. Hence Bhaskar fails to ask, what kind of freedom? For whom and for what? Surely a transformatory project would also have to impose constraints on certain freedoms (like the rights of capitalists)? The forms that freedom takes certainly cannot be assessed simply on the basis of absenting something. And complementing this dialectic of freedom is a faulty conception of agency and a universalistic conception of power. Dialectical critical realism moves away from the Marxist stress on the importance of class analysis in favour of ubiquitous (somewhat Hegelian) master/slave relationships. By failing to relate critical realist arguments to a Marxist analysis of the social formation, dialectical critical realism ends up with an abstract and universalised ethics and a social analysis which is often devoid of any specific content.

Hegemony

This book will be concerned with the concept of hegemony and its place within social science. In this sense there is no direct relationship between hegemony and critical realist philosophy. Indeed, we might criticise Bhaskar for conflating philosophical positions with his own brand of prescriptive politics (reflected in his concept of master–slave relations and the dialectic of freedom). However, critical realism will be used throughout this book in an underlabouring role and will be directed against various usages of the concept in order to give hegemony a realist basis. The consequences of critical realism's intervention will be political.

It is possible to make a strong link between the idea of hegemony and some of the claims made by critical realism. Both critical realist accounts and the conception and use of hegemony see society as structured and stratified in a certain way. Hegemony's role is to forge a political and consensual unity and direction out of this differentiation. Hegemony represents a multi-levelled social organisation that reflects the kind of multi-levelled reality suggested by the transcendental arguments of critical realism. Thus it would seem that critical realism can tell us something about the conditions under which hegemony operates and about the materiality of hegemony and the conditions of its emergence. The closest association lies with the reproduction and transformation of social structures. Bhaskar's transformational model of social activity gives our understanding of hegemonic practices a more developed theoretical basis. Rather than defining hegemony on the basis of political relations, or relations between dominant and subordinate groups, it can be defined in more structural terms.

However, theories of hegemony also modify our understanding of the transformational model. The nature of the working class means that a process of transformation must be carefully directed and focused, not just on the transformation of a structure, but on the capture of political power. Any meaningful transformative process will take place across a wide range of social bodies and maintenance must be directed through the state. A theory of hegemony would seem to be the best-suited strategy for such transformative praxis. It is concerned with how social structures interrelate with human agency and the class struggle. It clarifies the relationship between theory and practice, informing both how we analyse political processes and how we act upon them. Perhaps, after all, this is an alternative attempt to infuse critical realist philosophy with Marxist political ideas.

Part 1
A theoretical history

2 Gramsci's realist hegemony

Introduction

Antonio Gramsci has become synonymous with the concept of hegemony and many books have been written on this subject. His work has become the terrain for a constant war of positions between different interpreters. Difficult though it may be, the intention here is to avoid getting too caught up in the kind of debates that seek to find the 'true' Gramsci. As our interest is with the concept itself, this means, to some extent, prising the notion of hegemony away from an exclusively Gramscian reading. Of course, Gramsci's work is the natural place to start an investigation. But rather than trying to find the 'correct' interpretation, we will look to a more full-scale reconstruction based on critical realist guidelines. This chapter will therefore be concerned with analysing those ideas in Gramsci that can be utilised for critical realist purposes. The rest of the first part of this book will do the same for other theories and theorists. The second part of this book will then develop these insights in order to articulate a realist theory of hegemony that combines both structural and agential aspects.

Roy Bhaskar has thus far written only a few lines on Gramsci, but what he has written is significant. His critique makes three points (Bhaskar 1991: 165, 172–4), which although overly dismissive in tone are important as a guide to Gramsci's philosophical errors:

1 Gramsci sees objectivity in terms of a universal subjectivity asymptotically approached in history but only finally realised under communism. Gramsci rejects realism as 'religious residue' and sees Marxism in humanist terms, as the expression of a subject rather than as knowledge of an object.

2 Gramsci wrongly believes that Marxism 'contains in itself all the fundamental elements needed to construct a total and integral conception of the world, a total philosophy and theory of natural science' (Gramsci 1971: 462). This leads to (non-Marxist!) natural science being regarded as 'bourgeois ideology'. Against this, Bhaskar argues that the historicity of knowledge on which Gramsci properly insists, does not

refute but actually depends upon the idea of the otherness of its objects.

3   There is thus a double collapse in Gramsci's philosophy. His sub-jectivism, as expressed in the view that objectivity is really universal subjectivity, collapses the intransitive objects of knowledge (the independently existing world) into the transitive (historical) processes of knowledge. The real world gets conflated with the knowledge we have of it. Secondly, Gramsci collapses what can be called the intrinsic and extrinsic conditions of science, a *historicist* position that fails to differentiate between internal necessity and external contingency and which reduces science to an expression of the historical process.

These issues will be taken up later, although a distinction must be made, missing in Bhaskar's critique, between Gramsci's explicit philosophical positions (which Bhaskar rightly attacks on realist grounds) and Gramsci's more implicit realism. As Bhaskar says, all theories have an implicit ontology (Bhaskar 1989b: 2), a set of claims and assumptions about the nature of the world, and it is argued that in Gramsci's more political writings a more realist view of the world emerges. Again, it would be wrong to claim that a particular interpretation of Gramsci is the 'true' one, but it can be claimed that Gramsci's work is contradictory and multifaceted and that some of his analysis – particularly that associated with the concept of hegemony – is compatible with critical realism and can be developed in a realist direction.

The philosophical influences

The unique character of Gramsci's thought is revealed through a study of his influences. His work contains the kind of concerted study of practical, political, historical and 'superstructural' aspects so prominent in Italian culture from Machiavelli through to Croce, Gentile, Labriola, Mondolfo and Sorel. These influences reveal the strengths and weaknesses of Gramsci's own thought. He develops a strong grasp of the political and the historical without, however, acquiring the scope of Marx's synthesis of German philosophy, French politics and British economics. Gramsci's Italian theoretical development produces a strong sense of the political and historical but this is perhaps at the expense of the economic. Moreover, as Bhaskar suggests, Gramsci's sense of the political is accompanied by overly-subjective, voluntarist, historicist and even idealist influences. This is not necessarily to suggest that some of Gramsci's arguments flow directly from the errors of those who influence him, but it does help indicate the complex background to Gramsci's thinking.

To begin with the influence of Machiavelli, it can be said that there is a sort of practical realism in the work of the Florentine which Gramsci makes much use of. It also contains an emphasis on human action, and the importance of leadership and political craft, a praxis-based approach that Gramsci commends, writing that:

> In his treatment, in his critique of the present, he expressed general concepts ... and an original conception of the world. This conception of the world too could be called 'philosophy of praxis', or 'neo-humanism', in as much as it does not recognise transcendent or immanent (in the metaphysical sense) elements, but bases itself entirely on the concrete action of man, who, impelled by historical necessity, works and transforms reality.
>
> (Gramsci 1971: 248–9)

This passage indicates how Gramsci strives to get away from speculative and idealist philosophy by means of a practical realism. Like Machiavelli, Gramsci wants to 'bring everything back to politics' (Gramsci 1971: 249). He praises Machaivelli because his writings deal with concrete rather than speculative issues and they are very much focused on the actions of political agents, set in real historical situations. But by placing such a strong emphasis on human action, this realism will be limited to what we have called a praxis ontology, a position that tends to see reality simply in terms of human actions. To try and move beyond this, Gramsci draws heavily on the work of the Hegelian philosopher Benedetto Croce. This gives human action a deeper basis that ties it to a more general philosophy of history and also to a philosophy of the human will. This synthesis of the practical humanism of Machiavelli and the Hegelian arguments of Croce brings about a surprisingly realist product, as expressed in Gramsci's view that:

> If one applies one's will to the creation of a new equilibrium among the forces which really exist and are operative – basing oneself on the particular force which one believes to be progressive and strengthening it to help it to victory – one still moves on the terrain of effective reality, but does so in order to dominate and transcend it (or to contribute to this). What 'ought to be' is therefore concrete; indeed it is the only realistic and historicist interpretation of reality ....
>
> (Gramsci 1971: 172)

Machiavelli's ideas, while often limited to practical action, are important to a realist interpretation of hegemony. Machiavelli was the first theorist to really formulate questions that point in the direction of a theory of hegemony, something that flows from his approach to social reality where he is constantly looking at the possibilities for collective actions and attainable goals. If Machiavelli's work is an early example of questions of hegemony, then Gramsci's work represents a later example of questions raised by Machiavelli, indeed, as Croce notes, 'with the Marxians, Machiavelli returned to Italy' (Croce 1929: 52). Machiavelli and the

Marxians are brought together by a common desire to confront the problems facing Italy, problems concerned with forging a new leadership capable of leading society forward and lifting Italy out of its backwardness. In order to develop this leadership it is necessary to develop a set of ruling alliances that can draw together different sections of the population. To do so requires the politics and art of statecraft. Speculating on how a leader should behave, Machiavelli stresses the importance of using both force and consent, issues crucial to Gramsci's own understanding of hegemony, writing that 'it is desirable to be both loved and feared; but it is difficult to achieve both and, if one of them has to be lacking, it is much safer to be feared than loved' (Machiavelli 1988: 59). However, Machiavelli, showing his modern attitude, appears to move away from a stress on force, accepting that consent has become an essential part of leadership. It is interesting that he gives ancient examples of pure force, and more modern examples of consent, or what he calls a 'civil principality'. The need for a strong social hegemony indicates that cultural and civil ties must be made and that it is necessary to lay firm foundations for rulership. Otherwise,

> like all other natural things that are born and grow rapidly, states that grow quickly cannot sufficiently develop their roots, trunks and branches, and will be destroyed by the first chill winds of adversity.
> (Machiavelli 1988: 23)

It is clear that Machiavelli left a deep influence on Gramsci with his emphasis on practical and political matters, with the question of the need to unify Italy and forge a national will, and with his emphasis on the dynamics of force and consent. Gramsci often refers to the force and consent relationship as Machiavelli's centaur that is half human and half animal (Machiavelli 1988: 61), the human aspect representing cunning and intellect, the beast representing recourse to brute force. He also calls Machiavelli the first Jacobin, a man concerned with the practical problems of uniting the Italian state, culture and people, by giving spiritual leadership and forming a collective bond against the 'barbarian' forces. However, such a project requires specific strategies. For this reason, Gramsci turns to Machiavelli's *The Art of War*, making much of tactics and battle strategies, of the qualities of the generals and the people, and using the imagery of fortresses with walls and ditches.

However, Machiavelli's realism is limited to a practical realism, often tied to the politics and intrigues of statecraft and rulership, and Gramsci needs a broader conception of history and human will. The popular conception of Machiavelli as a schemer and manipulator is indeed a gross injustice, but it is true that he does concentrate his attentions on questions of a tactical and strategic nature. Gramsci's turn to the philosophy of Croce is made possible by practical realism's rejection of metaphysics, and we have noted that this synthesis of Machiavelli and Hegelian philosophy can have surprisingly realist consequences. But it also leads to more idealist statements, such as the famous passage where Gramsci claims that:

> in the case of a very common expression (historical materialism) one should put the accent on the first term – 'historical' – and not on the second, which is of metaphysical origin. The philosophy of praxis is absolute 'historicism', the absolute secularisation and earthliness of thought, an absolute humanism of history. It is along this line that one must trace the thread of the new conception of the world.
>
> (Gramsci 1971: 465)

This new conception of the world is in fact the old conception of the world as elaborated by Hegel and mediated by Croce. In relation to Hegel's philosophy, Croce's *What is Living and What is Dead in Hegel* states that:

> It was necessary to preserve the vital part of it, that is to say, the new concept of the concept, the concrete universal, together with the dialectic of opposites and the doctrine of degrees of reality; to refute with the help of that new concept and by developing it, all panologism, and every speculative construction of the individual and of the empirical, of history and of nature; to recognise the autonomy of the various forms of spirit, while preserving their necessary connection and unity; and finally, to resolve the whole philosophy into a *pure philosophy of spirit*.
>
> (Croce 1915: 203–4)

We can see in this passage themes which recur in Gramsci's writings: the concrete universal[1] (and world-views); a hostility towards empiricism and positivist sociology on the one hand and speculative thought on the other; and, above all, a philosophy of spirit as expressed in the conception of human will as the driving force of history. But despite this kind regard for Croce's Hegelian philosophy, Croce himself, along with other Italian idealists, would often express the view that while Marxism had revived a theory of history and a Machiavellian conception of political praxis, it succumbed to an economic reductionism and a crude materialism. In this way Marxism had lost the true insight of its Hegelian origins and the view of history as the unfolding of spirit (Croce 1929: 154–5; Croce 1949: 64).

Croce, Gentile and others developed their conceptions of history, in particular, in order to explain the Italian situation. The significance of the *Risorgimento*, the struggles of the new bourgeois class, and ultimately, the rise of populism and fascism, all indicated the need for moral, cultural and intellectual leadership. In such circumstances a specifically Italian form of voluntarism emerged. This can be explained as a particular conception of history that sees it, above all, as the product of the human will. It is a subjective conception viewing history as the outcome of peoples' actions and ideas. Croce's work advances the argument that history is essentially the struggle for the ideal of liberty, although the development of liberty must be fought for by people in actual historical situations. The history of liberty, synonymous with the development of Spirit, is not predetermined but resides in our every action, particularly in the actions of the intellectual elite. Again, this form of idealism can be seen as compatible with Gramsci's practical realism, his conception of action and his theory of the role of intellectuals in turning ideas into reality.

This voluntaristic conception of history is a complex product, combining a critique of Hegel's philosophy of Spirit with Machiavelli's political praxis, perhaps best synthesised in Vico's concept of human spirit as the passion that precedes the moment of reason – again conjuring up the Machiavellian image of the centaur, both animal and human. Italian voluntarism develops in different directions, from the idealism of Croce, who holds that all reality is merely mental activity, to the subjectivism of Mondolfo, who argues against the passive conception of the subjective, seeing it instead as the source of imaginative voluntary activity (Nemeth 1980: 37). Croce understands history as the dialectic between the practical and the ideal, unified by Spirit and historically represented by liberty. Spirit is divided into theoretical and practical activity, a position that shows the influence of Croce's one-time mentor, the Marxist Antonio Labriola.

Labriola's views show that voluntarism is not confined to idealism as he also argues that history is the product of people rather than 'the logic of things' (Femia 1981: 92). This may be so, but is it compatible with the view expressed in Marx that people may 'make their own history, but not of their own free will; not under circumstances they themselves have chosen' (Marx 1973d: 146)? Labriola, who was almost wholly responsible for the spread of Marxist ideas in Italy, first makes use of the term 'philosophy of praxis' to denote Marxism. Rejecting any strict mechanical science, Labriola develops a science of history and politics based upon human actions, but set within a materialistic framework. This might allow for Marx's view that humans must operate 'under the given and inherited circumstances with which they are directly confronted' (Marx 1973d: 146). However, the difficulty in carrying through such a synthesis of positions is reflected in the oscillations Labriola's thought takes between a more voluntaristic conception of the political superstructure, and a more determinist and mechanical conception of the economic. Despite brave attempts, Labriola is ultimately unable to break out of the straightjacket of Second International thinking.

Labriola's construction of a Marxist science based upon praxis and historicism obviously greatly influences Gramsci. It also reflects the irrealist trend to collapse the distinction between history and philosophy, also prominent in Croce, so that 'philosophy serves no other purpose than as a "methodology of historical thought"' (Croce 1941: 138). Gramsci takes up Labriola's conception of the self-sufficiency of Marxism and the scientific status of historical materialism in relation to what he saw as 'external philosophical ideologies' (hence Gramsci's statement that Marxism contains 'all the fundamental elements needed to construct a total and integral conception of the world') (Gramsci 1971: 462, 386–8). The assumption that Marxism is the only necessary science leads to a rejection of whole areas of scientific knowledge in favour of an intersubjective, all-inclusive Marxism. Yet the existence of different scientific disciplines is not simply a product of bourgeois thinking but has its basis in the structure of reality itself. The existence of different sciences and disciplines – not only physics, biology, etc., but also quasi-disciplines like economics and politics – is a reflection of the fact that the world itself is stratified and differentiated into distinct layers. The view that Marxism is the only necessary science is, in effect, a denial of this stratification and differentiation.

Georges Sorel also carries great influence because of his rejection of a cold, scientific theory of Marxism and his embracing of an ethical conception of revolutionary activity, inspired by a Bergsonian creative urge, to be found not in the heads of intellectuals, but in the spontaneity of the working class. Thus, in his *Reflections on Violence* (1975), Sorel embraces revolutionary syndicalism, seeing the ultimate creative event as the general strike. Discarding theories of economic catastrophism, he emphasises the moral and cultural collapse of society, something that struck a chord with Italian historicists who could see that the cultural crisis was actually matched with economic expansion. For Gramsci, Sorel's ideas easily fit with those of Machiavelli and Croce. The striving for an ideal would inspire the workers to rise above the decadence of bourgeois society. Sorel expresses these desires in the form of a myth and maintains that

> by means of them it is possible to understand the activity, the feelings and the ideas of the masses preparing themselves to enter on a decisive struggle; the myths are not descriptions of things, but expressions of a determination to act.
>
> (Sorel 1975: 32)

Gramsci was much influenced by the notion of myth, merging it with Machiavellian politics and its emphasis on the need to organise and unify the people so that:

> Machiavelli's *Prince* could be studied as an historical exemplification of the Sorelian myth – i.e. of a political ideology expressed neither in the form of a cold utopia nor as learned theorising, but rather by the creation of a concrete fantasy which acts on a dispersed and shattered people to arouse and organise its collective will.
>
> (Gramsci 1971: 125–6)

But Gramsci's feelings for Sorel are mixed, for he came to reject much of the syndicalist and spontaneist character of Sorel's thought. In particular,

Gramsci's experience of syndicalism in Turin and the failure of the factory councils, and his later break with *Ordine Nuovo*, meant that he came to rethink his earlier influences and the spontaneist and voluntarist humanism of Sorel. Gramsci turns instead to the struggle to form a revolutionary party based on the vanguard giving intellectual and political leadership.

These different viewpoints indicate the complex of influences that any study of Gramsci must deal with. This is not to suggest that the strengths and weakness of these thinkers and Gramsci's own strengths and weaknesses are one and the same, it is more the case that this diverse collection of thinkers helps shed some light on the tensions and complexities in Gramsci's work. The diversity of these influences makes it easy for different commentators to emphasise some aspects of Gramsci rather than others. Gramsci's relation to Croce, Gentile and Labriola is often counterposed to his Marxism. More recently, Laclau and Mouffe have offered a Sorelian reading of Gramsci in order to undermine the traditional Leninist reading. However, Gramsci's Marxism and Leninist politics cannot be dismissed so easily as they are central to his political viewpoint, and it is towards these very political viewpoints that we must turn if we are to develop the realist aspect of Gramsci's thinking.

Philosophy and hegemony

The above analysis indicates some of the philosophical influences behind Gramsci's thinking, but they are far from exclusive and it must be remembered that Gramsci was, above all else, a Marxist, interested in the actual issues of power, politics and class struggle. The above tends to emphasise some of the more irrealist influences on Gramsci's philosophical outlook, which does, to some extent, have a bearing on his conception of politics. In this way it is possible to understand some of the criticisms levelled at Gramsci, such as Bhaskar's claim that he sees Marxism as self-sufficient and that he embraces a historicist viewpoint, or indeed other criticisms of his tendency towards voluntarism and a praxis ontology. But as we move from Gramsci's more philosophical statements towards his political analysis we find that although it may be still be infused with these philosophical notions, it also counters some of them.

The process of extracting Gramsci's political analysis from some of his philosophical notions is a complex one. First, there are problems with Gramsci's (expressed) understanding of what philosophy itself is. At times, philosophy becomes subsumed by hegemony, becoming part of the worldview of the hegemonic groupings. It is related to common sense, although perhaps it represents a higher form of expression, but it nevertheless derives from the intersection of human praxis, organic expression and hegemonic struggle. Philosophy becomes entwined with the Machiavellian unity of thought and action. Indeed, hegemony comes to represent the coming together of philosophy (as Gramsci understands it) and politics. 'Philosophies', for Gramsci, are tied up with the leading role of intellectuals in shaping organic blocs and normative action. Above all, they are a particular elaboration of world-views, derived from hegemony in the sense that they are the expression of those groups who are seeking positions of authority or moral leadership. Gramsci's organic view of philosophy is connected to his theory of hegemonic leadership and political praxis, so that hegemony becomes the concretisation and realisation of the world-view of the philosophical subject.

Yet Gramsci is partly correct to say that philosophies exist in this plural sense, just as we might say that there are a plurality of ideologies and social practices. But the relativistic or overly-historicist implications of this must be guarded against. Philosophy is not simply something that is done by different groups and we cannot understand one philosophy simply by comparison with another. Philosophy and philosophical claims must be examined in relation to the world that produces such claims and with regard to the social and scientific knowledge we have of this world. Critical realism's epistemic relativism means that it recognises the social and historical character of knowledge and the fact that there are a number of different philosophies produced by various class positions. There is, of course, a danger of relativism here, in that ideas become related to particular groups or communities of people, but it is possible to offer some defence of Gramsci's position as Paggi has tried to do in saying:

> Gramsci's brutal assertion that philosophy is bourgeois or proletarian does not mean that there are two philosophies according to class perspectives, but that there are two ways of doing philosophy: one conservative and one revolutionary, depending on their acceptance or rejection of the symbiosis of philosophy and existing social conflicts.
> (Paggi 1979: 121)

But if there are different class 'philosophies', and if a bourgeois philosophical viewpoint is wrong or inadequate in some way, a 'proletarian' alternative will only be right if it can explain the real world of objects. It is not guaranteed correctness just because it is the expression of the working class. But the fact that it is the expression of the working-class, a class that has an interest in understanding and transforming society, could just mean that a working-class philosophy is in fact a better philosophy, or is capable, perhaps, of providing the basis for a better science of society.

Realism and social structure

Some commentators have tried to make the case that Gramsci is explicitly realist and that his idealist formulations have some other purpose – aimed at positivist sociology, speculative philosophy and so on. In his book on

Gramsci's historicism, Esteve Morera (1990) makes the best case for a realist reading based on Gramsci's attempts to analyse actual historical processes like passive revolution or the war of positions. Morera makes the point that Gramsci's historicist approach is not so much a questioning of the existence of an objective reality but simply emphasises the ways in which humans can gain an understanding of it. This knowledge is necessarily social and historical, but we still find Gramsci arguing that:

> it is difficult not to think in terms of something real beyond this knowledge ... in the concrete sense of a 'relative' ignorance of reality, of something still unknown, which will however be known one day ... when the technical and social conditions of mankind have been changed in a progressive direction.
>
> (Gramsci 1971: 368)

Morera finds an array of realist statements to quote back against the anti-realist ones, so for example Gramsci admits that the relations of forces, closely connected to the structure are 'objective, independent of human will, and which can be measured with the systems of the exact or physical sciences' (Gramsci 1971: 180).[2] However, it would be wrong to simply to draw the conclusion that Gramsci is a realist on the basis of such statements. The point is not to make claims as to whether Gramsci is a realist or not, but to note the serious tensions in his work which reflect his differing conceptions, interests and influences. This makes it possible to perform a realist reconstruction of some of Gramsci's ideas and concepts – something Morera does with the concept of historicism. To do this, though, it is necessary to move away from the philosophical aspects of Gramsci's work and to concentrate more on his social and political analysis, which is a more fruitful terrain for the excavation of implicit realist notions.

Whereas previous (mainly Russian) conceptions of hegemony were limited to the question of proletarian leadership, Gramsci extends the scope of hegemony so that it is applied not just to proletarian leadership but to political leadership more generally and to society as a whole. This extends the realist implications of the concept, for it is no longer restricted to the actions of a particular social group, but comes to refer to the general social requirement for the construction of rulership. The concept of hegemony also has internal and external aspects – it refers not only to external relations between dominant and dominated groups, but also to internal relations within groups or social blocs. If this is to be pushed in a realist direction it can be seen that hegemony is acquiring a complex character in that it refers to relations between an array of social groups and forces, straddling many social layers and cutting across many social structures. If a realist reconstruction of the concept of hegemony is to occur, then the construction of hegemonic blocs must be related to the need to secure the reproduction or transformation of society through a complex political strategy.

The realism implicit in Gramsci's approach is expressed through his analysis of social relations, the balance of class forces and the mechanisms of domination, coercion, consent and leadership. While this does not guarantee a realist explanation, it does allow for the possibility of setting some of Gramsci's theoretical concepts, particularly hegemony, within a realist framework. If Gramsci's concerns about political strategy, ideology, the articulation of interests and historical development can be dealt with in conjunction with a conception of objective reality as structured and stratified – which the very existence of hegemony implies – then a rewarding area of political analysis can be opened up. In this way, hegemony remains tied to the question of how different political groups operate, but it assumes that these groups operate on a diverse terrain of structures, practices and generative mechanisms; complex conditions that explain why rulership is not given but has to be constructed out of diverse elements in diverse locations.

However, the diversity and complexity of society also creates problems for how hegemony is theorised, problems that Perry Anderson's study of Gramsci is meticulous in pointing out. Where does hegemony operate, across what parts of the social terrain? In particular, Gramsci's analysis of hegemony is founded on the idea of the state contrasting with civil society, an idea which is particularly strong in his contrast between the conditions for hegemony in the East and in the West. But what is meant by civil society and what is meant by the state? In the work of Hegel and Marx the private sphere of civil society includes the economic domain, while Marx conceives of the state and politics as belonging to the superstructure. But in Gramsci there is not a clear idea of what is encompassed by either (a) civil society (the civil, social or private sphere), (b) political society (the public, political or state sphere) and (c) the economy (and whether it is part of civil society or separate from it). Moreover, Anderson points to three conflicting descriptions of the state that also lead to confusion (Anderson 1976: 12–13):

1   The state contrasts with civil society:

In the East the State was everything, civil society was primordial and gelatinous; in the West, there was a proper relation between State and civil society, and when the State trembled a sturdy structure of civil society was at once revealed. The state was only an outer ditch, behind which there stood a powerful system of fortresses and earthworks ....

(Gramsci 1971: 238)

2   The state encompasses civil society:

State = political society + civil society, in other words hegemony protected by the armour of coercion.

(Gramsci 1971: 263)

3   The state is identical with civil society:

> By 'State' should be understood not only the apparatus of government,
> but also the 'private' apparatus of 'hegemony' or civil society ....
>
> (Gramsci 1971: 261)

And:

> In actual reality civil society and State are one and the same ....
>
> (Gramsci 1971: 160)

This poses real problems if we are to try and understand where hegemony is located and how it operates. In fact it leads to three different conceptions of hegemony. One interpretation is that hegemony is located within civil society while coercion is confined to the state. This could be read into Gramsci's distinction between the East, where the state is everything, and the West, where there is a strong civil society and consequently a much stronger social hegemony. Strategy is likewise dichotomised into the war of manoeuvre and war of position, the war of manoeuvre or frontal assault is appropriate in taking the state, but a more patient war of positions is necessary where civil society is strong. However, while it is true to say that weaker societies rely more heavily on the state, while more advanced ones have a stronger civil society, any distinction that confines hegemony to civil society while defining the state exclusively in terms of a coercive body is a misleading one. For hegemony is not confined to civil society but does indeed operate through the institutions of the state, particularly through the process of legitimisation, as is shown through the operation of state bodies like parliament and the judicial system.

Another formulation is that the state includes both political society and civil society. In effect civil society loses its independence. The best expression of this position can be found in Althusser's later conception of Ideological State Apparatuses which argues that the state and civil society combine through the ideological function of such things as education, the church and the media, which exist alongside the coercive Repressive State Apparatuses. Such a position is criticised elsewhere.

The third and best formulation is that the state and civil society are distinct, but that hegemony operates across both. This is consistent with the view that the consensual aspect of hegemony combines with the more coercive role of the state. This is expressed in one of Gramsci's footnotes where he writes that: 'The "normal" exercise of hegemony on the now classical terrain of the parliamentary regime is characterised by the combination of force and consent, which balance each other reciprocally ... to ensure that force will appear to be based on the consent of the majority' (Gramsci 1971: 80, n. 49). This statement suggests not only that hegemony operates through the consensual, legitimising body of parliament (an institution of the supposedly exclusively coercive state), but also that hegemony itself combines both force and consent as opposed to the normally accepted view that hegemony is consent and that it contrasts with coercion.

The dominant hegemony operates through the state in order to best organise civil society. This leads to the view that the organisation and maintenance of hegemony is related to important social institutions and structures. This relates back to the question of structure and superstructure and it is found that, rather than confining hegemony to one of these, Gramsci's writings include a formulation which sees hegemony as related to both, in fact relating to the unity between structure and superstructure. Thus he writes:

> Structures and superstructures form an 'historical bloc'. That is to say the complex, contradictory and discordant *ensemble* of the superstructures is the reflection of the *ensemble* of the social relations of production.
>
> (Gramsci 1971: 366)

While this is no doubt a clumsy description, relying on Marx's overly crude base-superstructure distinction, Gramsci's formulation is still an important step towards a realist position. For the moment, Gramsci's term 'historical bloc' will be taken to mean hegemony, so that hegemony involves the process whereby structures and superstructures codetermine and relate to one another. Gramsci cites Fordist production as a clear example of this combined character – it concerns both the organisation of production and the development of a class project based on developments at the level of production. The historical bloc is being defined, not simply on the basis of the relations between groups, but on the basis of the relations between groups and structures (in this case the structures of the production process). This is again clear when Gramsci writes that:

> what is involved is the reorganisation of the structure and the real relations between men on the one hand and the world of the economy or of production on the other.
>
> (Gramsci 1971: 263)

So the organisation of hegemony at the level of social groups relates to the organisation of society at the political level and at the level of production. This means that for a group to become hegemonic, or for it to maintain its position, it must have behind it both the economic conditions and the political and cultural conditions which allow that group to put itself forward as leading. It also shows that a ruling hegemonic bloc must maintain itself through organising and reorganising social relations as well as social groups and that it needs, in fact, to organise those social groups in accordance with developments in social relations. According to the Fordism example, therefore, the ruling group should relate to changes in patterns of production and intervene into this process in order to strengthen its own position. This can be achieved because, by relating to changes in production, the hegemonic group can better organise those groups affected by them and it can relate to and develop the material interests of social groups that these conditions engender. A later chapter of this book will look at how the economic organisation of Fordism relates to the hegemony of the post-war period and to a set of political alliances and state strategies. In Gramsci's own work on Fordism a link is made between production methods and the 'Americanisation' of politics, culture and even moral, sexual and ethical values.

Inevitably, the combination of economic, political and cultural factors produces a number of different class determinations or fractions. Social classes have a heterogeneous character, comprising many different layers stratified over a number of different social structures. Hegemonic projects reflect this stratification in that they recognise that classes are not homogenous, but need to be brought together and unified. Hegemonic projects represent an attempt to construct alliances or blocs out of a diverse range of social groups and agents, each with different aims and interests, but this makes it all the more necessary to look beyond the actions of these groups and examine the various social structures and objective conditions that give rise to these divergent groups and interests. Hegemony may develop the process and modify, even help determine social agents, but it is not the primary origin of the differences between social groups and interests. Hegemony may take up and articulate these differences in various ways, but it acts upon a pre-existing raw material that is already stratified and differentiated because of its place in the nexus of social relations.

It is this complex nexus of social relations that means that ultimately the state is key to the organisation of hegemony. The ruling hegemony organises through the state, bringing together differing groups and interests and forging them into an economic bloc. Because of its organising capacity, the state provides the institutional framework for the implementation of hegemonic projects. Under capitalism the state must act to unite various fractions of capital in order to secure the best conditions for capital accumulation. This more functionalist aspect of the state as securing the unity of the ruling bloc in order to best facilitate capital accumulation contrasts starkly with the instrumentalist view of the state as a mere tool of the ruling class or 'executive committee of the bourgeoisie'. In fact it is not so much that the ruling class organises the state for its own purposes, more that it is the state that organises and shapes the ruling class. This, it shall later be argued, is the more functional or structural aspect of the hegemonic process. But how the state carries out its functions is another matter. If the state's function is to intervene in social processes, its strategies for intervention are dependent on the attitudes, beliefs, interests and behaviour of the ruling groups. So the state provides the framework for different social groups to attempt to implement their own projects and thus becomes a strategic terrain on which different groups compete to implement their hegemonic projects.

If the state combines the requirement for political leadership with the need to intervene in the most important social processes, then a hegemonic crisis, where classes become detached from their traditional parties or where there is a crisis of direction and leadership, is much deeper than a mere electoral crisis. It represents a real crisis of authority in the face of objective conditions. Gramsci makes the implicitly realist point that these parties are not always able to adapt themselves to new circumstances, to new tasks, thus showing that history is to be understood not simply in terms of the actions of groups and their organisations, but in terms of how these groups relate to underlying social and historical processes and conditions. A serious hegemonic crisis would therefore represent a crisis of the historical bloc as understood as the relation between structure and superstructure.

Finally, then, we will touch on the question of the passive revolution which reflects an attempt to organise the superstructure in line with structural developments. In this conception the ruling class compensates for any weaknesses it may have and attempts to combat any pressure coming from below by carrying through a reorganisation of civil society so as to pre-empt any activity from the masses themselves. This reorganisation must take the form of a modernisation which is in line with the structural developments that are taking place in the economy and which seeks to foster and cultivate these changes. In this way a ruling bloc can try and head off any potential crisis through a far-reaching reorganisation which creates the impression of progress. Gramsci's analysis of Italy points to how the bourgeoisie attempted to deflect from its own weakness by developing Fordist production techniques, the effect of which was widely felt, so that:

> through the legislative intervention of the State, and by means of the corporative organisation – relatively far-reaching modifications are being introduced into the country's economic structure in order to accentuate the 'plan of production'....
>
> (Gramsci 1971: 120)

Later we will study the notion of passive revolution in relation to developments after the Second World War. Again we see the realist implication of Gramsci's admittedly strange formulation of the historical bloc as a convergence of economic structure and politico-ideological superstructure.

The problems of historicism

Reaching an understanding of historicism is a key problem of social analysis. The typical critique of Gramsci's historicism, as exemplified by

Althusser's comments in *Reading Capital* (Althusser and Balibar 1979), is that he embraces a historical relativism that reduces social science to the expression of different groups at different stages in history. Underlying this, though, is a deeper problem that Althusser's opposite error of 'scientism' is unable to address, that is, how do we maintain some sort of scientific analysis of society while recognising the necessarily historical character of social theory and social practice? Esteve Morera in fact defends Gramsci's historicism on the basis that it is compatible with a realist conception of causality and that it manages to combine historical contingency with causal necessity:

> Gramsci's historicism is not a denial of the concepts of historical causality and laws, but merely an attempt to produce a conception of them that is suited to the complexities of the historical process and that takes account of the open character of that process. Furthermore, he seeks to give explanations for social phenomena that avoid reference to ahistorical entities, be they metaphysical laws, transcendental categories, or empirical constructions about the nature of the brain. Ultimately, historicism means precisely this: that all explanations of social phenomena should be based on strictly historical, or what he sometimes calls immanent, causes.
>
> (Morera 1990: 114–15)

Althusser's critique of historicism also accuses it of a lack of differentiation so that 'Marxism as an (absolute) historicism automatically unleashes a logically necessary chain reaction which tends to flatten out the Marxist totality into a variation of the Hegelian totality, and ... tones down, reduces, or omits the real differences separating the levels' (Althusser and Balibar 1979: 132). The particular conjuncture cannot be grasped by pretending that history is a simple mono-linear process that ends in the confirmation of the historical subject. But according to Morera, Gramsci does see historical reality as complexly structured and differentiated, a view that has also been expressed here in relation to Gramsci's political concepts. Particular conjunctures can only be understood as the coming together of different historical processes and mechanisms and the various groups of people who act within this context. Historically, these different groups, processes, structures, practices and contradictions move at varying speeds and in different directions, some more developed than others, some more progressive, some more conservative. To understand the conjuncture one has to grasp this wider historical field and know what historical forces are causing particular events and why. Morera applies these different criteria to Gramsci's historical analysis. Concepts are unavoidably historical:

> Theoretical concepts, such as class or hegemony, have a temporal dimension which defines them as much as their synchronic character-

istics. They are, in short, each of them an abstraction that holds for a series of inter-related phenomena over a period of time, not simply a matter of series of properties in a static whole.

(Morera 1990: 83)

In an interesting comparison with the Annales School and with aspects of structuralism, Morera argues that the concept of hegemony can bring together the synchronic notion of structure and the diachronic under-standing of historical development. We have argued that hegemony has a structural aspect that derives from its relation to various social processes and relations, but it also has a historical aspect that comes from actual conjunctural combinations of forces, groups, interests, activities and events:

> Structure, conjuncture, event: these are the elements of the situation, each with its specific rhythm, its temporality, and all linked together in a dialectical unity, a unity of contradictory forces.
>
> (Morera 1990: 91)

Complementing the concept of hegemony is the idea of the historical bloc which, as has been seen, creates a unity between structure and super-structure. The historical bloc should not therefore be reduced to the question of the relation between social groups, but should be seen as the relation between these groups and the underlying social conditions. The triumph of a hegemonic project is to be sought in the specific relation of forces that characterise a given structured situation. Against those who would have it that hegemony is purely an ethico-political concept, we can quote Gramsci's statement that hegemony 'must necessarily be based on the decisive function exercised by the leading group in the decisive nucleus of economic activity' (Gramsci 1971: 161). Further, the historical bloc represents the 'unity between nature and spirit (structure and super-structure), the unity of opposites and of distincts' (Gramsci 1971: 137). Leaving aside the Hegelian tone of such a statement we can see that hegemony is not regarded as purely an ethico-political phenomenon, but as the ethico-political aspect of the historical bloc, a bloc built on material (and economic) foundations.

A realist interpretation of Gramsci can also be developed from his analysis of 'the relations of forces'. First he talks of a relation of social forces closely linked to the structure. These relations are objective and reflect the development of the material forces of production and the emergence of social classes (Gramsci 1971: 180). The second moment concerns the relation of political forces, the degree of homogeneity, self-awareness and organisation of the social classes. The first level of this is the economic–corporate one, which is marked by an awareness of the unity of the group but lacks solidarity. After this comes consciousness of a solidarity of interests, but this is confined to economic or corporatist interests. The third and most political stage occurs when this corporate consciousness is overcome. An intellectual and moral unity arises and political parties emerge. This is, for Gramsci, the moment when structure passes into superstructure (Gramsci 1971: 181). Then, the third moment concerns the relation of military forces and relates to the strategic battle with the opposition forces.

Gramsci's notion of catharsis is in keeping with this analysis. Here, a process of realisation takes place, again concerning structure and super-structure, so that the subject comes to see the structure not simply as a constraint, but as a potential source of freedom:

> The term 'catharsis' can be employed to indicate the passage from the purely economic (or egotistic-passional) to the ethico-political moment, that is the superior elaboration of the structure into superstructure in the minds of men. This also means the passage from 'objective to sub-jective' and from 'necessity to freedom'. Structure ceases to be an external force which crushes man, assimilates him to itself and makes him passive; and is transformed into a means of freedom, an instrument to create a new ethico-political form and a source of new initiatives.
>
> (Gramsci 1971: 366–7)

It is possible to draw parallels here with Bhaskar's outline of the development of the dialectic of freedom as the satisfaction of desires and absenting, ills and constraints. This process of realisation is important, for it is both a process of self-awakening and a recognition of one's objective interests, out there in the world. Gramsci's arguments might usefully be compared to Bhaskar's idea of freedom as well-being – oriented to the satisfaction of needs and the absenting of ills, and as flourishing, based on the realisation of agential possibilities and potentialities (Bhasker 1993: 398).

Althusser's contribution

Louis Althusser writes that hegemony is 'a remarkable example of a theoretical solution in outline to the problems of the interpretation of the economic and the political' (Althusser 1977a: 114n29). But his notes on Gramsci in *Reading Capital*, and his critique of Gramsci's historicism in particular, say as much about Althusser's own weaknesses as they do about Gramsci's, and this in turn shows the advances that can be made by adopting an alternative critical realist approach.

Althusser develops a symptomatic reading of Gramsci's work. He rightly rejects a humanist analysis of Gramsci's 'absolute historicism' on the basis that Gramsci's arguments:

> are primarily critical and polemical in meaning; their functions are first and foremost: (1) to reject any metaphysical interpretation of

Marxist philosophy, and (2) to *indicate*, as 'practical' concepts, the site on which the Marxist conception should be established and the direction it should take.

(Althusser and Balibar 1979: 127)

As far as Althusser is concerned, historicism is valid if it corresponds to the practical role of Marxism or to the unity of theory and practice:

> By presenting Marxism as historicism, Gramsci is stressing an essential determination of Marxist theory: its practical role in *real history*. One of Gramsci's constant concerns is the practico-historical role of what ... he calls the great 'conceptions of the world', or 'ideologies' ... In this respect ... Marxism cannot claim to be the theory of history unless, *even in its theory*, it can the think the conditions of this penetration into history, into all strata of society ....

(Althusser and Balibar 1979: 127–8)

The problem here is that Althusser is reducing the historicism of Marxism to its actual practical application, while maintaining that the theory of Marxism should remain uncontaminated by such historical matters. It can be seen that Althusser's structuralism has a tendency to collapse into theoreticism or scientism, stressing intrinsic necessity at the expense of extrinsic historical contingency. Althusser considers theory to be scientific and practice to be historical, ignoring the important fact that theory is also inescapably social and historical, that it is created under specific social and historical conditions. Althusser allows Marxism to be historicist, but only in the sense that 'the historicism of Marxism is no more than one of the aspects and effects of its own theory, correctly conceived, no more than its own internally consistent theory. A theory of real history, too, must, as other "conceptions of the world" have already done, pass into real history' (Althusser and Balibar 1979: 129). The problem of Althusser's approach can be summarised thus – he sees the correct form of historicism as theory passing into history, but cannot tolerate the idea of history passing into theory.

It is certainly true that Althusser makes an important break from essentialist theories by emphasising through his concept of over-determination that the world is multiply determined by a complexity of social processes. This does give an element of contingency to his analysis in that social entities are a product of a coincidence of various factors, but this is done in a synchronic (structural) rather than a diachronic (historical) way. Althusser correctly points to Gramsci's (historicist) tendency to collapse science into history and blur the distinction between historical materialism and philosophy, but the charge of idealism levelled against Gramsci can quite easily by turned on Althusser; that his talk of the theoretical object of the science of history as distinct from 'real history', his rigid separation of the thought object and the real object, his tendency to stand the theory of history outside or above real history all suggest that we can only know knowledge and that this knowledge is somehow separate from and uncontaminated by the socio-historical world. While Gramsci's approach is too historicist, Althusser's is too internalised. Instead, to put it in critical realist terms, we must look at both how transitive knowledge itself is structured and differentiated, and how this transitive knowledge is related to the intransitive world of real structures and relations. We cannot rely on theories producing their own internal proofs of scientificity. Instead, we require an epistemological relativism based on a recognition of the inescapably historical aspect of knowledge. Thus Gramsci's historicism must be judged according to its potentially explanatory character and not just by a measure of its internal consistency.

A dual conception of hegemony

The transformational model of social activity tries to develop an explanation of the relationship between structures and agents. Society is both the ever-present condition (material cause) and the continually reproduced outcome of human agency (Bhaskar 1989a: 34–5). The various social structures are reproduced through human agency, although this is largely an unconscious process. However, the fact that the reproduction of social structures requires the activity of human agents means that the possibility exists, within very definite limits, that agents may transform such structures or that another group of agents may try to preserve existing structures or prevent transformative activity taking place. This is where the question of hegemony arises.

It can be seen that two concepts of hegemony are starting to emerge, one structural and the other more political or agential. The political usage is the normally accepted one – hegemony concerns the organisation of political agents around certain projects and winning consent to a set of ideas and interests. But hegemony is also defined in a structural sense in that it intersects with the process by which social structures are reproduced or transformed. There is an element of the automatic to this in that the agential reproduction of social structures is largely unconscious or is the unintended consequence of social activities. However, social structures exist in complex and contradictory combinations and because the world is open rather than predetermined and because different structures coincide and conflict, hegemony will always play an important role in securing the reproduction of these larger structural combinations. Hegemony, in its structural role, is related to the need to secure social cohesion and structural reproduction. Indeed, the necessary role that hegemony must play in securing social cohesion and structural reproduction is indicated by the fact that various hegemonic projects are possible at all and that their consequences are important. If the structures of the world operated in an automatically given way (as the functionalist sociology of Durkheim and Parsons suggests) then hegemony would be entirely redundant. The need to secure the unity of the social formation may not always seem apparent when supposedly automatic processes function smoothly, but it is all too evident in times of structural/hegemonic crisis or change.

If we bring together these structural and agential definitions of hegemony we can say that hegemony provides the political or class struggle moment in the interaction between structures and agents. This breaks from a humanist definition of hegemony that reduces it to the interrelations between groups of agents. By denying a structural ontology, the humanist approach cannot explain either what generates hegemonic processes or struggles, or what these struggles are about. We cannot understand the class struggle by simply referring to the proletariat and the bourgeoisie; ultimately, what determines both these forces are the objective structures of capitalist society. Likewise, hegemony cannot be understood simply in terms of the struggles between different agents; the material causes of hegemony must be sought. Agents are involved in relations, both with each other, and with social structures and practices. A hegemony or hegemonic project should therefore be seen as an articulated attempt to preserve or transform such structures and relations. It would be mistaken, therefore, to try and reduce Gramsci's analysis to simple political, ethical or strategic concepts. This is clear when Gramsci writes that:

> incurable structural contradictions have revealed themselves (reached maturity), and that despite this, the political forces which are struggling to conserve and defend the existing structure itself are making every effort to cure them, within certain limits, and to overcome them.
>
> (Gramsci 1971: 178)

In this quote, hegemony concerns the efforts of the political forces to conserve certain social structures. This hegemonic project is both motivated by structural contradictions, and limited or undermined by them. Gramsci also assesses the historical bloc, not simply as a historical relation between different social agents, but as the relationship between what he calls the economic structure and the politico-ethical superstructures, realised through the competing activity of different social groups and classes. This gives us a concept of hegemony as *emergence* – hegemony is not simply created by social groups; it is realised by them. It is dependent upon an underlying or lower level of social relations which allows for its expression. But the expression of hegemony does have its own character and dynamics irreducible to that out of which it emerges. The conception of hegemony as a conscious process of trying to conserve or transform social structures or relations, within very specific limitations, coincides with a critical realist perspective on social practice, outlined by Andrew Collier as:

practice tending to take over or destroy certain institutions (politics of change) or to defend them from such attacks (politics of conserving). The transformation of social structure is necessarily a political act, but their *reproduction* is not; the task of politicians who defend the existing order is not to cause its reproduction, since the system in a sense reproduces itself; it is rather to ward off threats to that reproduction.

(Collier 1989: 152–3)

From this it can be seen that hegemony implies a conception that the world is complexly structured with diverse human practices and intentional human activities. The concept, in attempting to explain the relations and conflicts between social groups, must analyse the social structures and practices through which human activity takes place or is enabled. It can show how articulated ideas and beliefs provide the causal motive present in Bhaskar's transformational model of social activity. It can provide a historical account of conjunctural moments without necessarily becoming overly historicist. It can examine the ethical and political aspects of processes while retaining an adherence to structural explanation.

Hegemony and strategy

What gives Gramsci's writings their realist nature is his attempt to theoretically analyse actual historical processes and to move from this analysis on to questions of appropriate strategy and tactics for the working class. Unlike theorists such as Lukács, Gramsci does not impose a burdensome philosophical framework on his conception of these tasks, but allows the political element to dominate. Bhaskar's pairing of Gramsci with Lukács is rather too much of a generalisation, considering that the theory of hegemony undermines the humanist notion of a universal class subject. As James Martin notes, while Lukács bestows upon the working class an a priori subjectivity, Gramsci understands that working-class consciousness is politically determined so that a process of political leadership and education is necessary if fragmented consciousness is to be overcome (Martin 1998: 152).

But even now, there are still problems. Gramsci's writings on political strategy have also become a battleground for competing tendencies. This is helped by the confusions that Anderson, among others, has outlined concerning Gramsci's positions on hegemony, the state and civil society. This has important political consequences and the Euro-communist movement, in particular, has been quick to seize on Gramsci in order to theoretically justify its own strategy. The slow battle of attrition that Gramsci describes as the war of positions has been interpreted by the Euro-communists as supporting a gradual capture of the institutions of civil society as an alternative to a full confrontation with the power of the state. It is certainly possible to support the Euro-communist position with arguments from Gramsci's writings and a critique of this reformist strategy would argue that he places too much emphasis on the ability of the working class to win sections of civil society *prior* to the revolution. Ernest Mandel writes the standard critique of Gramsci which is essentially correct (Mandel 1978c). He argues against the possibility of constructing and maintaining a hegemonic alliance through a long drawn-out process of a war of positions, believing that a strategy that seeks to capture civil society before any war of manoeuvre against the state ends up yielding to reformism. This can be attributed to the fact that the proletariat, while it is the agent of social change, is also economically – and thus to a large extent politically and culturally – disenfranchised. A hegemonic capture of civil society might have been possible for the property-owning bourgeoisie under feudalism, but it is not possible in the same way for the working class under capitalism. It is not possible, therefore, for the working-class bloc to maintain itself over a long period on such limited resources. Rather, Mandel argues, the revolutionary struggle comes quickly and decisively. Any attempt to maintain a bloc over a longer period cannot but become an accommodation to bourgeois society.

But while this is certainly true and must be stated against those who advocate such a strategy, this does not mean that the struggle for hegemony is not a valid strategy. Certainly a Euro-communist-type strategy that attempts to capture civil society without confronting state power will fail, or become bourgeois, but on the other hand, without some kind of strategy the 'decisive moment' that Mandel talks of will never arrive. Only a coherent strategy can give spontaneous developments a revolutionary outcome and this involves a struggle for political leadership across civil society in the here and now.

Mandel is not entirely correct when he suggests that Gramsci over-estimates the ability of the working class to achieve dominance. For Gramsci makes a very important distinction between dominance and leadership (or in other translations, rulership). The latter is a much more creative and flexible process which does not depend upon absolute dominance although it seeks to achieve it. This is made clear in Gramsci's quote:

> The politico-historical criterion on which our own inquiries must be grounded is this: that a class is dominant in two ways, namely it is 'leading' and 'dominant'. It leads the allied classes, it dominates the opposing classes. Therefore, a class can (and must) 'lead' even before assuming power; when it is in power it becomes dominant, but it also continues to 'lead'.[3]

This is the important strategic issue that should be taken up from Gramsci's work. It is not possible to reduce the struggle for leadership to the question of the ability to take power. The struggle for leadership is a constant process by which the working-class leadership advances its alternative proposals and fights for its political independence. Because the terrain on which the revolutionary forces fight is a complex and differentiated one, the question of leadership takes on different forms and nuances. For Gramsci, revolutionaries must be prepared to fight within each of these areas for leadership – *whether or not this can be achieved* – by advancing political demands and seeking to build up their own hegemony and to link the struggles across the board. Without such a strategy, spontaneous developments will simply pass by and a real mass base will never be created. The war of manoeuvre can only be reached after such wars of positions.

Such a hegemonic strategy takes account not just of the problems of organising revolutionary forces, but of the conditions under which this organisation takes place. Hegemony is not just a good idea, one plan among many, but the only realistic way of organising political forces given the nature of the social character of these forces. The working class is not a homogenous bloc. It is therefore necessary for a hegemonic project to unite these different groups, as well as the potential allies of the working class. But this can only be done through leadership.

3 Classical Marxism
Lenin and Trotsky

Introduction

The central argument of the last chapter is that while Gramsci often subscribes to an openly idealist or subjectivist philosophy, his political analysis embraces important aspects of realism derived, first, from Machiavelli's practical or empirical realism (which has an anti-speculative character), and second, from the notion, implicit in his conception of hegemony, of an open and stratified social totality. The argument, therefore, is that Gramsci's realism comes not from his explicit philosophical framework but from his analysis of actual political processes and the *implicitly* realist method he uses. Hegemony becomes a realist concept once it is separated from Gramsci's talk of human will and is instead linked to real material processes and class relations.

If it is the case, therefore, that Gramsci embraces a sort of realism through his sophisticated political analysis, then so too, this chapter will argue, do Lenin and Trotsky. Indeed, we can go further and argue that the way in which Lenin and Trotsky analyse concrete political situations allows us to extract an implicit notion of hegemony. This runs contrary to claims that Lenin and Trotsky's analysis is unsophisticated, wooden and dogmatic. Indeed, Euro-communists have made much of the fact that Lenin and Trotsky's analysis can explain, at best, only the situation in the East. Gramsci is seen, therefore, as an *alternative* to classical Marxism, a 'theorist of the West'. However, such a view does not square with an analysis of what these writers actually say. For example, Lenin acknowledged that:

> The whole difficulty of the Russian revolution is that it was much easier for the Russian revolutionary working class to start than it is for the West European classes, but it is much more difficult for us to continue. It is more difficult to start a revolution in West European countries because there the revolutionary proletariat is opposed by the higher thinking that comes with culture, while the working class is in a state of cultural slavery.
>
> (Lenin 1965b: 464)

It must be noted that much of Lenin and Trotsky's writings on the West are partial, sketchy, sometimes downright wrong, the point is not to take up these works, as many on the left have done, and use them as definitive statements. More interesting is that Lenin and Trotsky recognise the different conditions existing in these countries, as many on the left in fact do not, and they recognise that a detailed study of Western societies is necessary if the socialist movement is to gain any ground. This chapter will look at how Lenin and Trotsky, like Gramsci, distinguish between conditions in the East and conditions in the West, and how hegemony emerges as an important, though often implicit, concept. This chapter will also examine how such unpopular notions as the united front and democratic centralism flow from a keen understanding of how hegemony operates, and that in contrast to many more idealist alternatives, they may be said to contain a realist understanding of the world *as it is* rather than as many socialists would want it to be.

The early Lenin

Lenin's early writings develop the theme that the proletariat fights for its hegemony in the context of the struggle for bourgeois-democratic demands and he is influenced by older Russian writers like Akselrod who talks of 'the hegemony of the proletariat in the democratic revolution' (Harding 1977: 47). Lenin therefore associates the striving for proletarian hegemony with a principled and consistent struggle for radical democratic demands. In fact it is not the bourgeoisie but the proletariat that is best able to display these fighting qualities:

> From the proletarian point of view hegemony in a war goes to him who fights most energetically, who never misses a chance to strike a blow at the enemy, who always suits the action to the word, who is therefore the ideological leader of the democratic forces, who criticises half-way policies of every kind.
>
> (Lenin 1962a: 79)

According to Lenin's early view, the role of the working class is limited by objective circumstances – the stage of development of the Russian economy and civil society. However, it is still possible for the working class to play an active and radical role in fighting to extend the boundaries of political debate and struggle. Lenin makes this point in his *Two Tactics of Social-Democracy in the Democratic Revolution*:

> We cannot jump out of the bourgeois-democratic boundaries of the Russian revolution, but we can vastly extend these boundaries, and within these boundaries we can and must fight for the interests of the proletariat ....
>
> (Lenin 1975a: 47)

However, as Lenin developed his idea of class leadership, based on the vanguard of the working class and the struggle for political independence from other classes, his concept of hegemony gets more closely attached to the struggle for state power and the application of the leading role of the proletariat through the state. The struggle around national-democratic demands grows into a struggle for political independence and working-class forms of democracy. The context of national-democratic demands soon gets superseded by the need to take power, and working-class hegemony is secured during the course of this struggle. Lenin's theory therefore leads to an acceptance of a process of permanent revolution. In the same sense that Marx used the term,[1] the working class initially struggles to carry the bourgeois-democratic revolution to its conclusion, to make its demands permanent. But in doing so, the working class moves naturally into the struggle for its own demands and interests. This is in contrast to the mechanical materialism of Second International leaders who tend to give history an inevitability which opens the door to an opportunist political practice. This connection is best expressed in Kautsky's notorious declaration that: 'Our task is not to organise the revolution, but to organise ourselves *for* the revolution; it is not to *make* the revolution, but *to take advantage of it*' (quoted in Salvadori 1990: 21). Hence there is no need for any active revolutionary practice. Instead, the task of the workers' organisations is limited to the struggle for reforms that improve the conditions of workers under capitalism. This reformist practice is tied to a reliance on the capitalist state, and once those states had entered into world war, the Social Democrats followed with them.

Lenin's philosophical writings attempt to avoid this mechanical materialism by returning the active political element to history. It is true that Lenin's philosophical work *Materialism and Empirio-Criticism*, written in 1908, still has a rather crude and mechanical materialism. In fact, this more mechanical outlook matches Lenin's political positions and the view that the Russian revolution had to complete its bourgeois-democratic 'phase' before a workers' revolution was possible. Philosophically, Lenin argues in this early work that thought is a 'reflection' of reality (Lenin 1976b: 195, 218). However, the later *Philosophical Notebooks* displays a changed approach. Thought may still be a reflection of reality but this is given a more complex basis, developed through abstractions, concepts and laws, which act to mediate the process (Lenin 1961:182). Thought is given a more dynamic role, the active element is restored. Therefore, although thought–reality and politics–history are distinct relations, Lenin's philosophical shift gives both the former elements – thought and politics – a more dynamic character. In critical realist terminology, we could say that Lenin is giving more weight to the transitive domain of thought, knowledge and political practice.

Lenin has a basic realism that insists on the separation of thought and matter. But by breaking with the mechanistic view of history, Lenin is able to see these material processes as a specific combination of different contradictory factors. Lenin's theorisation of political practice flows from his analysis of the dynamics of the objective situation. The study of the dynamics of the imperialist phase of capitalism is therefore Lenin's starting point. Social concentration leads to monopoly. The ownership of capital is separated from the application of that capital to production. Finance capital is separated from productive capital. This makes capital more mobile and more parasitic. It also leads to an imperialist foreign policy reflected in wars and state rivalries.

Lenin's political concepts and ideas are given a very precise form based on the objective context. He takes up the matter of democracy not as some kind of abstract or universal ideal, but as a product of concrete circumstances. For Lenin, the question is not what is democracy, but what does democracy mean in the imperialist epoch? What does it mean in Russia or in Germany in this epoch? From this flow tactical and strategic questions concerned with how the working class should take up the struggle. For Lenin, the sell-out leaders of the Second International had failed to address these questions. Their general formulations were flawed by a failure to relate concrete demands to the reality of the objective context, the political and economic dynamics. Thus, in criticising Kautsky's reformism he writes that:

> Kautsky broke with Marxism by advocating in the epoch of finance capital a 'reactionary ideal,' 'peaceful democracy,' 'the mere operation of economic factors,' for *objectively* this ideal drags us back from monopoly to non-monopolist capitalism, and is a reformist swindle.
>
> (Lenin 1975b: 136)

However, Kautsky himself was not simply inventing his false concepts. His ideas were likewise a product of the objective situation. Social democracy, in its legal form, had come to represent certain privileges; first, the benefits gained by the Western European working class through the development of imperialism; second, the benefits gained by a particular layer of this working class, the labour aristocracy, who had more exclusive interests. Lenin's analysis of the development of the working class and its political parties saw it in this stratified or layered form. The revisionists were theorising objective developments: the development of a conservative layer of the working class, the labour aristocracy, the sectoral interests of the labour bureaucracy, the relationship of those parties to the state and so on. As Lukács puts it, revisionism is tied to realpolitik (Lukács 1971: 56). Lenin's cruder but more graphic explanation is that:

> The social-chauvinists are ... *bourgeois* within the working-class movement. They represent a stratum, or groups, or sections of the working class which *objectively* have been bribed by the bourgeoisie (by better

wages, positions of honour, etc.), and which help *their own* bourgeoisie to plunder and oppress small and weak peoples and to fight *for* the division of the capitalist spoils.

(Lenin 1971: 99)

We can therefore draw out Lenin's full position. The objective situation is dominated by the imperialist phase of capitalism and colonial exploitation, which gives rise to new social compositions. Ruling blocs can be strengthened by the incorporation of privileged sections of the working class, a project that also has the effect of undermining working-class hegemony. The task of revolutionary socialists is therefore to fight for the political independence of the working class and to break the alliances with the bourgeoisie and the state. Any alliance with the petite bourgeoisie must involve resolving the contradictions that oppose the petite bourgeoisie to the working class and winning them to the hegemony of the proletariat. This will be part of a general process in which the ruling class suffers a crisis of hegemony while the working class strengthens its counter-hegemony. A revolutionary situation emerges:

> when it is impossible for the ruling class to maintain their rule without any change; when there is a crisis, in one form or another, among the 'upper classes', a crisis in the policy of the ruling class, leading to a fissure through which the discontent and indication of the oppressed classes burst forth.
>
> (Lenin 1964: 213)

A revolutionary situation does not depend simply on the position of the working class. It requires a simultaneous crisis of bourgeois hegemony located within a structural crisis of society. Thus:

> for a revolution to take place it is not enough for the exploited and oppressed masses to realise the impossibility of living in the old way, and demand changes; for a revolution to take place it is essential that the exploiters should not be able to live and rule in the old way. It is only when the *'lower classes' do not want* to live in the old way and the 'upper classes' *cannot carry on in the old way* that the revolution can triumph ... revolution is impossible without a nation-wide crisis.
>
> (Lenin 1950: 69)

The totality of these objective changes is a revolutionary situation. Lenin allows for a regeneration of a concept of hegemony by breaking political analysis and strategy from the viewpoint of mechanical materialism and making the subjective factor once more a necessary component of the revolution itself. Lenin's implicit conception of hegemony is tied both to an analysis of the objective situation and to the tasks facing the working class.

The next section will look at how this relationship now develops through Lenin's understanding of the proletarian dictatorship.

Lenin and the dictatorship of the proletariat

The concept of the dictatorship of the proletariat can be found in Marx and his writings on the Paris Commune, but it is Lenin who really takes it up and develops it. According to Lenin, the need for the dictatorship of the proletariat is demanded by the nature of the objective situation – the social crisis and the need for restructuring and defence against hostile forces – and because of the disenfranchised nature of the working class and the difficulty it has in securing hegemony through the normal channels of civil society. Lenin's analysis of Russian society led him to the conclusion that a situation of dual power existed. In effect, two opposed hegemonies stood side by side. Alongside the bourgeois government stood what effectively amounted to a workers' government based on the soviets or workers' councils. These bodies had sprung up from below and developed their own rules and laws and other forms of proletarian democracy. Lenin's new position on permanent revolution led him to the conclusion that although state power was in the hands of the bourgeoisie, overall political power was passing over to the soviets. The March revolution prepared this situation and showed that two powers cannot exist together within the same state. The situation of dual power therefore represents a transitional phase in the revolution's development (Lenin 1971: 84). Consequently, the dictatorship of the proletariat was the only realistic course; power must go in one direction or another, the only alternative being bourgeois dictatorship. For Lenin, the idea that there might be a third way is petit-bourgeois utopianism that flies in the face of the objective situation (Lenin 1965a: 463–4). As Balibar has argued, the dictatorship of the proletariat is neither a tactic nor a strategy but a *reality* borne out of a historical tendency, rooted in the nature of capitalism and the painful transition out of it (Balibar 1977: 134).

Kautsky's opposition to the revolution and his talk of democracy is therefore meaningless. Lenin argues that Kautsky has become a liberal who talks of democracy but fails to ask for what class. Instead, Kautsky talks of pure, non-class or above-class democracy, formulations that fail to take into account existing reality (Lenin 1970: 29). In any case, the system of bourgeois democracy had itself been established through a violent dictatorship over the majority of the population while, in contrast, the proletarian dictatorship aims at repressing only the violent minority of the population – the counter-revolutionary bourgeoisie. However, the international situation means that the transition to socialism will take an entire epoch or as long as the bourgeoisie still cherishes the hope of restoration (Lenin 1970: 35). Consequently, the proletariat needs to establish its hegemony through state power. It is only after victory that it can hope to win the support of the majority of the population. Then state power can be used to win over the masses from the bourgeois and petit-bourgeois forces. Lenin writes:

> the proletariat must first overthrow the bourgeoisie and win *for itself* state power, and then use that state power, that is, the dictatorship of the proletariat, as an instrument of its class for the purpose of winning the sympathy of the majority of the working people.
>
> (Lenin 1965c: 263)

The proletarian dictatorship is therefore not simply a negative concept to keep control, but the most realistic way of using and directing state power to win over the masses and to demonstrate the superiority of working-class rule. Like all hegemonies, this is based on coercion and consent:

> The dictatorship of the proletariat means a persistent struggle – bloody and bloodless, violent and peaceful, military and economic, educational and administrative – against the forces and traditions of the old society.
>
> (Lenin 1950: 30)

Christine Buci-Glucksmann rightly argues that Lenin's concept of hegemony is not synonymous with the dictatorship of the proletariat. Hegemony is the function of the working class as a whole (Buci-Glucksmann 1980: 179). The relationship to the vanguard is a dialectical one. She likens Lenin's formulation to Gramsci's because:

> In both cases, what is involved is a concept closely linked to that of the dictatorship of the proletariat, without however being identical with this. Hegemony *qualifies* the proletarian dictatorship, in particular its expansive character.
>
> (Buci-Glucksmann 1980: 182)

This is reflected in Lenin's distinction between the party, the vanguard and the masses which is implicitly realist in the sense that it recognises the stratification of social structures, agents and activities. It argues that certain social agents, certain sections of the working class, are better positioned, more conscious and better able to play a leading role in the revolutionary struggle. But Lenin does not lose sight of the fact that although the party will play a leading and directing role, the aim is to establish the social hegemony of the working class as a whole. For example, Lenin disagreed with Trotsky's view that the trade unions should be brought under direct party control, as the trade unions, along with the soviets, represented the *social* hegemony of the working class as a whole. The dictatorship of the proletariat concerns the more specific *political* role given to the party and the vanguard. The latter role is one of direction and leadership, but its aim should always be to secure the hegemony of the working class in its broadest sense. If there is a problem with the Leninist legacy, it derives not so much from Lenin's actual arguments, but from the way in which the question of the social hegemony of the working class has been replaced with the leading role of the party. The degeneration of the Russian revolution brought about a situation where the party continued to lead, but where the social hegemony of the working class was broken up, fragmented and atomised.

Democratic centralism and the theory of hegemony

Democratic centralism is today regarded as an outdated product of Russian political conditions, while in a postmodern vein, former Marxists oppose democratic centralism claiming that because today's world is supposedly more complex and heterogeneous, political organisation must be founded on some sort of democratic pluralism. But it could be countered that it is precisely because reality is complexly structured and diverse that organisational discipline is necessary if any meaningful social change is to occur. To argue for a loose pluralism as an alternative to centralisation is to play the game on capitalism's terms. In fact the ideology of postmodernism could be said to be less of a coherent hegemonic ideology of the ruling class, more a deliberate attempt to de-hegemonise any potential opposition. As effective leadership and direction are removed, any attempt at a hegemonic project descends into incoherence. The pluralism of post-modernism soon passes over into fragmentation and the reinforcing of alienated identities. Lenin's theory, by contrast, attempts to connect a theory of organisation to a hegemonic project. His writings on democratic centralism should not therefore be viewed as mere organisational concerns, they are political matters relating to the organisation of the political vanguard and through them the wider social forces. Hence democratic centralism refers to the organisation of the party as a *vanguard party*. Recognising the stratified nature of social groups and classes, the Leninist theory of organisation seeks to relate first to the political vanguard and the most advanced workers and through them to the broader masses.

Although there are competing definitions, the vanguard can generally be defined as the most politically developed sections of the working class with good political instincts formed by participation in the class struggle. As opposed to the passivity of the mechanistic outlook, Leninism's historic break with social democracy is founded on an idea of the revolutionary party as an *active* and *organic* party which relates to the political vanguard by organising it. Democratic centralism therefore extends beyond the organisation of the party to the vanguard as well:

> The democratic centralism of the Communist Party organisation should be a real synthesis, a fusion of centralism and proletarian democracy. This fusion can be achieved only when the Party organisation *works* and

struggles at all times together, as a united whole. Centralisation in the Communist Party does not mean formal, mechanical centralisation, but the *centralisation of Communist activity*, i.e., the creation of a leadership that is strong and effective and at the same time flexible.

(Alder 1983: 235)

In this sense Leninism is conceived as a *more* democratic form of organisation than social democratic reformism. It rests on activity, organisation and participation. In contrast, social democracy rests on a passive relationship to its base, organising it socially, but keeping it separate from the political leadership. Leninism sees itself as organising the most conscious layers in society and directing them through hegemonic leadership. This means that the revolutionary party takes on an important role and status, hence Lenin's famous words:

Class political consciousness can be brought to the workers *only from without*, that is, only from outside the economic struggle, from outside the sphere of relations between workers and employers. The sphere from which alone it is possible to obtain this knowledge is the sphere of relationships of *all* classes and strata to the state and the government ....

(Lenin 1947: 75)

There have been lots of objections to this passage, accompanied by a tendency to forget the particular conditions under which Lenin was writing. What does seem clear is Lenin's rejection of adapting to spontaneous class consciousness, in particular, economism and syndicalism. It is not so much the matter of Lenin's supposed elitism, but the problem of organising under difficult conditions that seems to be the real issue here. Given these conditions, spontaneous struggles are not enough, clear direction and leadership are required. Thus Lenin writes: 'We must "go among all classes of the population" as theoreticians, as propagandists, as agitators, and as organisers' (Lenin 1947: 78). Lenin argues that although the party is involved in the day-to-day struggles of the workers, it stands above them in that its understanding of society is not reducible to day-to-day events. Lenin is saying that class political consciousness needs organisation and leadership, which cannot be established through adaptation to spontaneous consciousness or the sectoral interests of particular groups. Marxist consciousness must attempt to see things in their totality, and the party, therefore, is not simply an amalgam of different experiences, but represents an attempt to collectivise these experiences on a higher plane. By stressing the need for the most advanced theory (Lenin 1947: 27), Lenin rejects the empiricist view that the party represents the mere collectivisation of experiences. Experience alone is only partial and often misleading. The party must know something of the totality of structures, relations and conditions in which these experiences take place.

There are three dialectical relationships contained in the concept of democratic centralism. First is the differentiation between democratic centralism in theory – as a principle of organisation – and democratic centralism in practice – as related to specific tasks. The former is irreducible to the latter although the latter may modify and inform it. Second, democratic centralism needs to be seen as a specifically organisational question *and* as an eminently political matter. Political and organisational matters are both unified and distinctive. There are clearly dangers presented by both aspects – an overly formalistic form of organisation leads to bureaucracy, pedantry and possible dictatorship, while a form of organisation that becomes overly political or partisan loses its impartiality and even-handedness. Finally, there is the difficult relationship between the democratic and the centralist components of the concepts, where again one may undermine the other. The normal view is that centralisation undermines democracy, but this need not be the case. The centralisation of party discipline is often a product of particular circumstances that unfortunately friend and foe alike tend to regard as the norm, accepting, for example, the strictures of works like *What is to be Done?* as definitive statements. In actual fact, democratic centralism is supposed to act as a guarantee of democracy, seeking to allow for the fullest freedom of discussion and internal debate while recognising the need for the party to offer clear direction and leadership in action. This is based on the recognition that the revolutionary party seeks not merely to intervene, but to hegemonise. That such a means of organisation is necessary is derived from the role the party is required to play and the tasks that it faces. Of course, the very practical and political nature of these tasks means that it is possible to abuse democratic centralism. But again, a process such as the Stalinisation of the CPSU and abuse of power cannot be seen in isolation from the very real and material pressures being exerted.

Gramsci described the Communist Party as the 'modern prince', and the functioning of democratic centralism depends on a practical realist view of the world. It is based on the practical needs of the struggle for hegemonic power – as opposed to idealist notions of democratic plurality – and the tasks facing the working class. This is so precisely because the masses are seen as diverse rather than homogeneous. The real world is seen as a complex set of relations into which the party must intervene. This complexity requires that the party is unified in its activity and that it seeks to unify the vanguard around it. Given the complexity of the real world and the diversity of its terrain, the key political struggle is therefore to capture state power in order to organise and direct the necessary changes. It is here that the concept of democratic centralism flows into that of the dictatorship of the proletariat, but it should also be related to the wider struggle for political hegemony that seeks to organise the vanguard around the party and the masses around the vanguard, while recognising the need to secure the hegemony of the working class in its broadest sense. The party needs to be centralised in order to play a clear and leading role. Within the party there is freedom of discussion, but this discussion must be reconciled with clear leadership. Hence the slogan, freedom of discussion, unity of action (Lenin 1962b: 380).

Trotsky's understanding of difficulties

Gramsci and others are wrong to accuse Trotsky of favouring frontal offensives against a war of positions (Gramsci 1971: 236). Trotsky argues that a revolutionary situation does not develop uniformly, but by successive waves of ebb and flow. The possibility of a frontal attack on the Russian state is attributed to the peculiarities of Russian combined and uneven development. In the West, as Trotsky frequently states, a more careful war of positions must take place. It is therefore:

> necessary to understand that it will not be possible to overthrow the bourgeoisie automatically, mechanically, merely because it is condemned by history. On the highly complex field of political struggle we find, on the one side, the bourgeoisie with its forces and resources and, on the opposing side, the working class with its various layers, moods, levels of development, with its Communist Party struggling against other parties and organisations for influence over the working masses. In this struggle the Communist Party ... has to manoeuvre, now attacking, now retreating, always consolidating its influence, conquering new positions until the favourable moment arrives for the overthrow of the bourgeoisie.
>
> (Trotsky 1974a: 7)

This quote combines a sophisticated understanding of the complex field of political struggle with its different layers, forces and levels of understanding, and the complex tactics of manoeuvre. The situation in Russia is clearly not simply that of a frontal assault. In any case:

> The ease with which we conquered power on November 7, 1917, was paid for by the countless sacrifices of the Civil War. In countries that are older in the capitalist sense, and with a higher culture, the situation will, without doubt, differ profoundly. In these countries the popular masses will enter the revolution far more fully formed in political respects.
>
> (Trotsky 1974a: 221)

Trotsky repeatedly makes the point that an underdeveloped civil society makes the capture of state power easier. However, it also makes the maintenance of state power more difficult. The proletariat will have to slowly extend its hegemony through the development of a stronger civil base. In the West, on the other hand, the proletariat faces a more difficult initial struggle for power and it will be hard to build up its bases in civil society. However:

> after the conquest of power, the European proletariat will in all likelihood have far more elbow room for its creative work in economy and culture than we had in Russia on the day after the overturn. The more difficult and gruelling the struggle for state power, all the less possible will it be to challenge the proletariat's power after the victory.
>
> (Trotsky 1974a: 222)

Such statements are commonplace in Trotsky.[2] This chapter will therefore look first at his writings on the East and his understanding of the process of combined and uneven development in more backward countries, then look at his analysis of the West with its more developed conditions.

Combined and uneven development and permanent revolution

Trotsky's theory of permanent revolution flows from his analysis of combined and uneven development. For the purposes of a realist understanding – to avoid voluntarism or excessive objectivism – it is necessary to maintain the distinction between these two concepts. Combined and uneven development is an objective process and is a phenomenon of the more backward nations which are subjected to a peculiar combination of different stages of the historical process. Under pressure from external influences these countries are forced to modernise and develop capitalist features, to take up new forms of economic production and social organisation. This leads to a strengthening of the working class but these developments are combined with a backwardness of culture and a strong agrarian base. This gives the country's development an uneven character. The bourgeoisie is in a weak and compromised position and is almost entirely dependent on foreign capital and investment. It thus assumes a comprador character without establishing strong national roots. It cannot command a social base of support and is overly reliant on the power of the state. It is unable to play a hegemonising role due to its inability to give national and democratic leadership, and it suffers a chronic weakness, opening up possibilities for a working-class challenge to its authority.

> Living historic societies are inharmonious through and through, and the more so the more delayed their development. The fact that in a backward country like Russia the bourgeoisie had decayed before the complete victory of the bourgeois regime, and that there was nobody but the proletariat to replace it in the position of national leadership, was an expression of this inharmony.
>
> (Trotsky 1977a: 334–5)

From these features of combined and uneven development Trotsky develops the theory of permanent revolution. Objective conditions prevent the bourgeoisie from playing a leading role and render it incapable of uniting the nation around a set of national and democratic demands. It is caught between the peasantry, the feudal aristocracy, foreign capital and the developing working class. From this analysis Trotsky develops a new understanding of hegemony and the historical tasks of the working class. The bourgeoisie is unable to carry through the tasks of the democratic revolution. The peasantry, despite forming the majority of the population, is incapable of playing any kind of independent role. The rest of the petite bourgeoisie is similarly incapable of economic and political independence and is subject to deep internal division. Given that the bourgeoisie is unable to accomplish its national-democratic tasks, it is necessary that the proletariat hegemonises the masses under its own leadership. By doing so it takes the struggle beyond the limits of the specific democratic demands. The peculiarities of combined and uneven development and the dynamic of permanent revolution give the working class an *objectively* revolutionary role. However, while these possibilities are objective, the success of the working class depends on subjective factors of leadership and proletarian hegemony. The working class must be able to successfully construct and maintain its alliances and to resolve the problems being faced by the peasantry.

Here, Trotsky's notion of hegemony is highly developed. Leaving aside the matter of how the word itself is used, it is commonly argued that while Lenin and Trotsky had an idea of hegemony in relation to working-class leadership, they did not extend this hegemonic role to class leadership in general. Only Gramsci, it is argued, applied the matter of hegemony to the ruling class as well. Yet Trotsky argues:

> no historic class lifts itself from a subject position to a position of rulership suddenly in one night ... It must already on the eve of the revolution have assumed a very independent attitude towards the official ruling class; moreover, it must have focused upon itself the hopes of intermediate classes and layers, dissatisfied with the existing state of affairs, but not capable of playing an independent role. The historic preparation of a revolution brings about, in the pre-revolutionary period, a situation in which the class which is called to realise the new social system, although not yet master of the country, has already concentrated in its hands a significant share of the state power ... [But] If the new class ... [is] placed in power by a revolution which it did not want, [it] is in essence an already old, historically belated, class.
>
> (Trotsky 1977a: 223–4)

Objective conditions would allow the working class to seize power in Russia, but would also constrain the exercise of that power and its ability to maintain its alliances. The task of constructing a firmer socialist hegemony throughout society is dependent on the victory of the stronger, more developed proletariat in Western Europe. This is in line with the position that it will be easier to seize power in the East, but more difficult, owing to the deficiencies of economic and civil society, to maintain social control. The revolution must not just be permanent in the sense that it extends beyond the unsolved national and democratic demands, but must extend beyond the nation itself.

In advancing these perspectives, Trotsky struggles to break from pro-ductive forces determinism and the associated schematic view of history:

> But the day and the hour when power will pass into the hands of the working class depends directly not upon the level attained by the productive forces but upon relations in the class struggle, upon the international situation, and, finally, upon a number of subjective factors: the traditions, the initiative and the readiness to fight of the workers.
>
> (Trotsky 1969a: 62–3)

This is what makes possible a meaningful theory of hegemony. Although Trotsky often does succumb to economic determinism (particularly in his later views on the historical stagnation of the productive forces), it is also possible to find him arguing against such views. In the above passage he argues that history is not a predetermined process that passes from one period to another in a mechanical way. Rather, it combines different, often opposing, elements. In Russia these conditions seriously constrained the ability of the bourgeoisie to play a leading and dominant role. Its hegemony could be challenged by the working class due to the peculiar historical conditions. From these conditions, and from the objective needs of the workers and the peasants, Trotsky articulates the historical tasks facing the working class. It is necessary for the workers to lead an alliance with the peasantry and it is necessary to take up national and democratic demands. It is also necessary to go beyond these, and Trotsky's theory of hegemony therefore extends beyond the specific concerns of the working class to raise a number of questions pertinent to hegemony in general: What are the possibilities of assuming an independent role? How does a group relate to intermediate layers? When does a class exhaust its historic role and when can another class assume its?

Writings on the West

It is clear from an analysis of Trotsky's writings on Russia and China that the Eastern states are not to be dealt with by straightforward frontal attack. The peculiar objective conditions and the weakness of bourgeois hegemony gives the working class particular possibilities; however, taking state power is still a complicated tactical affair. In any case, the division between East and West should not be seen as a division between wars of manoeuvre and position. It should be seen in terms of different objective conditions, different levels of historical development, different degrees of class consciousness and specific hegemonic relations. These vary from one state to another and tactics must be assessed in relation to the particular situation, whether in the East or the West.

Trotsky's writings on Britain represent an analysis of a particularly stable and hegemonic situation which, nevertheless, is beginning to fall into decline. The working class is potentially very strong and its consent is therefore vital to the ruling class. Trotsky notes that 'the organised unity of the working class has long existed in England' but unfortunately this cohesiveness has been achieved through 'the political unity of the working class with the imperialist bourgeoisie' (Trotsky 1977b: 65). Of particular importance here is the role played by social democracy in relation to the interests of the ruling class and the struggles of the working class. A party such as the Labour Party is a workers' party by virtue of its base in the working class and its relation to the trades unions. Its politics, however, are those of class compromise. The interests of the social democratic leaders are tied to the capitalist state and the bourgeois nation. Through the complicity of social democracy the bourgeoisie is able to build a historical bloc which incorporates the labour bureaucracy as subordinate allies of the ruling class. The British state rests on the back of the working class through the intermediacy of this bureaucracy (Trotsky 1974d, vol. 2: 248).

With such an entrenched bourgeoisie, revolutionary tactics require patience and serious preparation. An important task in the struggle for leadership is to expose the labour bureaucrats in the eyes of the masses by revealing their subordination to the hegemony of the bourgeoisie. For Trotsky this is achieved through the tactic of the united front, which calls for united working-class action and in so doing seeks to put the labour bureaucrats on the spot, forcing them to choose sides. The united front attempts to mobilise the rank and file of workers while highlighting the weakness of their leaders. It is part of a wider strategy to win their base away from them.

There is no doubt that Trotsky's analysis has its schematic side. Britain is an economically advanced society which gives a firmer base to the 'superstructural' forms of civil society. The ruling class then makes use of this to secure consent through ideological means. In adopting this position Trotsky combines a degree of economic determinism with an instru-mentalist conception of class rule. At its worst moment this leads Trotsky to make wild predictions about the coming British revolution based on selected empirical evidence, mainly centred on various political crises. The fact that these crises did not lead to a revolutionary situation is often attributed solely to the crisis of working-class leadership. Its failure to materialise, a result of the treachery of the social democratic leaders. This ignores the real material forces, the ideological and political structures which, among other things, determine the role of the social democrats. Hegemony, for Trotsky, is given a more shallow, surface role concerned with the way in which classes organise and articulate themselves. When this organisation is seen to be in crisis, Trotsky mistakenly sees this as a crisis of the whole system. He fails to see that hegemony has a deeper, more material basis as inscribed into the structures of social life, as securing the cohesion of the social whole. Hegemony is seen in an instrumental rather than in a structural way.

However, it is also possible to find in Trotsky a partial rejection of crude determinism even if he does remain trapped within the base-superstructure metaphor. The relationship between the two is given a more complex character. It has its own particular forms rather than some universalistic basis. And determination, as Althusser might say, is only in the last analysis. Trotsky writes:

> the question itself boils down to the inter-relation between the basis and the superstructure and to the inter-relation of bases and superstructures of different countries with one another. We know that superstructures – state, law, politics, parties and so on – arise on an economic basis, are nourished and determined by this basis. Consequently, basis and superstructures have to correspond. And this happens in fact, only not simply but in a very complicated way. A powerful development of superstructure (the bourgeois state, bourgeois parties, bourgeois culture) sometimes holds back for a long time the development of the other superstructures (the revolutionary proletarian party), but in the last analysis – in the *last analysis*, not immediately, the basis reveals itself nevertheless as a decisive force.
>
> (Trotsky 1974d, vol. 1: 27–8)

Further, Trotsky's method at least allows for a concept of hegemony which is more than most deterministic analyses allow. Although this needs to be given a firmer basis, Trotsky is able to pick out the main features of a hegemonic crisis. The crisis of historical leadership has a particular importance regarding the petite bourgeoisie, the class historically caught between the two main classes and which looks to them for leadership. On the situation in France, Trotsky writes that:

> The political crisis of the country is above all a collapse of the confidence of the petty bourgeois masses in their traditional parties and leaders. *The discontent, the nervousness, the instability, the fluidity of the petty bourgeoisie* are extremely important characteristics of a pre-revolutionary situation.
>
> (Trotsky 1974c: 46)

The position of the petite bourgeoisie would be crucial to Trotsky's analysis of fascism in Germany and Spain. The failure of the working class to exert leadership over this layer would result in the petite bourgeoisie becoming the focus of reaction and counter-revolution. On Spain, Trotsky's subject-matter is similar to Gramsci's Italy. In particular, Spain is seen as an example of a weak bourgeoisie unable to provide national leadership and offer itself as a hegemonising force. In contrast to the hegemonic position of the British bourgeoisie:

> The history of Spain is the history of continual revolutionary convulsions ... The petty rivalry of the juntas was only the outward expression of the Spanish revolution's lack of a leading class. Precisely because of this, the monarchy triumphed over each new revolution. A short time after the triumph of order, however, the chronic crisis once more broke through. Not one of the many regimes that supplanted each other sank deep enough roots into the soil.
>
> (Trotsky 1973b: 71–2)

As in Italy, the left wing of the bourgeoisie, led by young intellectuals, set itself the task of converting Spain into a republic. Catholicism led the reaction against this. The bourgeoisie was too young and too weak to remove the influence of the old feudal order. Hence 'the cracks and gaps of bourgeois society are filled in Spain with declassed elements of the ruling classes, the numerous seekers of positions and income'(Trotsky 1973b: 72). Trotsky argues that the Spanish bourgeoisie cannot play the historic role associated with the French and British bourgeoisies. It appeared late on the scene, is dependent on foreign capital, and consequently is unable to establish for itself a sufficient social base. Its dependence on foreign capital and domestic feudal interests deprives it of independence and its ability to put itself forward as leader. In contrast to this slum leadership, at the bottom of society are slum proletarians and declassed workers. Starting from the objective situation and the position of the ruling class, Trotsky argues that the immediate task for the communists is not the struggle for power itself, but the 'struggle for the masses'(Trotsky 1973b: 128). Here is a clear case of hegemony being a prerequisite for revolution, and revolutionaries must avoid any 'premature attempts at decisive battle' (Trotsky 1973b: 130).

The struggle against fascism in Germany

Trotsky wrote that the emergence of fascism in Germany was due to a combination of factors. Underlying everything is a deep structural crisis along national and economic lines. There then exists a crisis of the ruling bloc. The working class is also beset by internal differences, a weakness that gives the petite bourgeoisie an elevated importance. Usually little more than a supporting class, the petite bourgeoisie does not have the social basis or the forms of organisation necessary to mount a challenge to the hegemony of the bourgeoisie. In particular, 'the petite bourgeoisie is *characterised by the extreme heterogeneity of its social nature.* At the bottom it fuses with the proletariat and extends into the lumpen proletariat; on top it passes over into the capitalist bourgeoisie' (Trotsky 1971: 212). It leans on various forms of production while lacking collectivity. However, despite this compromised position, the petite bourgeoisie is of immense importance to the functioning of the system:

> The economically powerful big bourgeoisie, in itself, constitutes an infinitesimal minority of the nation. To enforce its domination, it must ensure a definite mutual relationship with the petty bourgeoisie and, through its mediation, with the proletariat.
>
> (Trotsky 1971: 280)

In other words, while the big bourgeoisie may enjoy economic power, this is useless unless it can put together a political alliance which gets other classes to support its interests.

Trotsky is concerned with the moribund nature of social democracy. For him, social democracy or reformism is characteristic of petit-bourgeois influences within the workers' movement. Thus social democracy is founded on the material privileges of the labour aristocracy and on the narrow, sectoral influences of the bureaucrats and trade union leaders. It constitutes a political and ideological defence of these strata. In the case of the German SPD, its strategic relation to the capitalist state and its adaptation to parliamentary democracy meant it became increasingly tied to the interests of the system and hence to its subsequent failures. Economic crisis in turn leads to a political or hegemonic crisis in which all of the major political parties are discredited. Therefore, despite playing a subordinate role in the ruling alliance, the SPD also suffered from the crisis of leadership. And because of the SPD's relationship with the working class, the workers too faced a crisis of their own leadership.

Thus fascism arises as a mass movement as a result of a deep structural crisis which is reflected at a political level in the futility of parliamentary rule. Each of the traditional political parties suffers from a failure to give leadership. The ruling class maintains control at the economic level, but in the political sphere it suffers a crisis of political representation of these interests. The working-class organisations, in part due to their compromises with a system in decay, also fail to take control of the situation. Fascism assumes a *political* significance due to this paralysis on both sides of the class struggle. *However, it assumes this significance within the context of the ruling class maintaining economic power.*

The fascist programme is a product of the frustration of the petite bourgeoisie with the social and economic order. However, the fact that fascism can only come to power with the support of the big bourgeoisie means that this programme, as a programme aspiring to political independence, can never be implemented as intended. The fascist programme of the petite bourgeoisie becomes increasingly torn away from reality and is reduced to ritualistic acts. The illusions are reduced to a naked bureaucratic masquerade as fascism descends into Bonapartism (Trotsky 1971: 406). Consequently, Trotsky draws the conclusion that: 'Fascism is a specific means of mobilising and organising the petite bourgeoisie in the social interests of finance capital' (Trotsky 1971: 441). However, this mobilisation of the petite bourgeoisie and the demagogy of the fascists is of danger to bourgeois interests. The bourgeoisie does not therefore willingly turn to fascism. Rather, fascist rule is a last ditch attempt by the bourgeoisie to maintain power over the working class when all other means have failed. Consequently, fascism evolves out of the failure of the parliamentary system and the paralysis of social democracy, a failure of the traditional forms of political hegemony.

However, the above comments indicate that while Trotsky has the correct starting point – the structural crisis of society and the consequent crisis of social hegemony – his explanation of the role that fascism plays is increasingly an instrumentalist one. Fascism is seen as the means by which monopoly capital mobilises the petite bourgeoisie and the declassed layers against the organised working class. It attacks the parliamentary system. Fascism acts as a battering ram. It is used by the bourgeoisie to annihilate the organisations of the working class when traditional methods have failed. Once in power, the interests of finance capital predominate. A Bonapartist regime takes over (Trotsky 1971: 155–6).

This analysis is one-sided if the 'battering ram' theory is allowed to predominate. The ruling class does not simply take up fascism and decide to wield it against the working class. It is certainly true that the ruling class turns to fascism in despair, promoting it and financing it. This makes fascism's path to power all the more easy. But fascism has its own dynamics which grow out of the structural crisis. A crisis of legitimacy, of political parties, values and beliefs, reflects a deeper structural crisis. Fascism is not therefore an instrument to be used in crisis, its growth is a structural feature of the crisis itself and as such cannot be separated from it. The growth of fascism is not attributable to a hegemonic crisis at the surface level of political representation. Fascism grows out of a deeper material crisis although it manifests itself at the political and ideological level. From this, it is possible to understand the importance of achieving a social hegemony and the strategies employed by each class:

> The class itself is not homogeneous. Its different sections arrive at class consciousness by different paths and at different times. The bourgeoisie participates actively in this process. Within the working class, it creates its own institutions, or utilises those already existing, in order to oppose certain strata of workers to others. Within the proletariat several parties are active at the same time. Therefore, for the greater part of its historical journey, it remains split politically. The

problem of the united front – which arises during certain periods most sharply – originates therein.

(Trotsky 1971: 163)

This notion of class stratification could be read in an instrumentalist way as a simple case of divide-and-rule tactics. An alternative, realist analysis would instead start from the stratification and divisions that exist in society itself. Thus while divide-and-rule tactics may be a conscious project of the ruling bloc, the initial divisions are not simply a product of ruling-class actions, but are a product of real material processes and social structures that are made use of during the course of the class struggle. However, the particular nature of the dominant social structures and generative mechanisms allow for certain groups to become dominant and to construct their own hegemony out of these divisions, while placing limitations and restrictions of alternative hegemonic projects. Hegemony, given this objective casting, is about securing the cohesion of one's own side and of emphasising the divisions of one's opponent within the context of definite material relations. In this context, Trotsky's emphasis makes sense when he writes that:

Fascism is a particular governmental system based on the uprooting of all elements of proletarian democracy within bourgeois society. The task of fascism lies not only in destroying the Communist vanguard but in holding the entire class in a state of forced disunity ... It is also necessary to smash all independent and voluntary organisations, to demolish all the defensive bulwarks of the proletariat, and to uproot whatever has been achieved during three-quarters of a century by the Social Democracy and the trade unions.

(Trotsky 1971: 144)

From this analysis, Trotsky outlines the necessary strategy to confront fascism. Here, Trotsky is closest to Gramsci, whose own concept of hegemony is developed out of the need to confront the fascist threat and the disorganisation of the working class. He has a cautious approach based on the recognition that the coming struggle is principally a defensive one, albeit an active defence. He recognises that an offensive by the Communist Party would come up against the bloc between the state and the fascists and would lead to defeat. Therefore, a war of positions requires a strengthening of defences and support for the self-organisation of the working class and its institutions in society. The workers have built up their own bulwarks and strongholds – the trade unions, political parties and so on – working-class bases that social democracy has played a progressive role in building. With the fascists wishing to remove them as part of their strategy of smashing working-class power, it becomes necessary to unite with the social demo-cratic forces in a common struggle for the defence of these bodies.

This leads to the policy of the united front, which, as has been mentioned, has a dual character, for it both closes ranks with other forces against the common enemy, while at the same time raising questions of the ability of the social democratic leaders to carry through the struggle in the interests of the working class. For Trotsky, the united-front tactic is about pushing the social democrats as far as they can go in the struggle against fascism, while recognising that to fully remove the threat of fascism it is necessary to overthrow capitalism itself. This means that the united-front tactic must allow for both unity of action and the political independence of the forces concerned, or as Trotsky famously stated: 'March separately, but strike together!'

Unfortunately, Trotsky was almost alone in seeing the threat of fascism taking power. He was also alone in recognising the defensive character of the working-class struggle and the need to apply the united-front tactic between the communists and the social democrats. Trotsky criticises the Italian Communist Party, with the exception of Gramsci, for overestimating its own strength and possibilities and of underestimating the possibility of fascism coming to power. The Italian CP, including Gramsci, had always failed to understand the importance of the united-front tactic (Trotsky 1971: 191). In Germany, the Stalinists decided that there was in effect no difference between fascism and social democracy and that the condition of the working class was no better off whoever was in power. Instead of forming a bloc with the social democrats, Stalin's German puppets decided to call them social fascists and to cut themselves off from the majority of the working class. Trotsky noted with despair that:

> the proletariat is abandoning its positions without battle and is beating the retreat without plan, without system, and without direction. The enemy is unleashed to such a point that it does not constrain itself from discussing right in public where and how to strike the next blow: by frontal attack; by bearing down on the Communist left flank; by penetrating deeply at the rear of the trade unions and cutting off communications, etc. … The bourgeoisie enjoys full freedom of manoeuvre, that is, the choice of means, of time, and of place … The proletariat combines nothing at all and does not defend itself. Its troops are split up, and its chiefs discourse languidly on whether or not it is possible to combine forces.
>
> (Trotsky 1971: 350)

Bureaucratism

Although the bureaucratisation of the Soviet Union was the major theme of Trotsky's later writings, it will only briefly be dealt with here, from the point of view of its realist basis. Trotsky notes that the problem of the bureaucratic degeneration of a workers' state had not really entered into the heads of many Marxist theorists. Marx, for example, had not reckoned with a revolution in a backward country and Lenin could not have foreseen such a prolonged isolation of the Soviet state. The USSR, nevertheless, was gripped by a bureaucratically parasitic caste, a symptom of material want, cultural backwardness and the dominance of 'bourgeois law' (Trotsky 1972a: 55–6). Therefore, the force behind the Soviet bureaucracy is not Stalin or any other figure but the conditions of social and material isolation, of scarcity in objects of consumption (Trotsky 1972a: 112), of unproductive labour, of civil war and foreign intervention. Stalin arose as a Bonaparte, rising above a politically atomised society, a personification of social and material degeneration.

Trotsky links the rise of bureaucracy to 'the heterogeneity of society, the difference between the daily and the fundamental interests of various groups of the population' (Trotsky 1972b: 33). So bureaucracy arises because of a lack of hegemony in society, where it is not possible to truly reconcile the different interests of the various groups. The bureaucracy therefore rises above society imposing its own rule through the political apparatus. Its rule is based on the defence of privilege however, it is not class rule and the bureaucracy has no independent economic role or property rights. Rather, the bureaucracy feeds off the working class in parasitic fashion. Trotsky argues that to overthrow the bureaucracy a political rather than a social revolution is necessary. In making this distinction, Trotsky distinguishes between the exercise of power by a hegemonic group and the class positions that flow from the material basis of society. He defines the Soviet Union as a degenerated workers' state according to the material basis of that state and its relation to the dominant property relations, rather than according to its leadership whose own degeneration is a product of these material factors.

Culture

Trotsky's opposition to Stalin's attempt to impose a working-class culture on society was based on the recognition that socialist culture must be allowed to evolve through new social structures and material conditions. Such a process takes time and runs alongside the general transformation of society into a socialist one. Until this process is well under way, the dictatorship of the proletariat is seen as an abnormal period for art, in which it has difficulty in finding roots. It is a transitional phase born out of the fact that the working class is still unable to hegemonise all areas of social life The years of socialist revolution will be ones of fierce class struggle, in which most effort will be spent on taking and maintaining power. Only once power is achieved and established can culture start to take a new turn in its development. The working class, by definition, is culturally disenfranchised and alienated. It cannot be compared to the bourgeoisie who enjoyed a degree of cultural autonomy many years before assuming political power. Those who talk of proletarian culture in relation to bourgeois culture are therefore comparing two quite dissimilar things and are wrongly identifying the historical destiny of the proletariat with that of the bourgeoisie.

Trotsky first raised these objections in relation to the Proletkult movement which, under the influence of Bogdanov, was arguing for the development of an authentic proletarian culture. Bogdanov believed that the cultural revolution was a vital part of the social transformation, although, in keeping with his positivist materialism, he saw the process of cultural transformation in a rather mechanical way. The Proletkult movement established educational and cultural groups throughout the country, giving those involved a fair degree of autonomy. Ultimately this aroused the suspicions of Lenin and Trotsky who believed that Bogdanov was trying to build himself a power base. A directive of the Central Committee eventually closed the Proletkult down, but Trotsky (who opposed the closure) based his opposition to Proletkult more on a critique of the mistaken ideas behind the movement:

> It is fundamentally incorrect to contrast bourgeois culture and bourgeois art with proletarian culture and proletarian art. The latter will never exist, because the proletarian regime is temporary and transient. The historic significance and the moral grandeur of the proletarian revolution consists in the fact that it is laying the foundations of a culture which is above classes and which will be the first culture that is truly human.
>
> (Trotsky 1991: 50)

The proletariat, unlike other classes in history, does not have the same degree of access to property and the means of production. It cannot just make working-class culture; it must first make a revolution and hold power. This is different to the pattern of a classical bourgeois revolution where the bourgeoisie already holds a significant degree of economic and cultural hegemony. The weakness of the position of the working class in bourgeois society makes it impossible for it to establish its own hegemony to any great degree until it actually takes political power:

> The bourgeoisie came to power fully armed with the culture of its time. The proletariat, on the other hand, comes into power fully armed only with the acute need of mastering culture. The problem of a proletariat which has conquered power consists, first of all, in taking into its own hands the apparatus of culture – the industries, schools, publications, press, theatres, etc. – which did not serve it before, and thus to open up the path of culture for itself.
>
> (Trotsky 1991: 220–1)

This makes necessary the dictatorship of the proletariat – an exceptional period of crisis management where state power is held by a class still too weak to establish full social hegemony. Building up a socialist culture at a deeper material level is a long task. By the time the working class has been fully able to develop its own cultural basis, it will already have ceased to exist as a proletariat. Trotsky's analysis therefore represents a rejection of culturalism and its idealist implications of cultural autonomy in favour of a materialistic conception of art and culture. The working class is faced not with the matter of creating socialist art and culture but of creating the material conditions for these.

In this sense, Trotsky is able to move beyond the culturalism of some interpretations of Gramsci's analysis. It is not possible for the working class to establish full cultural hegemony prior to taking power because of the material conditions that determine the nature of that class and the conditions under which it exists. As a disenfranchised class:

> The proletariat is forced to take power before it has appropriated the fundamental elements of bourgeois culture; it is forced to overthrow bourgeois society by revolutionary violence for the very reason that society does not allow it access to culture.
>
> (Trotsky 1991: 223–4)

The weakness of the position of the proletariat within bourgeois society and the lack of an economic and cultural basis makes the question of working-class hegemony all the more dependent on revolutionary political leadership and direction. The period of the proletarian dictatorship should be seen as reflecting this need for leadership, extending from the leadership of the working class to the leadership of society as a whole. This period is a transitional, emergency period that reflects the weakness of the proletariat's material base in society and the need to begin to lay the necessary conditions for a future communist society. Only then can the matter of a socialist culture fully emerge.

Trotsky also resists the temptation – that attracts Gramsci – to give Marxist science an all-subsuming character. He separates out the different areas of life and culture giving each its own degree of autonomy, while maintaining the linkage between each social field and the totality which Marxism seeks to explain:

> It is unquestionably true that the need for art is not created by economic conditions. But neither is the need for food created by economics … A work of art should, in the first place, be judged by its own law, that is, by the law of art. But Marxism alone can explain why and how a given tendency in art has originated in a given period of history; in other words, who it was who made a demand for such an artistic form and not for another, and why.
>
> (Trotsky 1991: 207)

The point is therefore to maintain that things, whether scientific or artistic, have meaning and validity in themselves. They do not necessarily have an intrinsic class character. However, all things, as social products, are subject to class determination to a greater or lesser extent. This is the case with science where:

> All science, in greater or lesser degree, unquestionably reflects the tendencies of the ruling class. The more closely a science attaches itself to the practical tasks of conquering nature (physics, chemistry, natural science in general), the greater is its non-class and human contribution. The more deeply a science is connected with the social mechanism of exploitation (political economy), or the more abstractly it generalises the entire experience of mankind (psychology, not in its experimental, physiological sense but in its so-called 'philosophical sense'), the more does it obey the class egotism of the bourgeoisie and the less significant is its contribution to the general sum of human knowledge ... As a general rule, the bourgeois tendencies have found a much freer place for themselves in the higher spheres of methodological philosophy, of *Weltanschauung*.
>
> (Trotsky 1991: 226)

Scientific practice can therefore be seen as being its own distinct field with its own distinct object. However, how that knowledge is reached depends, to greater and lesser degrees, on the pre-existing social character of the knowledge and methods employed. In critical realist terms, the social conditions within which scientific practice takes place gives the transitive domain a class character which is then reflected in the ability that science might or might not have to explain the intransitive object of its study. Philosophy, in its practical, underlabouring role, should therefore be used to give us knowledge of the necessary conditions for the production of knowledge. Although Trotsky obviously never wrote in these terms, the critical realist theory of science can be matched up with Trotsky's views on art, where the task is not to try and 'create' some new form of art, but to create the necessary *conditions* for a new kind of art. In both cases the relationship is one that is concerned with the interaction between a particular social practice, the material conditions within which this practice takes place, and the social character of these material conditions.

Political investigation

Hegemony in classical Marxism emphasises the role of leadership, something that today's commentators often want to abandon. The post-Marxists and Euro-communists have liquidated the question of class leadership into the general concerns of 'popular struggle' and 'peoples revolution'.

These theories are no more than new editions of previous bourgeois ideas. Against this Lenin wrote:

> abuse of the word 'people' ... shall not be used to cover up failure to understand the class antagonisms within the people. It insists categorically on the need for complete class independence for the party of the proletariat. But it divides the 'people' into 'classes,' ... in order that the advanced class, which does not suffer from the halfheartedness, vacillation and indecision of the intermediate classes, may with all the greater energy and enthusiasm fight for the cause of the whole of the people, at the head of the whole of the people.
>
> (Lenin: 1975a: 122)

Lenin recognises the plurality of society. But from this fact he draws the conclusion that the different layers must be united behind the proletariat and its vanguard. The unity of the masses is based on a genuine struggle for hegemony, rather than on some irrealist notion of overcoming reification or achieving Lukácsian class consciousness. It is absolutely necessary, therefore, to return to hegemony some notion of leadership and direction. However, it is also necessary to recognise a weakness in theorists like Trotsky which tends towards an instrumental view of class, politics and the state. Hegemony is understood more as a tool of different classes and is often not given sufficiently deep structural roots. Consequently, Trotsky tends to see a crisis of political hegemony or of the authority of one social group as a crisis of the whole system. This might have been the case in Russia. But in Britain and France there are more developed fortresses and earthworks and more entrenched layers of the ruling class and its associates.

Lenin and Trotsky both held realist views of the layered and complex nature of the social world and a practical realist view of class struggle. However, they were also subject to the errors of their Second International upbringing and have tendencies towards mechanical materialism and class instrumentalism. The most fruitful exploration of their realism therefore lies, not with speculation over philosophical positions, but with their concrete engagement with the specific conditions of the class struggle and the ontology that flows from this. From this is left a strong legacy of strategy, method and tactics, crucial to a proper understanding of hegemony.

4   English debates and the structuralism of Poulantzas

Introduction

It took a while for Gramsci's work, and in a more general sense the concept of hegemony, to become influential in the English-speaking world. The *Prison Notebooks* were held by the Italian Stalinists, whose main consideration was to use them to justify their own positions. Gramsci's work therefore surfaced in a delayed, selected and distorted form, enveloped in the machinations of the PCI. However, the development of Euro-communism offered the possibility to re-launch Gramsci in his full splendour. The 'schizoid' Gramsci could now be permitted his moments of revolutionary exegesis on the understanding that he would give his final endorsement to the reformist strategy of 'capturing' the hegemony of civil society. In these circumstances, the new political Gramsci was born. But, theoretically, hegemony was open to a wider interpretation. In the debates of the 1960s, usually conducted through *New Left Review*, a competition began to see who could best apply Gramsci's concepts to British conditions. This chapter will examine these English debates and the wider context of Western Marxism. It will look at attempts to apply a Gramscian model to the English situation, while noting the limitations of empiricism, historicism and humanism, on the one hand, and a non-agential structuralism, on the other. It will then go on to look at the work of Nicos Poulantzas, starting with his assessment of the English debates and moving on to his views on class fractions, power blocs and hegemonic crisis.

Western Marxism

The Western Marxist tradition was an important influence on the attempts to develop a specifically Anglo-Marxism. The development of *New Left Review* is crucial. Under Stuart Hall and E.P. Thompson, the journal focused on problems of English culture and political tradition. However, it was already drawing upon Western Marxist theory before its new editor, Perry Anderson, made it more cosmopolitan. While both Thompson and Anderson attack Western Marxism for its theoretical elitism and its removal from popular struggles, both draw heavily from it.

As Anderson himself notes (1979), it is striking that Western Marxism is much influenced by a series of defeats and the twin triumphs of fascism and Stalinism. This in part explains the shift away from political matters towards more philosophical concerns. This is certainly the case with the writers of the Frankfurt School, whose concern with the effects of totalitarian society drives them towards philosophy and aesthetics as a form of critical protest. After Gramsci, praxis Marxism also moves in a philosophical direction, particularly in the work of Lukács and those who emphasise a subjectivist form of humanism that places its emphasis on the reification of consciousness and the struggle for a 'true' awareness. The Second World War caused a further wave of despair, while the Stalinist invasions of Eastern Europe gave increased support to a humanist alternative. But although it saw itself as responding to these situations, it would be more truthful to say that the effect of Stalinism and fascism was to drive Western Marxism further and further away from political struggles and the masses. Gramsci, posthumously claimed by the movement, is really the only political theorist of Western Marxism and, according to Anderson, hegemony is the only non-speculative Western Marxist concept (Anderson 1979).[1] But Gramsci too, with his general lack of economic emphasis, is used to justify a move away from analysis of economic structures towards cultural superstructures and philosophical concerns. In the 1960s, Marx's early works, in particular the *1844 Manuscripts*, and the newly available *Grundrisse*, reopened the question of Hegel's influence. European idealism, Anderson notes, began to make its mark as Western Marxism 'paradoxically inverted the trajectory of Marx's own development' (Anderson 1976: 53). The renewed concern with Hegel matches the turn (by theorists like Lukács and Marcuse) to class consciousness, mass psychology and the struggle for human liberation.

The English debates do have a number of important features that break from normal Western Marxist ideas – allowing Anderson to write the highly condemning *Considerations on Western Marxism* (1979). First, while cultural analysis plays a central role on both sides of the English debates, there is also a full-scale analysis of historical factors. Second, the debate is shaped by the need to understand the politics of the present – Anderson and Nairn examine British history in order to analyse the 'origins of the present crisis', while Thompson's political analysis is very much concerned with building up a protest movement. Finally, and most importantly for this chapter, the debates are centrally concerned with the concept of hegemony, a political rather than a speculative concept, and one that opens up debate around such issues as structure and agency, structuralism and historicism.

Hegemony and the human base

The overriding concern of Raymond Williams, E.P. Thompson and those around them is for an active humanist Marxism that rejects dogmatism and schematism and the politics of Stalinism. Thompson, a dissident from the

Communist Party, seeks a restatement of Marxism as an emancipatory project. Williams too is concerned with the creative potential of human situations and experiences. Together, Williams and Thompson were part of a New Left which sought to respond to the political situation by creating a new sort of British Marxism that was eminently humanist. This movement also marked the coming together of cultural and historical analysis as a powerful alternative to social scientific theoreticism, economic schematism and political dogmatism.

An important article in support of this perspective is Williams's 'Base and Superstructure in Marxist Cultural Theory' (1982) which opposes the classical schema. But Williams's contribution is novel in the sense that while the trend against determination and the primacy of the economic base usually emphasises the political, cultural and ideological superstructure element, as has been the case with many readings of Gramsci, Williams instead proposes to extend the concept of the base. He moves it away from a narrow economic conception towards a broader definition that includes a whole range of human relationships and processes. Williams extends the idea of the base so that it is no longer confined to economic actions, but in fact relates to a wider range of human activities. The base is no longer simply an economic domain and it is no longer a fixed or static entity, it becomes humanised. This makes is possible to bring base and super-structure into alignment through the key humanist notion of praxis.

This is not meant to be reductive, and Williams does criticise Lukács, for example, because he feels his notion of the totality lacks structuration and differentiation. This is where hegemony achieves its prominence, for it goes beyond a simple notion of totality in that it presupposes something total, something lived at a depth (the human base), rather than being merely superstructural or manifold. The system of meanings and values that Williams associates with hegemony runs deep into society. Hegemony is deeply saturated in the consciousness of a society. Above all, it is not something that is given but is a relation that is actively lived, and thus meaningful:

> Hegemony supposes the existence of something which is truly total, which is not merely secondary or superstructural, like the weak sense of ideology, but which is lived at such a depth, which saturates society to such an extent ... We have to emphasise that hegemony is not singular; indeed that its own internal structures are highly complex, and have continually to be renewed, recreated and defended ... it is a set of meanings and values, which as they are experienced as practices appear as reciprocally confirming.
>
> (Williams 1982: 8–9)

The problem with this view is that the base tends to get *reduced* to this system of meanings and values while hegemony tends to become associated with their cultural dominance so that 'in any society, in any particular period, there is a central system of practices, meanings and values, which we can properly call dominant and effective' (Williams 1982: 8). This represents a form of culturalism, for instead of being incorporated into a model of social structure, these practices, meanings and values replace social structure as the primary focus. Whereas in Gramsci the notion of hegemony represented the unity of structure and superstructure, in Williams there is a tendency for hegemony to reduce structure to 'super-structural' practices, meanings and values. This is evident when Williams talks of the need to focus less on the question of social 'fact', more on the question of social intention (Williams 1982: 7). While social intention, as represented in meanings and values, is indeed important, it cannot form an adequate basis for a study of society. As critical realism has argued, many social actions have unintentional consequences. This is due to the fact that human agents act within a set of powerful social structures that exert a determining influence over agents. To overemphasise intentionality, practices, meanings and values is to overemphasise the power of agents and to ignore the powerful influence of social structure.

There are, however, possibilities of developing some of Williams's points on human intentions and the spatio-temporal possibilities of the location of agents, provided that this is taken in a realist direction. This is to examine the nature of experience, identity and beliefs in relation to space, place and time. Emancipatory projects can be assessed in terms of the broadening or universalising of experience or identity through conflicts of feeling, knowing and situatedness. In Williams's subjectivist terms, we might examine how, through struggle and changed perception of one's place, a coal miner might pass from wage labourer to class militant, transcending many of the limitations of the localised role of wage labour by universalising other aspects of class experience. However, it is necessary to insist that Williams's key concept of the structure of feeling is linked to the objective conditions which give rise to those experiences. The deepening or development of experiences is the result of the dialectical nature of reality which gives rise to certain possibilities. Economic and social positions and relations have a determining influence that cannot be avoided by focusing on cultural conditions instead. Williams's position sees too much in terms of experience and too little in terms of structure, hence the lack of an objective consider-ation of the possibilities and limitations derived from those material con-ditions. Without this kind of analysis of structural conditions there is no way of assessing the potentials of different social groups. By focusing on our shared humanity, Williams's argument suggests that the key question is one of numbers rather than influence and it fails to properly assess the different potentials that groups possess according to their different relationships to social structures and mechanisms. By reducing social positions and potentials to a shared humanity, such a theory is less able to differentiate between various groups and classes. Not only is the historical role of mobs and eccentrics wildly over-exaggerated in the works of Williams and Thompson, but in theory, the humanist position is unable to tell the difference in potentiality between the peasantry and the proletariat. Humanity should not be seen as constitutive of the base – rather, there is a complex social base which ascribes different positions and abilities to different humans.

But while Williams identifies hegemony with a lived cultural process, imposing a certain flatness on the social totality, he does allow that hegemony might be emergent in some way. In distinguishing between practical and abstract senses of the concept, Williams writes that a lived hegemony is a realised complex of experiences, relationships and activities. Although the emphasis is again on experience rather than structure, the use of the word 'realised' is important as there is clearly some sort of (unformulated) recognition that hegemony also exists at a deeper level and that the various practical, lived 'hegemonies' are somehow emergent or 'realised' out of this. This leaves the door open for a theory of hegemony that can incorporate the kind of experiences, relationships and activities that Williams highlights, while still remaining committed to a theory of hegemony at the level of social reproduction.

So Williams's conception of hegemony emerges as one that emphasises the lived conditions of human agents from a cultural and historical perspective. Williams is keen to emphasise complexity, plurality and differ-entiation, but he is hostile to any social scientific abstraction of mechanisms and structures that denies a proper role to human experience and agency. His is a concern with a more human form of social complexity, a position that can also be found in the writings of E.P. Thompson.

Thompson's theory

The historical works of Edward Thompson stand out proudly against static theoretical analysis that lacks a conception of agency. Thompson acts as like an archaeologist, re-examining history from the point of view of the oft forgotten masses. His is a history from below, of popular movements, customs and traditions, common experiences, quiet dissatisfaction and open revolt. It rejects the view that history is created from the top down, whether this is done by the ruling class or dominant power, or else by some abstract mechanism or structure. Above all, Thompson sees history as the embodi-ment of the class struggle which is an active, dialectical process in which classes interact and evolve. This is very much on display in Thompson's famous work *The Making of the English Working Class* (1968). However, the book also contains an assault on theoretical Marxism – something that is continued in *The Poverty of Theory* (1978). Yet, as a Marxist, Thompson does have a largely implicit, but occasionally elaborated theoretical position on what history is and how it should be studied. Also, he does get involved in debates with other Marxists over theory and methodology, and these will now be studied in order to assess the implications for a theory of hegemony.

The general theme of *The Making of the English Working Class* is expressed in the open lines where Thompson explains his choice of title:

> *Making*, because it is a study in an active process, which owes as much to agency as to conditioning. The working class did not rise like the sun at an appointed time. It was present at its own making.
>
> (Thompson 1968: 9)

There is something laudable in Thompson's approach, especially when he writes that class is not a thing but a relation. This can be directed against those attempts to impose simple categories on the social world, to enforce a form of identity, thinking or categorisation, to fail to see that history studies dynamic relations not static or neatly formed entities. Class must be seen as a dialectical entity; socially and historically it is defined through complex and changing social relations. However, Thompson's aim is not just to shift the study of class from the simple to the complex, but also to move from objective to more subjective factors. As a Marxist, Thompson must accept some form of structural analysis, hence he does write that 'class experience is largely determined by the productive relations into which men are born – or enter involuntarily' (Thompson 1968: 10). However, Thompson is less subtle than Raymond Williams, for while Williams tries to explore the complex interrelation between objective processes and subjective human factors through the workings of hegemony, Thompson prefers to admit that objective processes are important but then seems to discard them. Having rightly noted the complexity of social relations, Thompson concludes that class can only therefore be known through people's actions and experiences:

> If we stop history at a given point, then there are no classes but simply a multitude of individuals with a multitude of experiences. But if we watch these men over an adequate period of social change, we observe patterns in their relationships, their ideas, and their institutions. Class is defined by men as they live their own history, and, in the end, this is its only definition.
>
> (Thompson 1968: 11)

This begs the questions: How do people live their own history? Why do they live it in one way rather than another? What gives structure and meaning to history and the way that people live it? As Bhaskar might ask, given that history, as it is lived, is meaningful and open to concrete analysis, what does this tell us about the nature of historical relationships? The point is whether or not history contains analysable structures, processes and mechanisms which provide a set of conditions in which individuals and groups act, rather than being reducible to the actions of individuals or groups. Thompson's conception of class suggests that he sees social relations less in terms of structures and more in terms of the ways that individuals and groups get together and relate:

> By class I understand a historical phenomenon, unifying a number of disparate and seemingly unconnected events, both in the raw material of experience and in consciousness. I emphasise that it is a *historical* phenomenon. I do not see class as a 'structure', nor even as a 'category', but as something which in fact happens (and can be shown to have happened) in human relationships.
>
> (Thompson 1968: 9)

If this is taken as a definition of class, then class lacks any clear objective basis outside of lived human relationships. Class is no longer defined according to the model of base and superstructure, nor, really, from the basic relations of production. Yet Thompson cannot give the basis on which these relationships are constructed, or why these occur, nor what they are, other than on simple empirical and human grounds. He never gets to grips with what these relationships really are because he reduces relationships to the experiencing of them:

> class happens when some men, as a result of common experiences (inherited or shared), feel and articulate the identity of their interests as between themselves, and as against other men whose interests are different from (and usually opposed to) theirs.
>
> (Thompson 1968: 9–10)

Thompson does go on to mention objective productive relations. But this reference is merely incidental. The key thing for Thompson is not class itself, but class consciousness and experience. Class must ultimately be constituted subjectively. The existence of a class is reduced to its expression. Perry Anderson notes that it is possible to distinguish between the objective composition of class as a social force and its subjective outlook as a political force (Anderson 1980: 46).[2] But it can be seen that Thompson's definition is overly subjective, indicating that class is constituted by common interests that are expressed in opposition to another group. This relates to the humanist view of hegemony as the relation between groups, with their opposing ideas and world-views, rather than the view of hegemony as based on the relation between groups and social structures. In Thompson, the question of class is effectively reduced to that of class consciousness and experience.

E.P. Thompson's attack on Althusser in *The Poverty of Theory* is based on similar themes to those outlined in the preface to *The Making of the English Working Class*. Above all, Thompson is concerned to argue that active historical processes cannot be reduced to static theoretical categories. Althusser's error is to de-historicise and de-socialise these relations so that class becomes a static category. For structuralist Marxism, people 'are not the makers but the vectors' (Thompson 1978a: 46). This criticism, in its limited way, is correct. Althusser's use of Marx's term *träger* (reducing people to the mere 'bearers' of structures) is rightly notorious. However, Thompson turns this correct criticism into an argument that makes class struggle the prior concept to class so that classes arise out of such struggles, or perhaps, more to the point, they are formed through the collective experience of such struggles. This position is decidedly anti-objective, and immediately raises the question, if class arises out of struggle, then how do we explain what struggles arise from?

Thomson sees Althusser's work as a system of closure and he attacks the various 'levels' of Althusser's system from a humanist viewpoint writing that

> all these 'instances' and 'levels' are in fact human activities, institutions and ideas. We are talking about men and women in their material life, in their determinate relationships, in their experience of these, and in their self-consciousness of this experience.
>
> (Thompson 1978a: 97)

Thompson rightly criticises Althusser's 'self-generating conceptual universe' (Thompson 1978a: 13), and structuralism's self-regulating, self-validating systems. But Thompson's return to the openness of experience ignores the need to develop a more abstract theory that investigates the kind of underlying structures and generative mechanisms that might plausibly account for these experiences. Surely the point is not to have to choose between abstract theory and a history based on human experience, but to find a method that can combine both. Critical realism attempts to do this by asking what experience presupposes. But although this rightly shifts focus to underlying structural processes and gives this some sort of historical primacy, it also recognises the need to return to the concrete world of everyday experience in order to examine how these structural processes are manifested. A history based on experience alone cannot explain society, but then neither can abstract theory. The point is to look at what experiences presuppose, then to look at how what is presupposed is manifested. This method is in keeping with Marx's process of abstraction (concrete–abstract–concrete). And it is in keeping with the view that while social structures and generative mechanisms have causal primacy, they give rise to emergent processes that cannot be reduced to these underlying conditions, but have their own features and dynamics. This is surely the basis on which an open rather than a closed system can be acknowledged. For Thompson attacks 'systems of closure' by claiming that 'if we return to "experience" we can move, from that point, once again, to an *open* exploration of the world' (Thompson 1978a: 167). But surely the open system comprises more than just experiences; it represents the way in which a whole range of structures, mechanisms, practices, institutions, apparatuses, traditions, experiences and feelings come together in a complex and contradictory way, a way that cannot be reduced to the workings of abstract structures alone. Thompson equates open systems with experience; the point, however, is to see how experience is just one of the irreducible features of an open system that nevertheless rests on some fundamental structural conditions.

History as humanism

For both Thompson and Williams, the foundations of socialism reside in human relations and experiences or what critical realists would describe as transitive processes. Intransitive processes such as those concerning economic structures are subsumed into human relations as is reflected in Williams's idea of the human base, an idea that Thompson also suggests when he writes that '[e]ven if "base" were not such a bad metaphor we would have to add that, whatever it is, it is not just economic but human' (Thompson 1978a: 294). Part of the struggle socialists face is to resist 'capitalism's innate tendency to reduce all human relationships to economic definitions' (Thompson 1978a: 294). This means embracing a more moral line of reasoning as expressed in Thompson's statement that 'there is an economic logic and a moral logic and it is futile to argue as to which we give priority since they are different expressions of the same "kernel of human relationship"' (Thompson 1961, II: 38). But as Marx makes clear in his criticism of Feuerbach, we cannot come to terms with the social by starting with the human, we must come to terms with the human by starting with the social:

> Feuerbach resolves the religious essence into the *human* essence. But the human essence is no abstraction inherent in each single individual. In its reality it is the ensemble of the social relations.
>
> (Marx 1975b: 423)

Rather than describing history in terms of a human essence, Marx looks at how the material conditions for human existence are expressed in historically specific social forms. It is clear from the following passage that Marx's focus is on social rather than human relations and that these are based on specific economic and historical relations of production:

> We have seen how the capitalist process of production is a historically specific form of the social production process in general. This last is both a production process of the material conditions of existence for human life, and a process, proceeding in specific economic and historical relations of production, that produces and reproduces these relations of production themselves, and with them the bearers of this process,

their material conditions of existence, and their mutual relationships, i.e. the specific economic form of their society ... Those conditions ... are on the one hand the presuppositions of the capitalist production process, on the other its results and creations; they are both produced by it and reproduced by it.

(Marx 1981: 957)

Williams's position is more complex than Thompson's since the human base is broadly defined to include a number of socio-economic 'human' relations, bound together by a hegemonic process that combines 'objective' human relations and 'subjective' human intentions. Thompson's position is more schematic, inverting the base/superstructure relationship and giving hegemony a superstructural role. In both cases, the tendency is to reduce the social to the human, rather than seeing the social as including both human practices and relations, and the sort of material conditions that Marx describes above. By conflating objective social structures with the human practices that these structures contain, a humanist focus shifts away from the belief that society can be analysed scientifically. Marxist analysis becomes an analysis of the expressions of the subject rather than a study of the object. This is reflected in Thompson's historiography of suffering and resistance. Social formations are judged, not so much scientifically, but morally. Historical analysis becomes a process of championing popular expression, common struggle and human enlightenment. But there is a danger that the primary focus is romantic rather than materialist.

History is viewed by Williams as 'the long revolution' for human self-expression:

It is a genuine revolution, transforming men and institutions; continually extended and deepened by the actions of millions, continually and variously opposed by explicit reaction and by the pressure of habitual forms and ideas.

(Williams 1965: 10)

But there is a danger of this long revolution becoming ahistorical in the sense that it is given a universal human character, acting upon history rather than derived from it. Williams and Thompson draw inspiration from the romantic movement, the intellectual dissent of those Thompson terms the 'free born Englishmen'. This makes up part of Thompson's history, along with the heroic resistance of the masses in creating their own customs and values and in resisting aspects of ruling-class hegemony. This hegemony becomes the historical terrain of struggle while history becomes the peoples' resistance to intrusion from above on their way of life:

hegemony is not just imposed (or contested) but is articulated in the everyday intercourse of a community, and can be sustained only by concession and patronage (in good times), by at least the gestures of protection in bad.

(Thompson 1993: 345)

Certainly, hegemony is a lived experience subject to complex mediations and negotiations. As we shall see below, Thompson is right to accuse Anderson and Nairn of seeing hegemony too much as an all-or-nothing relationship between the hegemonic or dominant class and the dominated or 'corporate' masses. Hegemony is more subtle than this; it is indeed something that is lived and contested, not something that is more or less imposed. But neither can hegemony be reduced to the way it is lived and experienced. It exists, as Williams hints, at a deeper more fundamental level as a necessary function of the structures of society. Hegemony is derived from the actions of people, but it is also derived from the intransitive structures of society. It is in reducing these structures to people that Thompson is fundamentally wrong. It is true that Thompson's historical analysis implies that social structures and mechanisms do exist. But Thompson is always concerned to move away from such a position and to emphasise the transitive elements of human practice, such as customs and conceptions, as if they have primacy over the intransitive social structures. As the following passage indicates, the development of the English working class is a result not of structural processes, but of collective self-consciousness:

> Collective values are consciously held and are propagated in political theory, trade union ceremonial, moral rhetoric. It is, indeed, this collective self-consciousness, with its corresponding theory, institutions, discipline, and community values which distinguishes the nineteenth-century working class from the eighteenth-century mob.
>
> (Thompson 1968: 463)

By analysing history and society from the perspective of working-class and oppositional traditions and culture, Thompson gives this level of expression a totalising character, thus losing sight of the complex historical processes and social structures which underlie these expressions. A conception of hegemony remains, but it is not one based on political leadership and direction, but a more diffuse notion of a politics 'from below', based on the spontaneous consciousness of the working class and radical masses. This is a politics drawn as much from William Morris as from Karl Marx; a politics founded upon the primacy of human practice and moral argument. It attempts to avoid a more theoretical, materialist analysis of society and as a consequence tends to reduce the concept of hegemony to its concrete expression in human practice. This leaves no place for a theoretical conception of hegemony as a necessary and complex connection between these human practices and the more intransitive social structures. Hegemony is reduced to its expression.

Arguments about the English revolution

> By its eternal compromises gradual, peaceful political development such as exists in England brings about a contradictory state of affairs. Because of the superior advantages it affords, this state can within certain limits be tolerated in practice, but its logical incongruities are a sore trial to the reasoning mind.
>
> (Engels 1962: 529)

The problems that Engels had with analysing the development of English society meant that he never wrote the planned follow up to *The Condition of the Working Class in England*. As time drew on, the problem became more pronounced – having the earliest bourgeois revolution was not, in the long term, the best way to ensure the most advanced capitalist society. This was the theme that was to surface in the 1960s as the consequences had apparently reached crisis point. It is developed in the historical research of Perry Anderson and Tom Nairn, whose position can be sketched out as follows. The English revolution allowed for the growth of capitalism in Britain; however, because it occurred so 'early', the bourgeois class in England was in a weaker position than in subsequent bourgeois revolutions abroad. In fact, Anderson and Nairn argue, the revolution was primarily a fight between sections of the aristocracy which overshot its political intentions, creating a vacuum into which the emerging bourgeoisie stepped. But the bourgeoisie was still too weak to carry through the revolution on its own terms and was forced into a compromise with the old aristocracy. In this fused bloc, it was the aristocracy which remained hegemonic. It was 'a bourgeois revolution by proxy' (Anderson 1993: 17).

It is argued that because the political revolution came long before the process of industrialisation, the bourgeoisie was unable to develop a true ideological legacy to reflect changing material conditions. Likewise, the English working class grew up without clear ideas; in contrast with the rest of Europe it had neither bourgeois nor socialist ideology to turn to or interact with. As Anderson puts it: 'In England, a supine bourgeoisie produced a subordinate proletariat. It handed on no impulse of liberation, no revolutionary values, no universal language' (Anderson 1993: 17). The British working class thus developed a practico-corporate consciousness, enshrined in the structures of British labourism and wedded to the ideas of gradual reform and piecemeal change.

The influence of imperialism meant that domestic interests were tied to foreign interventions. That Britain remained unoccupied and undefeated after two world wars meant that the old social structure was preserved but with the labour aristocracy now incorporated into it. The old aristocratic forms, combined with the decline of the Empire, thus define the nature of the crisis facing an antiquated but unchallenged social formation. For

Nairn, British society was neither feudal nor modern but 'obstinately and successfully intermediate' (Nairn 1981: 19). From such a situation develops a peculiar hegemony of the elite, for many years untroubled by social conflict, but now totally inadequate at dealing with political and economic crisis. Its ideology and world outlook is dominated by traditionalism and empiricism. This is compounded by the historical dominance of the City institutions over the state and of an overseas mercantile sector over national industry. Anderson and Nairn aim to expose the archaic nature of a ruling patrician elite whose 'amateurish' personnel and conservative traditions stretch back to an aristocratic and agrarian past. Its continued existence is owed to the half-heartedness of the industrial bourgeoisie, and the defensive, subordinate character of labour. Thus the traditions of the conservative agrarian aristocracy not only persisted, but in many ways dominated and shaped the ruling bloc; it was the hegemonic fraction of a hegemonic class bloc.

In contrast, the working class has had no socialist or even bourgeois ideology to take up as its own. As the earliest mass working class, it was acutely aware of itself, but found no adequate means to develop its revolutionary potential. Instead, it developed a subordinate, corporate consciousness. In a Gramscian sense, it is a group that is aware of its own immediate interests, but has yet to move beyond them. It is conscious of its class, but its acceptance of this means that it is unable to transcend it. In effect, it reproduces and reinforces its class subordination. This polarity of hegemonic and corporate is central to Anderson's thesis:

> If a hegemonic class can be defined as one which imposes its own ends and vision on society as a whole, a corporate class is conversely one which pursues its own ends within a social totality whose overall determination lies outside it. A hegemonic class seeks to transform society in its own image, inventing afresh its economic system, its political institutions, its cultural values, its 'modes of insertion' into the world. A corporate class seeks to defend and improve its own position within a social order accepted as given. The English working class has been characterised since the mid nineteenth century by the distinction between an intense consciousness of separate identity and a continuous failure to set and impose goals for society as a whole ... The very intensity of its corporate class consciousness, embodied in a distinct, hermetic culture, has blocked the emergence of a universal ideology in the English working class.
>
> (Anderson 1993: 29)

Thompson's response, 'The Peculiarities of the English' (in Thompson 1978a: 245–301), raises some important questions about Anderson's analysis. He argues that the model of hegemonic class and corporate class is too schematic, leaving one class as ruled and one class fraction as ruling, with little in between. The notion of hegemony is unstratified and seems to exist at one all encompassing level in a one-way direction that leaves little room for resistance, for localised hegemonies, or non-dominant relations. Rather than being a set of complex and mediated relations, hegemony is often reduced to being the property of the class or group that dominates, leaving little room for struggle, opposition, contestation or negotiation.

Anderson admits that his analysis is only intended as an initial attempt which must by its very nature make assumptions and be schematic. There is at least a potentially correct position in Anderson which highlights the reasons for the dominance of a traditionalist conservative elite and an inert and anti-intellectual labour movement. The chief reason that Thompson objects to this 'model' is that it attempts to analyse British history from a position that does not try to claim that this history is a long line of heroic resistance. However, a lot of Thompson's criticisms are valuable, even if his alternative is less plausible. He correctly links Anderson's schematic conception of hegemonic–corporate relations to the overemphasis of the political moment of revolution:

> I am objecting to a model which concentrates attention upon one dramatic episode – *the* Revolution – to which all that goes before and after must be related; and which insists upon an ideal type of this Revolution against which all others may be judged.
>
> (Thompson 1978a: 257)

Anderson's conception seems to be that revolution is usually decisive and that the peculiarity of the English situation lies with its indecisiveness. Maybe this represents a case of Gramscian analysis being stretched too far, for Gramsci's key concern, like Anderson's, is the peculiar nature of the (Italian) social formation, the incompleteness of the bourgeois revolution, the lack of a hegemonic intellectual class, the 'superstructural' functioning of civil society and so on. In order to analyse Italian history, Gramsci used a basic model – the French one – and looks at its social forms, hegemonic blocs, civil society and revolution. Given the lateness of the *Risorgimento*, he is more entitled to use this as a basic starting point than is Anderson, who imposes the French model on an English revolution many years previous to it.

In comparing France and England, Anderson contrasts maturity with prematurity. Anderson believes that the more 'complete' nature of the revolution in France has led to a more enlightened and combative working class. But in some senses, Anderson is making the same error as Thompson, in that he is holding to an impressionistic conception of political struggle and ideas. This does not take into account the matter of organisational forms, an aspect in which the British labour movement is ahead of France. As Anderson's later essay 'The Light of Europe' (in Anderson 1992a) starts to acknowledge, the political traditions may have been stronger in France, but the organised movement is weaker.

Anderson's Francophilia is also questionable on political and ideological grounds. The more 'complete' bourgeois character of the French revolution and its richness of legacy has left a fairly satisfied and comfortable bourgeoisie that has had no real need to rebel, or to produce a radical ideology. The 'progressiveness' of the French revolution is therefore just as likely to produce a rather stagnant theoretical legacy, which Althusser calls 'French misery'. The initially revolutionary character of the French bourgeoisie meant that:

> it had long been able to assimilate intellectuals to its revolution and to keep them as a whole at its side after the seizure and consolidation of power. The French bourgeoisie had successfully carried through a complete, clear revolution, driving the feudal class from the political stage ... it had set the seal of its own command on the unity of the nation in the process of revolution itself, it had defeated the Church and then adopted it, but only to separate itself at the right moment and cover itself with the slogans of liberty and equality .... With a few important exceptions ... French intellectuals accepted this situation and felt no vital need to seek their salvation at the side of the working class ....Thus it was that the forms of bourgeois domination themselves long deprived the French workers' movement of the intellectuals indispensable to the formation of an authentic *theoretical* tradition.
>
> (Althusser 1977a: 25)

Furthermore, the most clear cut and simple bourgeois revolution, that of the United States, has perhaps the most unorganised 'corporate class' of all the advanced social formations. The absence of an aristocratic rump has not prevented the US working class from being fully co-opted. So Anderson's theme of English peculiarity does not really hold.

The Nairn–Anderson 'models' are also faulty in their use of the base-superstructure equation. The most striking example is Anderson's point that:

> After a bitter, cathartic revolution, which transformed the structure but not the superstructures of English society, a landed aristocracy, under-pinned by a powerful mercantile group, became the first dominant capitalist class in Britain ... the bourgeoisie won two modest victories, lost its nerve and ended up by losing its identity.
>
> (Anderson 1993: 29)

Certainly this is a strange formulation. If the base-superstructure metaphor is to be used, then is it possible for the base to change without the superstructure changing? Even if the superstructure appears to remain the same, it is different by virtue of its relationship to a changed base and consequently a new institutional–functional arrangement. The point of the base/superstructure model is surely to argue that the base is, to some extent determining of the superstructure. But, in any case, the whole base/superstructure schema is clumsy and imprecise. Critical realism can enable us to move away from such schematism and conceive of a set of structures, some with more primacy than others, with non-deterministic relationships that are codeterminant, dialectical and stratified. The base analogy can be maintained by virtue of the concept of mode of production which exists within the broader social formation, but which cannot be reduced to the only determining factor. It is necessary to uphold a dialectical conception where the mode of production entails relations of production whose reproduction entails complex social structures which thus re-enter into the equation.[3]

Anderson's theme is that the structure changes due to the development of capital and a bourgeois class, leading to a revolutionary confrontation with the landed aristocracy. However, revolution comes too early and forces a compromise. The old superstructural forms of the aristocracy are maintained and much of civil society remains in the grip of aristocratic hegemony. The superstructure is then out of synchronisation with the base, rendering it vulnerable to subsequent crises. The consequence of such a theory of aristocratic backwardness is to argue for the extension of bourgeois hegemony as part of some unfinished, modernising process. Anderson finishes his account by writing that: 'The international pressures of contemporary capitalism require a radical adaptation. The unfinished work of 1640 and 1832 must be taken up where it was left off' (Anderson 1993: 46–7).

An alternative position to this would be to argue that what should be emphasised is not the persistence of a hegemonic aristocratic fraction, but aristocratic and feudal *residues* which endure within the hegemonic bloc and throughout society. This is not to argue, as Anderson and Nairn are prone to do, that these aristocratic residues determine the character of the dominant bloc, rendering it incapable of dealing with 'modern' problems, but rather, that they have some bearing, as indeed they do in other countries.

Similarly, Nairn and Anderson are right to stress the weaknesses of the British labour movement, but they overemphasise its corporateness, rendering it almost incapable of playing any progressive role. Nairn takes the rather ultra-left view that the working class was granted its own political organisations in order to give it its own paternalist, self-policing regime (Nairn 1970: 19). Such a position moves from a structuralist concept of hegemony to an instrumentalist, conspiratorial one. Taken to its logical extreme, this position would say that the establishment of working-class organisations, particularly the Labour Party, was actually a defeat for the working class because it only acts to integrate the working class and reinforce corporate consciousness. In reality, the establishment of a labour movement was a hard-fought victory and an expression of collective potential. One need only compare the situation in Britain, even now under New Labour, to that of the USA where no such party exists. Nairn and Anderson take a non-dialectical view of this matter, unable to see that the organisations of the labour movement represent contradictory structures. These are both a functioning part of capitalist society, restraining working-class activity and susceptible to the hegemony of the ruling class, yet at same time, provide the best means by which the working class can express itself in action and develop its own counter-hegemony. In rightly challenging Thompson's glorification of the labour movement, Nairn and Anderson allow themselves to be trapped in an extreme counter-position which leaves no space for the radical potential of these structures and organisations, or of the possibility, in some cases, of their transformation.

As for Thompson's theory of hegemony, it tends to emphasise human praxis as primary over social situation, cultural practice over economic mechanisms, and common sense over social science. Similarly, Williams takes up the concept in order to reject economic primacy in the base/superstructure model so that

> hegemonic has come to include cultural as well as political and economic factors; it is distinct, in this sense, from the alternative idea of an economic *base* and a political and cultural *superstructure* ....
>
> (Williams 1976: 118)

The result is that hegemony comes to be associated with only one level of expression with no underlying causes. Although Williams's position is more complex, it reduces the underlying structures to human structures. A realist position must counter this with the argument that hegemony can only operate under conditions of social and material causality. Thompson's history tends to see hegemony simply as a relation between social agents, whereas really hegemony is a relation between social agents based upon a relation between agents and social structures and mechanisms.

Further, hegemonic relations presuppose a political battle over the reproduction, conservation and transformation of these structures. It is thus an eminently political rather than a simply cultural concept. Anderson's strength is that he emphasises a political reading of hegemony founded upon questions of power, civil society and the state. Whereas Thompson tends to argue that hegemony generates its own conditions – just as the working class was present at its own making – Anderson's work does seem to pay more attention to what hegemony presupposes – objective interests, social processes, human practices, generative mechanisms, material conditions and historical relations. In contrast to a realism that starts from what is, Anderson quips that 'Thompson's work is haunted by political or intellectual junctures that failed to occur' (Anderson 1980: 206). Ultimately, Thompson's work is of an idealist nature.

The structuralist contribution

Althusserian forms of structuralism can play a positive role in challenging the humanist view of history which advocates a mono-linear expressive totality and a universalised history. Instead, structuralism argues for a complex totality of different structures, each with their own specific particular histories. However, the contribution of Nicos Poulantzas to the English debates – 'Marxist Political Theory in Great Britain' (1967) – also highlights structuralism's tendency towards one-sidedness. Rightly, and insightfully, Poulantzas argues that Anderson and Nairn also display a tendency to reduce the notion of hegemony to the class consciousness or world-view of a particular group or subject. This is clear from the emphasis that they place on the role of aristocratic tendencies and corporate consciousness in shaping English history. As Poulantzas argues:

> It is clear that the 'unity' of a historically determined social formation, the global social 'totality', is referred to the social class which imposes its 'hegemonic' structuration ... which becomes the unifying principle of a determinate social formation.
>
> (Poulantzas 1967: 61)

So the peculiarity of the English social formation is explained by Anderson and Nairn in terms of the peculiarities of the English ruling class, in particular, its influences and outlook. Poulantzas believes this yields too much to class consciousness and proposes a more structural explanation – that the peculiarities of the English social formation are a product of the overlapping of different modes of production. This contrasts with the volutarist view that objective reality is the product of the consciousness of the politically dominant class. That Nairn and Anderson also end up moving towards a position that sees history according to world-views (or more to the point, the peculiarities of world-views) is indicative of the Gramscianism and culturalism that clearly influences both sides of the New Left divide. Poulantzas's article challenges the humanist notion of hegemony which reduces it to Gramscian world-views and cultural expressions. But it is not clear that Anderson and Nairn are wholly guilty. Their analysis of world-views and ideologies, although couched within a reductive hegemonic–corporate relationship, does presuppose the social structures, processes and generative mechanisms which give rise to them. Poulantzas's oversight is indicative of his own weaknesses. While accusing Anderson of overplaying the conscious element of hegemony, Poulantzas emphasises the structural element of hegemony almost to the exclusion of any conscious application:

> The domination of these classes or fractions in the 'power bloc' relates to *relatively macrochronic objective structures* – to 'phases' – *of the relations of*

production as a whole (not, therefore, to tactical 'compromises' or 'alliances'). This *contradictory unity* is realised *under the aegis of the hegemonic fraction.*

(Poulantzas 1967: 70)

In arguing this, Poulantzas separates the notion of political hegemony from class consciousness. Political hegemony becomes an 'expression' of a purely objective process mechanically derived from the unity of the social formation:

The internal unity of the dominant ideology derives from the fact that it 'expresses' the 'Marxist' unity of a social formation as a whole founded as a determinate mode of production ... its internal coherence, comprehensible if related to the overall unity of the formation, corresponds to the 'political hegemony' – not to the class consciousness – of the bourgeoisie.

(Poulantzas 1967: 67–8)

'Political hegemony' is reduced to an expression of structural determination, with no dynamics of its own. Hegemony comes to represent the intransitive way of things, devoid of any transitive development. Poulantzas's picture is of a closed system which mechanically reproduces itself until it breaks down. Hegemony, likewise, is a non-historical closed process that is unaffected by the class consciousness of social agents. As Ellen Wood notes: 'Purely "structural" conceptions of class do not require us to look for the ways in which class actually imposes its logic, since classes are simply there by definition' (Wood 1982: 50).

Hegemony does have its roots in the socio-economic structure of society. Against humanists like Thompson, it must be stressed that hegemony is not reducible to class consciousness, expression or world-views. Poulantzas is right to argue that hegemony is rooted in the way things are, in the objectivity of social structures and interests. But he is wrong to deny all else. Intransitive structures form only the material basis upon which hegemony develops. These structures enable and define the nature of hegemony (as they do class), but hegemony is then actualised when classes become conscious or partially conscious of their interests and powers and seek to act upon them. Hegemony is equally a conscious process that develops its own characteristics according to social consciousness, world-views and, most fundamentally, class struggles. The hegemonic process reflects in some way, agent, group and class conceptions of the processes in which they are involved. Hegemony does not simply represent a certain structural way of things – although social structure is its material prerequisite – it is above all a certain recognition of social processes and social interests, leading to conscious attempts to act upon this situation. Conscious actions to defend, transform or conserve social interests, embodied in social structures, themselves generate different dynamics. Hegemony has a dual nature and location – transitive and intransitive, structural and manifest.

Comparing Poulantzas's arguments with the humanist positions shows that they tend towards opposite weaknesses. Thompson and Williams emphasise the actual social expression of hegemony and its relationships, while not developing its structural role in securing the cohesiveness of the complex social formation. Poulantzas, however, emphasises a structural–functional notion of hegemony without allowing for its emergence in the concrete, historical interactions of intentioned social agents. Having said this, however, while hegemony has a conscious expression, this must primarily be explained by reference to the structures rather than the agents. Agents, particularly in the process of reproduction, act upon conscious intentions, but the outcomes and effects of these actions are very different to the intentions. This indicates the power that structure enjoys over agency. Consciousness is limited and is social and ideological in character. It is subordinate to wider material developments that lie beyond the conceptions that agents hold. In this respect, Poulantzas's insistence on structure over agency is necessary.

Nicos Poulantzas

Poulantzas's position on the English debates is characteristic of his early work and the structuralist ideas he was later to abandon. In this earlier work he places great stress on the specificity of the capitalist mode of production and its relationship with the state. His analysis of the capitalist mode of production emphasises the importance of the separation of the producers from the means of production. Exploitation is thus realised through the relations of production and exchange rather than through any extra-economic coercion. This means that the capitalist state enjoys relative political and institutional autonomy from the production process. Consequently, the state can play a unifying role by setting itself up as a national–popular body. The institutional and functional separation of the political and economic spheres gives the capitalist state this univer-salising ability. Political struggle takes place for control of this universalising instance. The capitalist state thus comes to represent not the economic interests of the dominant classes, but their political interests, giving the hegemonic process a central importance.

Poulantzas (1967) argues that hegemony involves more than simply securing the consent of the dominated classes, it is central to the organ-isation of the dominant power bloc. This is done through the institutional ensemble of the state itself, its functional role being to organise the hegemony of the power bloc and mobilise consent to this. It is not an easy task since, as the debates about the English revolution and, indeed, Marx's own writings illustrate, we cannot talk of monolithic, cohesive classes, but rather of distinctive class fractions, as well as different social strata and categories. Hence there is also a dominant class fraction inside the dominant power bloc; a hegemony within hegemony.

Poulantzas develops these points in his famous polemic with Ralph Miliband, again conducted through *New Left Review* (Poulantzas 1969). Miliband's view is that the state is the instrument of a particular class. This is based on a simplistic reading of the famous remark in the *Communist Manifesto* that the 'executive of the modern state is but a committee for managing the common affairs of the whole bourgeoisie' (Marx and Engels 1973: 69). Against this, Poulantzas argues that the state is capitalist not because it is controlled and used by the capitalist classes, but rather because of its objective place or function in the reproduction of the economic mode of production. The state enjoys a relative autonomy from any one class precisely because of its role in organising different classes and fractions into a power bloc under the hegemony of a particular fraction. The state would not be able to perform this function if it was simply the instrument of one particular class. However, just because the state is not reducible to a particular capitalist class, this does not mean that the state has a neutral or non-capitalist character. The state assumes a capitalist character in relation to its objective place in capitalist society. Its role is to secure the social cohesion and unity of class society necessary for capital accumulation. This presents a fundamental contradiction. The state is required to secure the reproduction of class domination necessary for capital accumulation, while at the same time presenting itself as a universalising, national–popular entity – i.e. excluding class struggle from its centre (Jessop 1985: 64).

But if the state contains this contradiction, so too does Poulantzas's work. There is a clear and evolving conflict between an analysis of the state's structural–functional role in securing the cohesiveness of a social formation and the state and its institutions as the effect of the class struggle. Poulantzas gradually abandons structuralism so that in his final book, *State, Power, Socialism*, he argues that the state should not be regarded as an intrinsic entity, that 'it is rather a relationship of forces, or more precisely the material condensation of such a relationship among classes and class fractions' (Poulantzas 1978: 128). There is no longer mention of the structurally determined role of the state in securing the unity of the capitalist social formation. Rather, the state comes to be regarded as embodying class positions and class practices, thus allowing the dominated classes to build up centres of resistance within the relatively independent apparatuses of the state itself. As Bob Jessop notes (Jessop 1985: 134), the structural determination of hegemony or the class unity of the state as a functional imperative of the reproduction of the social whole gives way to the view that these are simply structural–institutional effects of the class struggle. In fact, Poulantzas ends up taking positions not that dissimilar to E.P. Thompson:

> Just as the relations of production and the social division of labour do
> not constitute an economic structure outside (before) social classes so

they do not belong to a field external to power and class struggle. There are no social classes prior to their opposition in struggle.

(Poulantzas 1978: 27)

This shift towards a view of the state as an institutional condensation of social relations and the class struggle affects Poulantzas's conception of hegemony. This is noted by Jessop who writes that Poulantzas sometimes bases his view of hegemony on the structural determination of political class domination and state form, while at other times he moves towards the more strategic view that relates hegemony to political class positions (Jessop 1985: 186). Jessop in fact argues that hegemony does not belong to Poulantzas's most abstract levels but rather to the level of juridico-political institutions and the class struggle. Hence the structural determination of hegemony is grounded in the particular form of political class domination existing in a given state system (Jessop 1985: 139).

The problem is that Poulantzas is unable to satisfactorily combine the structural determination of hegemony with its political expression and class development. In terms of critical realism's transformational model of social activity, Poulantzas cannot reconcile the social structures from which the functional role of hegemony is derived with the processes of reproduction and transformation that necessarily reflect class positions and class practices as they are concretely and consciously expressed through hegemonic projects. Instead, we find in Poulantzas a dualism, a division between an overly structural account that is contained in his main writings, and a less structural, relational approach found in his late work. If in his early work the effects of class struggle is missing, it returns later on as a replacement for, rather than a complement to, a structural account. With Poulantzas we either get a structural or a relational approach to hegemony, but he never manages to properly combine the two.

There are three particularly prominent trends in the development of Poulantzas's thought which can be questioned. The first is the shift in the conception of the state and hegemony from a structuralist to a relational analysis. Moving away from the Gramscian distinction between political and civil society, Poulantzas comes to see the state and its apparatuses (Ideological State Apparatuses and Repressive State Apparatuses) as cutting across all aspects of social life. However, these apparatuses and institutions are only the effects of the political class struggle. It is through the state that hegemony operates, a representation of political and ideological class practices. Particularly noticeable is the importance Poulantzas attributes to the ideological class struggle. The battle for control of the general interest, and the juridico-political apparatuses whose role is to interpellate class subjects as individuals.

Poulantzas's second trend is to overemphasise the tendency towards interventionist and exceptional forms of state. This is connected to his view that the state cuts across all forms of life and that institutions and apparatuses are embodiments of class relations and practices. This, we can say, is a reflection of Poulantzas's error in rejecting the distinction necessary (at least at a theoretical/analytical level) between political and civil society. There is a tendency for Poulantzas to over-politicise his theoretical analysis, marked also in his notion of the interventionist state whose role is not only to secure the political and ideological conditions necessary for capital accumulation, but also to intervene in the economic processes themselves, particularly in securing the reproduction of labour power. There is clearly some correctness in this position which implies a more dialectical relationship between the political and the economic. But it leads to the view that monopoly capitalism requires an 'interventionist' state of an authoritarian or strong character. These 'exceptional' states are marked by their increased control over social life and the economy, and the rise of bureaucracy and administrative apparatuses. These developments are never concretely explained by Poulantzas. For example, the 'exceptional' form of state is exceptional from what? Why should Western bourgeois democracies be considered by implication to be normal? Poulantzas's economic arguments, tending towards a theory of state monopoly capitalism, likewise fail to substantiate themselves. In fact, the arguments concerning the development of monopoly capitalism and interventionist states are still inextricably tied to a political problematic increasingly motivated by a rejection of Leninism, the third trend in Poulantzas's work.

The trend towards economic intervention necessitates authoritarian states. However, the paradox involved here is that while state power is strengthened, the ability to hegemonise is weakened. This occurs both within the power bloc, which is now dominated by a fraction of monopoly capital, and between the power bloc and the dominated masses. Since Poulantzas's position is now that the state and its apparatuses are the effects or institutional embodiment of class relations, the weakening of hegemony means that the whole set of state apparatuses are now also vulnerable, making it possible for the dominated classes to capture state apparatuses. Thus the class struggle takes place within the state itself. In effect the state becomes a strategic terrain.

This represents Poulantzas's first break with Leninism. Since the state, and in particular the 'exceptional' state, intervenes into all areas of social life right up to securing the reproduction of labour power, then the class struggle is reflected and condensed within the state. Thus Poulantzas rejects the traditional idea of 'smashing' the state, instead arguing that it is possible to capture the state by means of a war of positions rather than by any frontal attack. This is quite clearly a Euro-communist position, a rejection of the necessity of revolution in favour of the democratic road to socialism. But it is combined with another trend in Euro-communism, the 'popular' struggle which, as we shall see, also attracts theorists like Ernesto Laclau. The justification for the popular struggle lies in Poulantzas's belief in the rise of authoritarian states. The strengthening of the state necessarily weakens the ruling hegemony. Direct involvement in the economy sharpens the divisions within the power bloc and weakens the structures of consent. The authoritarian nature of this process thus defines the mass struggle as a popular–democratic struggle. The logic of this position, as we shall see in the next chapter, is that the working class should subordinate itself to the popular masses, giving up its specific economic demands in order to articulate the national–popular consciousness of the masses. Hence the role of the vanguard is lost and the struggle for working-class dual power is replaced with a struggle for popular power within the existing apparatus. This whole position is clearly outlined at the end of *State, Power, Socialism* where:

> the real alternative raised by the democratic road to socialism is indeed that of a struggle of the popular masses to modify the relationship of forces within the state, as opposed to a frontal, dual power type of strategy.
>
> (Poulantzas 1978: 259)

Fractions, strata, social categories and bureaucracies

Perhaps Poulantzas's most useful contribution is his concern with breaking social classes down into fractions and other social groups. Clearly there are potential dangers involved in taking this process too far, for it can end up overstressing social divisions among the struggling classes rather than their potential revolutionary unity. But this analysis of social groups and fractions adds another dimension to the cohesive, unifying role of hegemony. Poulantzas's strength is to stress that hegemony is not simply about gaining consent from the dominated classes, but is also a matter of unifying the dominant power bloc as well as competing blocs, alliances and projects. This is made clear in Poulantzas's brief essay on the English revolution:

> Since the commercial bourgeoisie was insufficiently developed and the industrial bourgeoisie was almost non-existent, neither could take over the leadership of the process. This revolution might therefore appear *premature*, when regarded from an exclusively political point of view. But if we consider the ensemble of the relations of the formation, the revolution happened *at the right time*, since it made possible to dispose of the problem of the dominance of the CMP [capitalist mode of production] over the other modes in agriculture; i.e., to liquidate small-scale production … In the transition from feudalism to capitalism in Britain, this problem could be solved only by initiating the revolutionary process in an apparently *impure* form under the leadership of a fraction of the land-owning bourgeoisie which was already on its way to establishing its independence from the feudal nobility. In

other words, the revolutionary process had to be initiated on the political plane and under the leadership of a fraction which, politically speaking, was still a fraction of the nobility.

(Poulantzas 1973b: 169)

Poulantzas distinguishes between different social groups and fractions on the basis that concrete social formations contain within them 'an over-lapping of several modes of production, one of which holds the dominant role' (Poulantzas 1973b: 71). This allows Poulantzas to develop his important distinctions between fractions, categories and strata.

Fractions correspond to different interests, powers and relations within classes, they are the substratum of eventual social forces. These differences must again be related to structures and generative mechanisms, for example, fractions exist within the bourgeois class based upon finance capital and industrial capital.

Social categories are defined as social ensembles with 'pertinent effects', with a specific overdetermining relation to political and ideological structures. Social categories do not have the same autonomy as class fractions and are comprised of various classes and fractions, but are unified by their structural relations and functions. The most notable examples of social categories are the bureaucracy and the intelligentsia.

Finally, Poulantzas refers to *social strata*, the secondary effect of the combination of modes of production in a social formation. Poulantzas here specifically refers to the labour aristocracy. The key distinction, therefore, is that fractions are determined by economic differentiations whereas social strata are defined by political and ideological structural determinants. Social categories are a result of a drawing together of diverse agents who are united by their function, for example, the various bureaucracies.

The potential danger in Poulantzas's categorisation is that it might overemphasise political and ideological differentiations, perhaps leading to the kind of fragmentation and difference characteristic of the theories of Foucault and post-structuralism. It also shifts the emphasis away from economic factors, and Poulantzas grants certain fractions, and even perhaps social categories such as the bureaucracy, a political autonomy that tends to undermine the more basic economic distinctions. Nevertheless, these distinctions do help clarify the nature of political alliances, strategies and blocs, elevating hegemony to a crucial significance. Against economic determinism, Poulantzas's analysis allows a genuine role to be given to political processes. Due to the fact that classes and social groups have many different determinations – political and ideological as well as economic – an important significance is given to the construction and maintenance of political blocs. These blocs unite the various social groups through a negotiation of interests. An economically dominant class is thus not immediately assured of political power. This must be achieved through a power bloc which 'constitutes a contradictory unity of *politically dominant* classes and fractions *under the protection of the hegemonic fraction'*. This unity is never assured since the class struggle and the particular rivalry of interests is constantly present. Thus the bloc is far from being a fusion; indeed the specific interests of the hegemonic fraction within the bloc ensures a certain polarisation (Poulantzas 1973b: 239).

Poulantzas goes on to talk of supporting classes, comprised of those groups who lend their support to the power bloc while requiring no real sacrifices from that bloc. The classical case is the petite bourgeoisie. However, such a vague notion of supporting classes is rather unsatisfactory. Maybe the petite bourgeoisie is not offered any real political concessions and does not form part of the power bloc, but it certainly gains a number of social concessions which can then be defended through certain appara-tuses. The 'support' of such supporting classes must be maintained, therefore, through continuing hegemonic relations. The notion of sup-porting classes is also inadequate since it seems to be confined to the petite bourgeoisie. However, there are many other groups who may support the power bloc and who gain clear concessions for doing so. The problematic position of the labour aristocracy is one example. It is clearly not a supporting class because its class determination lies within the working class. However, one of Poulantzas's important insights is to argue that class determinations and class positions do not necessarily correspond. Thus, in a particular conjuncture, a section of the petite bourgeoisie may take up a working-class position without actually becoming a part of the working class. The labour aristocracy, representing an economically privileged stratum of the working class, can clearly be seen to be taking up the positions of the dominant classes and defending them ideologically and politically. We can thus term the labour aristocracy a supporting stratum.

In lending their support to the power bloc, the labour aristocracy is granted a number of concessions. As well as economic privileges, it is also rewarded with the necessary ideological and political powers to maintain its status as a privileged stratum over the mass of unskilled and semi-skilled workers. In Britain we can see that the post-war hegemony is very much a product of these sort of concessions to sections of the working class as well as the petite bourgeoisie. Thus we require another distinction. The labour aristocracy is clearly not integrated into the power bloc itself; however, its status as a supporting stratum is not a passive one as Poulantzas seems to suggest. There is a clear hegemonic relationship between the forces of the power bloc itself and the most active supporting elements. This relation-ship is based upon the granting of a number of concessions and a maintenance of certain privileges, however small. A group like the labour aristocracy lies neither within the power bloc itself, nor simply with the dominated masses. It thus forms part of a broader, more historically motivated alliance.

The distinction that is necessary is therefore between the ruling *power bloc*, and the *historical bloc*. The historical bloc is made up of the power bloc and the supporting classes and strata. These supporting elements do receive a number of small concessions but do not enter into the actual power bloc. They are part of a broader hegemonic order which controls and pacifies the masses, again through certain concessions if necessary. As Chapter 9 will later examine, the post-war hegemonic order saw the ruling class rebuild and reconstruct its hegemonic relations through incorporating sections of the working class and the labour bureaucracy into a closer historical bloc, while granting major concessions to the working class in general. Welfarism and consumerism provided the ideological cement for this new hegemonic order.

The question of the labour bureaucracy is more problematic. These leaders are not simply bureaucrats of the labour movement, although this is quite clearly their social base. By taking office, the labour bureaucracy becomes part of the state bureaucracy as well. There does not seem an adequate way to classify the labour bureaucracy based upon Poulantzas's definitions. In a sense, it is a privileged stratum of the working class. But through the unifying function of bureaucratic interest and governmental office, the labour bureaucracy could also be defined as a social category. And the actual interests that the labour bureaucracy has in defending capitalism and lending support to the ruling class suggests that it actually gains an autonomy from the working class if not from its organisations, thus giving it more the character of a fraction.

This example suggests that Poulantzas's categories need to be employed in a more flexible manner, allowing that social groups may be constituted in a number of different ways, a combination of different determinations which are not fixed but are continually being reproduced. In a certain sense, the labour bureaucracy has actually risen above the ranks of the working class in parasitic manner, to the point where it actually enters the ruling power bloc itself, albeit as a junior partner. This certainly gives the labour bureaucracy a bourgeois character, although it is not a fraction of the bourgeoisie. However, it is clearly necessary to acknowledge the divisions within the labour bureaucracy between left and right elements, and the social and political bases to which these elements belong.

There are two structural factors that give the labour bureaucracy its peculiar character. First is the contradiction contained within the structures of the labour movement which are at the same time both structures of the working class – and hence sites for a working-class counter hegemony – and, also, structures of capitalist society – and hence also integrated into bourgeois hegemony. The second structural determination of the labour bureaucracy lies in its contradictory relationship to both the labour-movement structures of the working class which are its power base, and the structures of the capitalist state. We can therefore say that often the labour bureaucracy straddles the working class and the bourgeoisie, but that it does so in a political and functional sense, rather than in a full social sense. This does, however, give the labour bureaucracy a sort of autonomy which allows it to participate in the power bloc despite the fact that it is a privileged section of the working class. However, the precariousness of this social position means that the labour bureaucracy is vulnerable to a challenge from the organised rank and file, as must be the case if the trade unions are to be turned into more militant bodies.

This recalls Lenin's description of the Labour Party as a bourgeois workers' party that is organically related to the working class but which has bourgeois politics. A reworked Poulantzian analysis is clearly compatible with this position, for Lenin is effectively arguing that the labour bureaucrats derive their power and social base from the organised working class, but through their political and functional relation to the capitalist state, take up bourgeois class positions. This contradictory class position compromises the labour bureaucracy. Its working-class base means that it can play only a secondary role within the ruling power bloc, chiefly called upon to discipline its own ranks, but with a degree of bargaining power. Its status within the ruling bloc depends upon the balance of class forces and the state of capitalism. Following the onslaught of neo-liberal government policies, the labour bureaucracy no longer enjoys the kind of privileged position it held during the golden age of the post-war period.

We can therefore develop a concept of *contradictory political location* of which the labour aristocracy and labour bureaucracy are both variants. This is in contrast to the notion of contradictory *class* locations which according to theorists like Erik Olin Wright accounts for the bureaucracy and other state positions. The distinction that we are making here is a determination of a more 'superstructural' or political nature. The notion of contradictory political locations, rather than contradictory class locations, implies that class is determined at a more fundamental level – in relation to the means of production – but that class position is a more fragile construct by virtue of its more 'superstructural' or political determination. Perhaps more to the point, the development of contradictory locations is testament to the power of the hegemonic process itself in shaping and reshaping classes, fractions and social groups.

Fascism and bourgeois crisis

Poulantzas's analysis of hegemonic blocs and political processes is also helpful in developing an understanding of fascism. Poulantzas rightly sees the main weakness in Trotsky's account of fascism as a tendency to see fascism in terms of an economic rather than a political crisis. Such a position can easily degenerate into an instrumentalist conception which sees fascism simply as a 'battering ram' to be used against the workers' movement in times of economic difficulty. Thus Poulantzas adds the necessary analysis of the political and ideological crisis under which the hegemony of the ruling classes suffers a crisis of legitimacy.

However, Poulantzas's arguments should be incorporated into Trotsky's analysis rather than being posed as an alternative, for the overall arguments are wrong. First, it is not correct to say that fascism is representative of a political crisis rather than an economic crisis. The sort of political crisis necessary to empower fascism is inevitably going to be connected to an acute economic crisis. Second, Poulantzas presents fascism as an exceptional form of the capitalist state. This implies that democratic bourgeois states are normal – a position which displays the Euro-communist illusions in bourgeois democracy. Thus, for Poulantzas, the struggle against fascism takes the form of a struggle against an authoritarian state, rather than assuming a particularly revolutionary or anti-capitalist character. This struggle takes the form of the popular–democratic struggle, the Euro-communist form of the popular front, rather than Trotsky's united front. Such a policy fails to offer adequate leadership, instead tail-ending the social democrats and bourgeois forces, the very people who, as Trotsky's analysis shows, contribute to the rise of fascism.

However, some of Poulantzas's arguments are worth developing. The most important point is to develop an understanding of fascism as intimately linked to a crisis of hegemony, and hence a product of specific political, ideological and cultural factors as well as the more general economic ones. It is therefore necessary to distinguish between the dominant classes in an economic sense – objectively derived from the mode of production – and the hegemonic classes and fractions in the social formation. These, in certain conjunctures do not always correspond – fascism is precisely such a moment.

The growth of fascist parties corresponds, as Trotsky rightly notes, to the weakness of the left and the failure of its leadership. However, Trotsky perhaps underestimates the political weakness of the traditional parties of the bourgeoisie, instead focusing more on the economic weakness of the ruling class. We can say, therefore, that fascism begins to grow at a time of structural crisis, taking advantage of the ensuing crisis of hegemony of the bourgeoisie. The most striking aspect of this situation is the crisis of the political representation of the bourgeoisie. The role of the traditional bourgeois parties in securing the necessary political, ideological and cultural conditions necessary for capital accumulation is undermined. This crisis of representation is no mere electoral crisis, but a serious crisis of hegemony, reflecting political, cultural and ideological weaknesses.

The crisis of legitimacy that affects the bourgeois parties reflects a crisis of hegemony at quite a deep structural level. Thus fascism is no mere instrument to be used in times of crisis. Rather, it is very much a part of this crisis, organically linked to the political, ideological and economic spheres. It has its own dynamics and represents an organic development based on structural dislocation. Given that fascism reflects the political weakness of the bourgeoisie, it is wrong simply to ask whether or not the ruling class will look to fascism to solve its problems. Fascism grows under conditions of structural crisis. Seen in this more organic sense, it must therefore be asked, what ability and desire do the sections of the bourgeois class have in trying to *resist* the rise of fascism?

It is true that the classical conditions of full economic crisis and the revolutionary threat of the working class need to be in place if fascism is to stand a chance of coming to power. In this case, of course, the bourgeoisie turns to fascism as a last resort, financing the movement and giving it a cover of legitimacy to rule on its behalf. These conditions also secure the petit-bourgeois mass base necessary at both electoral and organisational levels. But even if these conditions are not in place, fascism as a movement is still a threat. It highlights a crisis in the hegemony of the bourgeoisie, hence, in a structural sense, it fills a vacuum vacated by bourgeois politics. This hegemonic crisis can mean that fascist parties are in the position to set the political pace. Even today, although talk of fascism in Europe is overstated, a smaller-scale crisis of political representation and legitimacy is evident and the far right has been able to encourage a less liberal agenda. Although such parties in Austria, Italy, France and Belgium are not fascist in the classical sense, being more of an authoritarian–populist nature, it would certainly be wrong to ignore the neo-fascist aspects of these organisations and the forces behind them.

5 Posts and structures

Introduction

An interesting recent development has been the unfolding relation between various so-called 'post-Marxisms', post-structuralism and deconstruction. This is often specific to the development of British theory and represents the fallout from the Althusserian and culturalist (often Gramscian) turns of the 1970s.[1] What is often retained from this is the central role of hegemony. This trend has been given official sanction by Jacques Derrida's recent turn to Marx.

Deconstruction has not been at all sympathetic to Marxism. This can be said at both a theoretical and an institutional level. Sections of American academia have taken it to the forefront of their assault on emancipatory discourses, while at a theoretical level, deconstruction claims radicality all for itself. It argues that true subversion lies in undermining the text and the radical use of word-play. Politics and identity become textual, or at least interpretive, matters. For deconstruction, to make any claim beyond this is to risk descending into metaphysics. It is natural, therefore, that deconstruction should be hostile to Marxism, a materialist theory which claims to represent a social scientific outlook. Marxism is ontological and tries to establish a basis for meaning that lies beyond the text. For deconstruction this is impossible. Meaning can only be conferred through the text. To try to move beyond the text is to try to move beyond the sole basis for meaningfulness.

Yet various 'deconstructors', including Derrida himself, have claimed an interest in Marxism. This chapter will investigate Derrida's recent arguments as set out in *Specters of Marx* (1994) along with those of the discourse theorists Ernesto Laclau and Chantal Mouffe, who have tried to link deconstruction to radical politics, invoking in different ways strategy and thereby hegemony.

Derrida's spirit

The starting point for Derrida's deconstructive project is his opposition to the 'metaphysics of presence'. He is not choosy about his targets – the transcendental ideality of Husserl, or subjective identity are just as much targets as any materialist thesis. For Derrida they all commit the same error of foundationalism, whereby traditional notions of presence always rely on the foundations of origin or final cause.

From the structuralism of Saussure, Derrida takes up the notion of the negativity of language. Signs have no positive meaning in themselves but derive their meaning through their relations with other elements. Identity and meaning are products of a system of internal differences so that meaning is never identical with itself but is the result of difference and articulation. Structuralist linguistics therefore severs the connection with the referent or real external object referred to by a sign. The word 'book' does not refer to a real book; the relationship is an arbitrary one based on social convention. Meaning becomes differential rather than referential. However, while structuralism is correct in suggesting that words derive meaning through their relations with other words, there is a danger of taking this too far and it would be wrong to suggest that words do not, or have only an accidental relation to anything outside of language. Words may derive their meaning from relations with other words, but they refer to things outside language by virtue of their relation to these other words (Collier 1994: 5).

Structuralism points to the unstable, arbitrary nature of meaning. Derrida's project of deconstruction argues that Western metaphysics has sought to impose an identity by seeking a transcendental signified which could stabilise meaning around a fixed point. This process he describes as logocentrism, and the logocentric tradition has elevated certain terms over others and is based on the imposition of a dominant political framework. It is here that we find the first connection between deconstruction and a theory of hegemony in that the fixing of meaning is a political process based on relations of power and domination. Deconstruction, as a political project, seeks to subvert these hierarchies and through the concept of *differance* tries to re-open the uncertainty of language. Derrida's concept of *differance* has a double meaning, indicating both spatial differing and temporal deferring. The purpose of the concept is to highlight how identity is only established according to how it differs from or delays something else. Meaning is relational and within an articulatory system the connection between the signified and the signifier is never fixed. The deferral of meaning leaves a chain or trace which indicates displacement, dislocation and effacement. Derrida uses the concept of trace to show that meaning is about the endless play of signification and that an identity can be overcome by showing how it has had to be imposed. Logocentrism is attacked for seeking to impose a fixed identity or presence; it is under-mined by showing how this presupposes a set of power relations and how those relations might be other than they are.

Derrida continues this attack on presence in his recent book *Specters of Marx*, whose very title attempts to undermine the certainty of appearance and meaning. Instead of representing the certainty of the present, the ghost represents the trace of the past and the anticipation of something to come. The ghost is playful and elusive, it rejects identity and presence for subversion, it is the visibility of the invisible. The bodiless and ungraspable character of the spectre might also be applied more widely to a field of spectrality, a whole domain that Derrida calls hauntology. And such a domain, Derrida believes, is well described by certain Marxist concepts, in particular those that analyse the phantom-like commodification of the world and the way that social relations take a ghostly fetishised form: 'In other words, as soon as there is production, there is fetishism: idealisation, autonomisation and automatisation, dematerialisation and spectral incorporation, mourning work coextensive with all work, and so forth' (Derrida 1994: 166). Thus Derrida draws out the spectrality of Marx's account of the phenomenology of capitalism and wider society and the dominance within this society of spectral forms like commodity fetishism. These spectral forms have a mystifying effect. First, '[t]hese ghosts that are commodities transform human producers into ghosts', but then this process acts as a 'mysterious mirror' so that 'the returned (deformed, objectified, naturalised) image becomes that of a social relation among commodities' (Derrida 1994: 156) and the spectral becomes real.

If capitalist society is spectral, it is nevertheless haunted by an alternative – the spectre that is haunting Europe, the spectre of communism. When Marx and Engels wrote these words, communism did not yet exist, but its spectre held Europe in fear. Now, after the fall of the so-called communist regimes, Marxism, Derrida believes, can never exist as a system. But contrary to fashionable thought, its spirit will live on:

> The spectre that Marx was talking about then, communism, was there without being there. It was not yet there. It will never be there. There is no *Dasein* of the spectre, but there is no *Dasein* without the uncanniness, without the strange familiarity ... of some spectre. What is a spectre? What is its history and what is its time?
>
> (Derrida 1994: 100)

Denying the *Dasein* of the spectre means that communism will never come into being or acquire the presence of a system or a coherent movement. Derrida finds any such attempts to come into being as undesirable in that they produce such things as totalitarian states, authoritarian parties and rigid doctrines. However, our being-in-the-world will continue to be affected by the spirit or trace of Marxism, and this true, critical spirit of Marxism, as opposed to its distorted bodily forms, is what should be maintained.

Derrida is being mischievous in two ways. First, he is 'conjuring' up the spirit of Marx against the 'present' world order (the spectrality of capitalism, the New World Order and the claims of the 'new' right). But he is also 'conjuring' up the spirit of Marx to undermine what we might call the corpus of Marxism. For Derrida is dragging the spirit of Marx out of the body of Marxism which as a tradition he almost totally discards (very humbly professing himself not to have much compentence in this field). Of course, Marx's thought is cleansed of the 'metaphysics' of presence and identity. Derrida prefers Marx's spectre because it has a floating, translucent, bodiless nature (Derrida 1994: 99).

An appropriate new neologism is found – that of ontology/hauntology. Thus to invoke the 'spirit of Marxism' is necessarily to undermine its ontological body. The bodily remains are left to 'the work of mourning'. It is a farewell to 'ontological Marxism' and its dialectical materialism, its concepts of labour, mode of production and social class (Derrida 1994: 88). So why, without any of these things, should Derrida still be interested in Marx? Quite simply because: '"The time is out of joint": time is *disarticulated*, dislocated, dislodged, ... *deranged*, both out of order and mad. Time is off its hinges ...' (Derrida 1994: 18). And in recognising this situation, Derrida wishes to confront its main apologists the smug theorists of neo-liberalism, the New World Order and the End of History.

Even if it is only in a 'spiritual' or critical sense, Derrida is at least defending something in Marx and making some sort of stand against the triumphalism of the new neo-liberal right. Given his theoretical location and the reputation of his followers, it would have been far easier for Derrida to join the reactionary march. So, importantly, Derrida attacks the postmoderns lined up behind Fukuyama's theory of the end of history. Despite its complexities, Fukuyama's work can only end up by endorsing the new neo-liberal right, the Cold War victory and the barbarism of the New World Order.

Derrida, despite his postmodern following, does have a commitment to reason insofar as he wishes to examine the limits and errors of this reason. His aspirations are in this sense closer to Kant's project of a critique of reason than to the attacks most of the postmodernists have launched on reason itself. He wants to explore the limits and boundaries of reason from within. So Derrida has to defend something of the Enlightenment and something of Marxism. He wants to defend those who resisted reactionary, conservative, anti-scientific or obscurantist temptations, did not renounce an ideal of democracy and emancipation, but who in a deconstructive spirit, believe in an Enlightenment to come (Derrida 1994: 90). Rather than defending the 'dogma' of Marxist or Enlightenment politics, Derrida, once more, defends a certain spirit of Marxism and the Enlightenment:

> if there is a spirit of Marxism which I will never be ready to renounce, it is not only the critical idea or the questioning stance ... It is even more a certain emancipatory and *messianic* affirmation, a certain experience of the promise that one can try to liberate from any dogmatics ....
>
> (Derrida 1994: 89)

This conception of the messianic must be thought of as a promise that is made now even though what is promised is not here. Derrida sees an intimate link between the promise and the question of democracy while at stake is 'the very concept of democracy as concept of a promise that can only arise in such a *diastema* (failure, inadequation, disjunction, disadjustment, being "out of joint")' (Derrida 1994: 64). Democracy is not so much a future democracy as a democracy to come. This promise of a new messianism plays a central theme for Derrida. Thus he criticises Althusser for dissociating Marx from both eschatology and teleology rather than separating them. Eschatology is for Derrida a positive thing, a promise to come. But democracy is not here. It will not even arrive in the future. We are back to the play of the spirit, back to the ungraspable elusiveness of spectrality. In a similar vein, Derrida talks of law not in terms of actual law but the 'undeconstuctibility of a certain idea of justice'. He shifts from the world of politics to the spirituality of ethics. And finally he talks of an oppositional movement: 'Barely deserving the name community, the new International belong[ing] only to anonymity' (Derrida 1994: 90).

Unfortunately, the playfulness of his approach leaves us with nothing concrete. Derrida's concept of a new International is little more than a linguistic gesture, a spontaneous thing, based on critical opposition to the state and international law, and on an unspecified ideal. Anything more prescriptive than this would be a cardinal ontological sin. By raising the idea of the new International he is haunted by the spectres of other Internationals – some of which actually did things. In comparison, Derrida's politics represent no more than a liberal consensus or minimum programme. There is opposition to unemployment, homelessness, economic conflict, the free market, foreign debt, the arms industry, nuclear weapons, inter-ethnic wars, capitalist phantom-states and international law. But, predictably, nothing positive in its own right; interesting and broadly agreeable aims, but hardly a radical hegemonic project. Above all, what Derrida's International lacks is the concrete question of methods, direction and leadership. Unsurprisingly, Derrida has no class analysis. Instead he offers us a 'link of affinity, suffering and hope' (Derrida 1994: 85). He fails to offer any relationship to those who can and will fight for these aims. Instead we are left with a community of intellectuals.

If Derrida is really offering a hegemonic project that seeks to articulate radical elements around a certain progressive discourse, he is doing so in a mythical rather than a concrete way. Against Gramsci's organic intellectuals, we have non-organic intellectuals with political roots not in reality but in ideality. Georges Sorel seems to be an absent ghost here. His emphasis on the moral, cultural and intellectual collapse of society can only be overcome by an ideal. Hence mythos replaces logos. Sorel's 'reflections on violence' offer a parallel with the work of Derrida's mentor, Emmanuel Levinas, whose conception of violence is marked by an attempt to free the self from the *il y a* (there is), of anonymous being. Levinas connects this to the promise of justice, the messianic. But if Sorel's call to arms is based on an expression of a creative, almost poetic urge, there must be a historical warning. For if Derrida is ridding Marxism of its scientific metaphysics and offering a Sorelian poetics of myth instead, then who decides on the politics?

This emphasises the central importance of a correct notion of hegemony. Derrida has a narrow, one-sided usage of the concept which relates it exclusively to the act of (discursive) domination and suppression. However, the post-Marxists around Laclau and Mouffe have been quicker than Derrida to see that the play of *differance* and the indeterminacy it creates provide a terrain for a new reading of hegemony. Thus Laclau and Mouffe develop a conception of political strategy based on the coincidence of *differance* and hegemony. Not surprisingly, they pick out the liberal themes of democracy and pluralism which are tied to the indeterminacy of their terrain. But we can see that Derrida has the same implicit notion of hegemony when he talks of the emancipatory promise of the new International and democracy and justice to come.

Unfortunately, this concept of hegemony in Derrida, and in Laclau and Mouffe, is really little more than another word for articulation with an element of decision thrown in. It is true that there is a close relation since articulation around a certain centre is connected to domination and suppression as well as a certain fusion or cohesion of the elements that are articulated. But surely hegemony loses its true meaning once it is separated from its material location in social practices and structures and is confined to the role of a discursive articulator?

For critical realists, hegemony retains its functional role as a factor of social cohesion and its strategic role as an articulator of action within the context of the preservation or transformation of social structures. The discursive is important in terms of the role of ideology, the mediation of language and the transitive conditions of knowledge, but these can only be properly understood by reference to the material conditions within which they are set. Why one discourse is more powerful than another is an extra-discursive question. Deconstruction may help us analyse the social and the political in discourse, but we also need a theory capable of analysing the place of discourse in the wider socio-political world.

An inability to act

Derrida is rather changing the script when he praises Marxism as the radical spirit behind deconstruction, claiming that deconstruction only has sense or interest as a radicalisation '*in the tradition* of a certain Marxism, in a certain *spirit of Marxism*' (Derrida 1994: 92). Whatever Derrida's own intentions, academics have largely used deconstruction to attack Marxism and other emancipatory discourses, resulting in a justification of the world as it is. There may be something radical in the questioning stance of deconstruction but there is nothing intrinsically progressive about it, for it attacks all discourses, not just oppressive, dominant discourses, but any discourse, emancipatory as well.

Some form of deconstruction, in itself, is not necessarily a bad idea. So long as the philosophical arguments against metaphysics and ontology are challenged and so long as deconstruction is regarded as a historicised critique of power, privilege and presence within the Western metaphysical tradition, it can be a useful tool for textual analysis. Derrida's grammatology is hard to refute. Indeed, it is surely compatible with Marxism (or realism for that matter) to say that, within writing, the 'play of differences supposes, in effect, syntheses, and referrals which forbid at any moment, or in any sense, that a simple element be *present* in and of itself, referring only to itself' (Derrida 1981b: 26). This analysis can incorporate something akin to overdetermination, as well as dialectics and the notion of things as relations and processes. Indeed, in some respects, Derrida's conception of writing may be considered an advance on Althusser, since it incorporates a temporal or diachronic element against the fixity of synchrony, based on an 'interweaving of elements', each element 'being constituted on the basis of the trace within it of the other elements of the chain or system' (Derrida 1981b: 26).

The irrealist error of deconstruction (that of the followers if not necessarily Derrida himself) is to raise these insights above their station, promoting textual practice not as one practice among many, but as the only practice of significance (or the all-constituting terrain of practice). Everything else is bracketed off from enquiry as 'outside the text'. So although these things outside the text might exist, we might say, following Wittgenstein, that 'a nothing would serve just as well as a something about which nothing could be said' (Wittgenstein 1958: 102). We can see the effect of such a move in the evolution of Barry Hindess and Paul Hirst, where history, for them, no longer refers to actual historical processes, practices and events, but to historical texts, as if actual historical events could themselves just be bracketed off because the account has become more important than the event.

Deconstruction is no *substitute* for radical politics. By claiming exclusivity, deconstruction inhibits the power of its own insights. What is striking about Derrida's *Specters of Marx* is its inability to offer any coherent political message. This is because of its anti-ontological stance. Derrida's project is to rouse the spirit of Marxism as a critique in the same manner that deconstruction itself can be a subversive critique. However, this is a critique that is deprived of its most important category (not to mention agent), namely class:

> one may thus, for example, speak of a dominant discourse or of dominant representations and ideas, and refer in this way to a hierarchised and conflictual field without necessarily subscribing to the

> concept of social class ... this ultimate support which would be the
> identity and the self-identity of a social class by means of which Marx
> so often determined ... the forces that are fighting for control of the
> hegemony.
>
> (Derrida 1994: 55)

Class is therefore identified as a foundational concept, a metaphysical presence, an identity principle which must be exorcised from Marxist thinking. As an alternative to class, Derrida suggests the idea of a 'hegemonic force' represented by a 'dominant rhetoric and ideology'. However, this counterposition is wrong. Instead, by *combining* the idea of class with the idea of hegemonic force we move away from the brutal, simplistic, self-identity of class which Derrida presumes Marxism to defend. And, conversely, by combining the idea of hegemonic force with the idea of class we can at last provide some content to the politics that Derrida is patently unable to provide.

But instead of taking this simple path, Derrida moves to politics by embracing eschatology and the messianic, reducing social emancipation to a mystical and symbolic status. His anti-ontological position means he cannot say anything concrete about a project of social emancipation for to do so would be to embrace concepts like presence and identity. It would be too much of an imposition of meaning, of closure, it would undermine the cherished play of *differance*. Emancipation has to be given a more elusive character. It is a promise based on a creative and poetic urge. Logos is replaced by mythos. Politics assumes a creative, aesthetic character.

But politics cannot be based on some kind of creative urge alone. Attempts to do so have ended up embracing spontaneity at the expense of direction. Prescriptive politics is often accused of being elitist and the Bolsheviks and the Jacobins were both attacked for insisting on the need for political direction and leadership. But embracing spontaneity is far more likely to lead to an elitist political position. Georges Sorel, so much admired by Laclau and Mouffe, based his politics on the creative urge. His supporters began by advocating the spontaneous syndicalism of the revolutionary movements in Northern Italy but many of them ended up as fascists. Heidegger, mentor of Derrida, likewise based his politics on the moral, cultural and intellectual collapse of society and also became a fascist. There is also the elitism of a whole number of writers – Nietzsche, Lawrence, Yeats, or the Italian Futurists – for whom art, culture and politics merge into a symbolic form of expression. All these writers emphasise spontaneity and the power of the will. All of them embrace the symbolic. And, ultimately, the spontaneity of the many is replaced by the symbolic acts of the few. So, at stake is really what politics is all about. Does it move in an explanatory direction, making certain claims about the way society is and offering practical solutions to these problems? Or does the struggle for liberation take on a spontaneous, artistic and expressive form? Derrida's philosophical position – his attacks on metaphysics, identity or indeed of any ontological claims – commits him to political symbolism.

So while Derrida is keen on the idea of democracy as representative of the promise, his interest is not with any particular form of democracy, but with an open-ended, pluralistic system of differences intimately connected to the play of discourse. But because of this it becomes no more than a regulating ideal, an abstract, neutral play of differences which avoids any commitment to any particular democratic process. As far as the actual, concrete, political nature of democracy is concerned, Derrida is trapped. He wants to say something but he cannot. He wants to talk about social issues, but why should we listen? He is opposed to poverty, the free market, the arms industry and international law. But he cannot offer anything positive. He would be committing an ontic fallacy if he were to make any claims about the non-spiritual world.

But on the important issue of whether Derrida believes there is anything beyond the text, he is not saying, as is commonly stated, that only the text exists, and he makes the point that 'it was never our wish to extend the reassuring notion of the text to a whole extra-textual realm and to transform the world into a library by doing away with all boundaries' (Derrida 1979: 84). Rather, Derrida argues that everything we come across is mediated textually. We cannot step outside of this and see things 'as they are'. To say we cannot get outside the text is to say that we cannot escape from context.

Critical realists should have no problem in supporting such a position insofar as it recognises the social and transitive character of knowledge. It should not mean that knowledge becomes more important or significant than the real world, only that our knowledge of the world is always mediated through discourse or the text. We cannot step outside these relations – they shape our conceptions of the world and mediate our relationship to it. Where Derrida errs is to turn from this correct position of epistemic relativism, to an incorrect attack on ontology, calling upon us to question all attempts to explain how the world is. Certainly such knowledge cannot be guaranteed, but Derrida goes a stage further and gives up on most claims to understanding or explanation. This is why, in *Specters of Marx*, he turns his back on the scientific Marx, and adopts, instead, a messianism. It may be that there is an intransitive world out there, but Derrida is unwilling to make any theoretical claims about it. It may have been notoriously hard to translate the first time, but in practice, if not strictly in meaning, *il n'y a pas de hors-texte* comes to mean that there is nothing beyond the transitive.

Deconstruction limits itself to epistemological questions concerned with the functioning of language or the text, and the status of meaning within it. To the extent that everything is mediated through language, we are not allowed to go beyond it and develop an ontology. This makes it impossible to locate any fundamental human needs or interests. It leaves Derrida unable to make any kind of convincing case for socialism.

Another attempt

The relation between hegemony and socialist strategy is taken up by Laclau and Mouffe, but in a post-Marxist, irrealist form. They open their book *Hegemony and Socialist Strategy* with the claim that:

> It is no longer possible to maintain the conception of subjectivity and classes elaborated by Marxism, nor its vision of the historical course of capitalist development, nor, of course, the conception of communism as a transparent society from which antagonisms have disappeared ... we have constructed a concept of hegemony which, in our view, may be a useful instrument in the struggle for a radical, libertarian and plural democracy.
>
> (Laclau and Mouffe 1985: 4)

In the authors' opinion, Marxism contains an essentialism which emphasises class and the economic in a foundationalist way. The growing importance of the concept of hegemony indicates a recognition (although not a resolution) of the problems of this view. Laclau and Mouffe seek to exploit the use of hegemony to subvert and deconstruct the Marxist discourse. Freeing hegemony from essentialism allows it to operate within conditions of radical contingency. It becomes defined as the articulator of discourse.

To escape essentialism, discourse theory draws on Derrida, Heidegger and Wittgenstein. However, Laclau and Mouffe's project cannot be explained purely in philosophical terms. It is a product of a journey through and out of Marxist theory and politics. This journey, for all its theoretical posturing, can be given a simple name. It is, to use Ellen Meiksins Wood's (1986) description, 'a retreat from class' and it starts with Laclau and Mouffe's first contact with Gramsci.

The ideological road to idealism

In an earlier essay, 'Hegemony and Ideology in Gramsci' (in Mouffe 1979), Chantal Mouffe has argued that a concept of hegemony can deal with some of the problems in Althusser by bringing political autonomy to ideology while leaving determinism in the last instance to the economic. But unlike most Althusserian analysis, hegemony is seen not so much as a structured and differentiated alliance, but as a complete fusion of political, economic, intellectual and moral objectives through the intermediary of ideology. Thus ideology is given primacy as a practice producing subjects.

Mouffe's analysis does stress the importance of Gramsci's conception of leadership, but emphasis is laid upon the intellectual and moral aspects of leadership. This, according to Mouffe, takes Gramsci's analysis beyond Lenin's 'instrumental' conception of class alliances, which focuses too narrowly on a 'fundamental class'. Rejecting the view of hegemony as the articulation of class interests, Mouffe sees it as a 'higher synthesis' of many elements that fuse into a 'collective will' which becomes the new protagonist of political action. Tying these points together, we can see that Gramsci's notion of a collective will is used by Mouffe to denote the outcome of the hegemonic articulation of ideology. Ironically, though, Mouffe, who sees hegemony as a concept which challenges various forms of reductionism, commits precisely such an error, only instead of economic reductionism she reduces her analysis to the ideological. While she is quick to stress the material nature of ideology, this is limited to its inscription into social practices and apparatuses rather than to economic and political structures. In her striving against class and economic reductions, Mouffe ends up giving ideology primacy over the economic and political, the very basis on which ideology's materiality depends. Ultimately, groups are reduced to the hegemonic articulation of ideological practice. In such an equation the relationship of a group to the mode of production or to social structures means practically nothing. From here it is only a short step to discourse theory, idealism and post-Marxism.

Ernesto Laclau has a similar fascination for ideology. Again taking up the Althusserian debate his book *Politics and Ideology in Marxist Theory* (1977), he criticises Poulantzas for failing to see ideology as the primary determinant of class. As Meiksins Wood notes, class, for the time being, maintains its theoretical purity but loses its historical significance. Ideological divisions become more significant than class contradictions, the identity 'people' becomes more important than class (Wood 1986: 49–59). Laclau over-exaggerates the significance of Althusser's concept of interpellation (the recognition of self when hailed) as the basis for the constitution of subjects. By focusing on the idea of interpellation through ideology, Laclau opens the door to a discursive conception of hegemony and a Euro-communist rejection of class:

> The notion of the specific autonomy of democratic interpellations is implicit in the concept of 'hegemony', of democratic ideology as the domain of class struggle and, consequently, it permits Marxist theory to overcome class reductionism.
>
> (Laclau 1977: 141n56)

The role given to the working class is to 'disarticulate' the 'interpellations' and offer its own hegemonic project around the 'democratic–popular' interests of the 'people'. Laclau introduces these arguments in an essay on fascism, but it soon becomes clear that he is more ambitiously attempting to dissolve class interests into bourgeois democracy. As Wood notes:

> For Laclau, the appropriate strategy is not to stress the specificity of socialism, not to reclaim democracy for socialism by challenging the limits of bourgeois democracy with alternative socialist forms, and,

finally, not to pursue the specific interests of the working class, but to dilute them in an indeterminate 'stew'. We now have a theory of ideology to accompany the theories of class and the state which are needed to underpin the strategy of popular alliance and the building of socialism by the extension of bourgeois-democratic forms, all bypassing the direct opposition between capital and labour.

(Wood 1986: 53)

By means of theoretical trickery, Laclau still tries to uphold the importance of economic and class relations. But 'classes exist at the ideological and political level in a process of articulation and not of reduction' (Laclau 1977: 161). Thereby, Laclau separates the economic from the ideological and political, and reconceptualises class as determined by the hegemonic interpellation of politics and ideology:

If class contradiction is the dominant contradiction at the abstract level of the mode of production, the people/power bloc contradiction is dominant at the level of the social formation.

(Laclau 1977: 108)

Given that Laclau accords the ideological level almost total influence, the existence of class at the level of productive relations is really of little importance. This is doubly so since Laclau has previously (in a postscript to his essay on feudalism) stated his new doubts about the concept of mode of production – a concept which is soon abandoned altogether. Already, then, hegemony is being developed as an alternative way of seeing determination, in opposition to the role of the economy.

Laclau and Mouffe's common interests become clearer and clearer. Both are rejecting the fundamental concepts of Marxist theory and socialist practice. In particular, they reject a class analysis, which they describe as 'reductionist', and a Marxist politics which they call 'sectarian'. Thus the concept of ideology becomes more and more important. But Laclau and Mouffe's escape from class is achieved at a terrible price. Rejecting class interests means rejecting objective, material class relations (or at least the idea that they have significance). In shifting emphasis to ideological articulations, Laclau and Mouffe slip further and further into the world of ideas. The real world is denied any importance outside of ideological discourse. Ultimately Laclau and Mouffe become idealists.

Euro-communism

Laclau and Mouffe's theoretical views owe a lot to the political influence of the Euro-communist movement. Based on an impressionistic analysis of capitalist development, the movement rejected the contention that the working class retains a central, strategic position within capitalist society.

The displacement of the working class from the socialist project is therefore connected to the belief that we are living in 'new times'.

Of course, the abandonment of class by the world's Communist Parties is hardly new. The Stalinists abandoned the class struggle years ago, replacing it with the popular front and with international support for the Soviet Union (which really meant support for the Soviet bureaucracy). However, in the past, the Stalinists have always seen the need to intervene in working-class struggles, to contain them, so to speak. Euro-communism, by contrast, proclaims the death of this traditional working class. In Britain the key examples have been the defeat of the 1984–5 miners' strike (note Laclau's disdainful reference to Arthur Scargill (Laclau 1990: 162)), the impact of Thatcherism and social democracy's corresponding 'New Realism' and 'Modernisation', and internationally, the collapse of the Soviet Union. As such, Stalinism no longer feels the need (or perhaps more to the point, no longer has the ability) to constrain class activity. Instead it offers a meek 'popular–democratic' project. The bad old days of class struggle are over.

For Laclau and Mouffe, the structural transformation of capitalism has led to the decline of the classical working class in the post-industrial countries (Laclau and Mouffe 1990: 97). Just what 'structuctual trans-formation' means is difficult to say, given that Laclau and Mouffe do not believe in structures. And surely they do not intend to suggest themselves that there was once such a thing as a 'classical working class'? Nevertheless, the point they are trying to make is that the working class, as others understand it, is no more and that we live in a new, (post-) society where the project must not be class struggle but the extension of bourgeois democracy. Like their more original predecessors, the Frankfurt School, Marcuse, Gorz, they seek new agents in the 'new social movements', preferably those rooted in the popular–democratic, liberationist milieu, who show hostility to class politics. The new leaders are the intellectual elite who, having spotted that material class interests no longer inspire people, take it upon themselves to convince them of bourgeois democracy instead.

An idealist form of discourse

With *Hegemony and Socialist Strategy*, the priority Laclau and Mouffe give to ideology is shifted to the all-encompassing realm of 'discourse'. Hegemony is given a central role because of its ability to articulate discourse, creating and modifying social identities. It becomes crucial to the maintenance of Laclau and Mouffe's discursive reality. All social objects are constituted according to their discursive articulation, which indicates their purely historical and contingent character. It is not so much that objects do not exist outside of discourse, but that they have no significance outside of it. Obviously this might bring accusations of postmodern idealism, and Laclau and Mouffe are keen to defend themselves against such charges. They claim:

What is denied is not so much that objects exist externally to thought, but the rather different assertion that they could constitute themselves as objects outside of any discursive condition of emergence.

(Laclau and Mouffe 1985: 108)

But, for critical realism, the idea that an object only acquires an identity through discourse is a clear example of the epistemic fallacy or the reduction of intransitive being to transitive knowledge. To say that without discourse the object is meaningless is to say that its natural properties are insignificant until discursively articulated, that it is in fact discursively rather than physically constituted. And this leads to the idealist notion that changes in description lead to changes in the object itself. Changes in our idea of the object are seen as altering the actual being of the object.

In a bad-tempered exchange with Norman Geras, Laclau and Mouffe stress that they are not idealists. They make a (rather Heideggerian) distinction between a thing's being (which depends on discourse) and its existence (which does not). This allows them to argue that:

What actually distinguishes idealism from materialism is its affirmation of the ultimately conceptual character of the real; for example, in Hegel, the assertion that everthing that is real is rational. Idealism... is the affirmation not that there do not *exist* objects external to the mind, but rather that the innermost nature of these objects is identical to that of mind – that is to say, that it is ultimately *thought*.

(Laclau and Mouffe 1990: 106)

But this is a very specific sort of idealism that Laclau and Mouffe are defining – either solipsism or else, as the above quote suggests, a sort of objective idealism like Hegel's. Their own idealism, drawn as it is from Wittgenstein's language games, is of a more intersubjective nature. Laclau and Mouffe's world of forms is inextricable from the community of 'we' and reduces material things to the conceptions, not of an individual or a *geist*, but of a community. Material objects *are* reduced to the conceptions we have of them, albeit that these are conceptions that we develop inter-subjectively, in communities, where it 'is evident that the very material properties of objects are part of what Wittgenstein calls language-game, which is an example of what we have called discourse' (Laclau and Mouffe 1985: 108).

The distinction that Laclau and Mouffe make between the *being* of the object (in or through discourse) and the *existence* of the object (outside it) reduces being to discursive description/re-description and renders existence meaningless. They are under the impression that mere existence is meaningless and that a 'move away from idealism cannot be founded on the *existence* of the object, because nothing follows from this existence' (Laclau and Mouffe 1990: 111). Once more shifting the terms of the debate and redefining concepts to suit their needs, Laclau and Mouffe argue that materialism no longer concerns what exists, but is about how objects are articulated through discourse. That an intransitive realm exists is insignificant compared to the object's transitive 'being'. This cannot but end up as cultural relativism, giving full power to the hegemonic battles within discourse. If the hegemonic view within a society is that earthquakes are acts of God, then so be it. Geras replies to this position by arguing that:

> a pre-discursive reality and an extra-theoretical objectivity form the irreplaceable basis of all rational enquiry, as well as the condition of meaningful communication across and between differing viewpoints. This foundation once removed, one simply slides into a bottomless, relativist gloom, in which opposed discourses or paradigms are left with no common reference point, uselessly trading blows.
>
> (Geras 1990: 99)

Of course, we know that in social practices such as science, people do not simply trade blows with other people's ideas. Rather, they can only assess these ideas by investigating the real objects that lie behind these ideas or to which these ideas refer. The transitive practice of description depends on the intransitive status of things as independent of our knowledge of them. This can be turned into an incommensurability argument. For if Laclau and Mouffe want to sustain their conception of a hegemonic struggle between competing, descriptive discourses, then for this to be a dispute, the theories must have a common referent outside of themselves, or else the contestation is meaningless. But by denying extra-discursive reality any significance, Laclau and Mouffe sever the reference relation. Therefore, any clash or rivalry between discourses becomes incomprehensible since there is no intelligible way of comprehending either discourses themselves or conceptual transformations.

Anti-Marxism

Laclau and Mouffe's reaction against Marxism is present in almost every aspect of their theory, whether it is in rejecting economic determinism, class politics, any notion of relatively durable interests and identities, dialectical analysis, or the conception of a structured totality. They reject science in favour of what is effectively ideology, offer us discourse in the place of material structures and practices, replace dialectical relations with atomised externality and replace objective interests with hegemonically articulated subject locations. But if Laclau and Mouffe conceive of hegemonic articulation as a game, then in their own efforts to articulate a theory they give their Marxist opponent a set of cards by which it cannot fail to lose. The fact that Marxism has to be set up in such a way only highlights the hollowness of discourse theory's victory.

Marxism is set up as monolithic, totalising, mono-linear, reductionist, determinist, essentialist, devoid of any richness or diversity. When it comes to discussing *economics*, Laclau and Mouffe present Marxism at its most narrowly reductionist. Rather than looking at productive relations, they focus on productive forces. To attack such a deterministic approach might be permissible if applied to the work of Plekhanov, or more recently G.A. Cohen. But if we are to read someone like Althusser, let us judge him by the standards of Geras who can see that:

> what Althusser put forward was neither the single, omnipotent cause nor the mere multiplicity of meanings. It was a conception of the primacy of one type of structure within a group of structures, of a *hierarchy* of causalities of uneven weight.
>
> (Geras 1990: 62)

That the economy has a certain privilege in the structural hierarchy can be justified on the basis of the centrality of production and distribution within every society. As Derek Sayer argues:

> Essential relations can be said to comprise any society's 'economic structure', not by virtue of any innately 'economic' qualities they might possess but because of their entailment in the production process without which that society could not exist.
>
> (Sayer, D. 1979: 81)

The fact that productive forces require organisation means that they have a specific social character which is very different from the mechanical definition presented by Laclau and Mouffe. This complexity is stressed by Marx who argues: 'How, indeed, could the single logical formula of movement, of sequence of time, explain the structure of society, in which all relations co-exist simultaneously and support one another?' (Marx 1963: 110–11).[2] On this basis we will argue for a theory of society based on the centrality of the mode of production, but not reducible to economic relations. That class enjoys a privileged status is due to its grounding in these relations although they also confer upon class a complex character. Rather than reducing an analysis of hegemony to 'subject articulation', it is necessary to give it a material content based on the nature of these social conditions and the role it performs in relation to them.

This takes us to the next question, which is that of class or group *interests* and the matter of their objectivity. But since Laclau and Mouffe deny that the material world has any significance outside of discourse, interests are deprived of any intransitive status. This is clarified by the passage:

> Ours is a criticism not of the notion of 'interests' but of their supposedly *objective* character: that is to say, of the idea that social agents have

interests of which they are not conscious. To construct an 'interest' is a slow historical process, which takes place through complex ideological, discursive and institutional practices ... 'Interests', then, are a social product, and do not exist independently of the consciousness of the agents who are their bearers.

(Laclau and Mouffe 1990: 118)

If interests are a social product, and yet these interests are not objective, then accordingly, it is difficult to see the social as objective either. Realism holds the position that ideas are a social product and that they are based on real material relations. An interest represents a relation with the world. For this to be meaningful, we must say that people have an interest *in* something. Interests cannot just be reduced to subjective wants, needs or desires. They must correspond to something real which is an issue for them. To argue that interests are purely subjective and that agents are always conscious of their interests is to argue that interests are products of the mind (here, in fact, Laclau and Mouffe retreat from the Wittgensteinian 'we' back to the 'I', and from discourse to ego). Realists, by contrast, would argue that our interests come from our interactions with objective things (or relations). They vary according to these relations. Therefore a worker will develop an interest in performing wage labour in order to feed the family. But workers also have an interest in overthrowing property relations, the primary source of their enslavement. There is nothing wrong with saying that this is an objective interest despite the fact that workers only move towards such positions in extreme situations. That this is so is because agents are mostly engaged in the *unconscious* reproduction of social structures and only in certain situations do agents become aware of the need to transform these structures. It is therefore a basic materialist position that interests and ideas are not the same thing. The ruling ideas in society derive from its material structure and assume an ideological, mystical and fetishised character. It is precisely such ideas that prevent a realisation of objective interests, until, that is, there is a movement of struggle or a crisis in the material structure that underlies such ideas. It is only when a crisis develops in this system of structural relations that agents become aware that they have an interest in transforming these relations.

The concept of hegemony allows that particular groups or classes may articulate what they see as their interests through a hegemonising project or historical bloc. But interests are not reducible to this process as Laclau and Mouffe would argue. That a hegemonic project can articulate interests at all presupposes that there are objective interests that can be articulated. There is no doubt that the two become intermeshed so that hegemonic projects develop interests in their own way. But there still remains the crucial difference between the articulation process and that which is articulated. Hegemony represents not the primary origin of interests but their mediation under particular conditions by certain groups. A progressive or radical hegemonic project would seek to make agents aware of their interest in transforming social relations, while a conservative hegemony would promote the interests of a privileged group and the conservation of social relations.

On the question of *essentialism* we should turn to the concept of *conatus*, which Spinoza describes such that the 'endeavour (*conatus*) wherewith a thing endeavours to persist in its being is nothing else than the actual essence of the thing' (Spinoza 1993: 90). Taking up the critical realist concern with the relatively enduring character of social processes, Andrew Collier employs this concept to consider a thing's essence simply in the sense of being 'the set of mutual relations of motion and rest without which the complex would fall apart' (Collier 1989: 72). This allows us to conceive of the necessary and contingent aspects of a structure or mechanism in a non-essentialist and non-teleological way. By contrast, Laclau and Mouffe, by repudiating 'essentialism', end up denying any necessary internal nature. All relations are understood as external, contingent, extrinsic, not-necessary or accidental. It might be wondered how anything can hang together, persist or endure.

Further, the *conatus* allows us to conceive of human interests in a non-essentialist way. Collier combines the *conatus* theory – a tendency to persist in its being – with the idea of the inorganic body (from Marx and Heidegger[3]) so that the human *conatus* will possess interests that are not just inside the physical human body but also external, objective interests. On this basis we must surely admit that the highest form of a person's interest (or the development of the *conatus*) will come through a project of social transformation of society, so that we can enjoy a more meaningful relationship with the world around us. This is praxis theory without the essentialism of humanism, a view of human beings as driven by informed desire, concern and considered being. A far cry indeed from the atomised, self-interested individuals of *Hegemony and Socialist Strategy*.

Political and strategic implications

The position developed in *Hegemony and Socialist Strategy* is one of absolute relativism. All notions of relatively enduring, intransitive structures, mechanisms, interests, identities, needs, relations or even things, are denied. Because of this, it might be wondered on what basis discursive and hegemonic practices might be said to exist. We find, in fact, that Laclau and Mouffe totally alter the notion of hegemony to suit their own relativism. It will be recalled that Gramsci developed a conception of the historical bloc that saw it as the unity of structure and superstructure. This structural element in Gramsci's conception of historical bloc, despite being noted by Laclau and Mouffe (Laclau and Mouffe 1990: 111), is completely ignored. Theirs is a celebration of fragmentation and dispersal. Gramsci conceives of the historical bloc in relation to structures; Laclau and Mouffe define it in terms of the dispersal of discrete atomistic elements

> A social and political space relatively unified through the instituting of nodal points and the construction of *tendentially* relational identities, is what Gramsci called a *historical bloc*. The type of link joining the different elements of the historical bloc – not unity in any form of historical a priori, but regularity in dispersion – coincides with our concept of discursive formation.
>
> (Laclau and Mouffe 1985: 136)

The status of discourse theory is another problem. Either it has the status of a meta-discourse (in which case Laclau and Mouffe are themselves guilty of essentialist, metaphysical, logocentric privileging), or discourse theory is merely one discourse among many, in which case there is nothing to stop us ditching Laclau and Mouffe for something more exciting. While many advocates of discourse and deconstruction would be quite happy to exist in this playful state of contradiction and non-commitance, this will not do for a book supposedly dealing with hegemony and socialist strategy. So Laclau and Mouffe are forced to make a Rortian turn to pragmatism in order to try and break free of an absolute relativism. The result is the worst possible concept of hegemony, whereby it effectively ends up defining the bounds of reality. This hegemonic reality, according to Laclau, 'is a question of pragmatically constructing a hegemonic centre which articulates a growing range of social discourses and logics around it, and thus gives rise to a relative "universalism"' (Laclau 1990: 219).

We might add, following Wittgenstein, that 'the limits of my hegemony are the limits of my world'. By making such a shift, Laclau and Mouffe commit themselves to a praxis ontology, whereby they reduce the world (or our conception of it) to the occurrence of action within it. This actualistic praxis ontology is therefore unable to give any grounds by which we might identify a progressive political project or even the 'popular–democratic struggle' that Laclau and Mouffe constantly refer to. They have already ruled out the possibility of a progressive hegemonic project transforming existing social relations. In fact we can develop this further and say that Laclau and Mouffe's theory has an ontological flatness which ends up ushering back in a form of atomistic empiricism. Their theory lacks any ontological depth because structured, stratified, dialectical, intrinsic or necessary relations, connections or mechanisms are denied through the all-encompassing hegemonic articulation of contingent, external elements. It is only through hegemonic articulation that things acquire an identity, governedness or gatheredness. With no scientific investigation of underlying relations, we must observe empirically the arbitrary moments of the atomistic parts.

A political side effect of this atomistic conception of social elements and the denial of their intrinsic natures is that Laclau and Mouffe argue for the essentially neutral character of these elements prior to their hegemonic articulation. This conveniently allows them to deny that there is anything essentially bourgeois about bourgeois democracy. Thus workers and the oppressed have no intrinsic interest in developing their own forms of democracy, but must instead concentrate on developing democracy as it actually is. *Hegemony and Socialist Strategy* not only defends bourgeois democracy, it also articulates the bourgeois ideology of neutrality. No strategy is offered even to the new social movements, never mind the class struggle. At best what is on offer is only some sort of discursive ameli-oration of a contingent moment. The nature of the project requires a denial of any scientific understanding of society. With no points of reference and no way of defining what socialism and democracy are supposed to relate to, and with a denial of the conditions under which hegemony operates, there is no coherent reason why strategy should be possible at all.

A return to Althusser

There is no doubt about the influence that Althusser has had upon Laclau and Mouffe and other post-structuralists. But it is also possible to see the ways in which Althusser's more troubled statements have been exploited and abused. We will set out three such areas:

1 There is the problem of Althusser's separation of the thought object from the real object and a corresponding separation of theory from its social and historical conditions. Such a position allows an easy escape route to idealism and the idea that we can only know knowledge, and that the real world is somehow insignificant unless discursively consti-tuted. Against this, critical realism poses the relation between transitive thought or knowledge and the intransitive objects of that thought. Therefore, while our knowledge of the world is transitive, it is knowledge of the intransitive. The intransitive domain exists independently of the knowledge we have of it but is the condition for the intelligibility of transitive knowledge. Therefore, just because intransitive objects are relatively invariant to our knowledge of them, this does not mean that our knowledge is relatively independent of the objects.

2 It is necessary to reject the exclusivity of Althusser's conception of practices and structures. These must be recognised in their distinctive-ness, but must also be seen as interconnected and dialectically co-determined. This means rejecting the path that leads from 'relative autonomy' to absolute autonomy and the schematic notion of 'determination in the last instance' (see Chapter 8). Such a position allows for the economy to be determinant in no instance and has led to a rather easy abandonment of the concept of mode of production (as for example, with Hindess and Hirst 1975). By contrast, critical realism

insists on the interconnected and stratified character of the social and natural worlds. It also upholds the dual determination of intrinsic and extrinsic factors and the dialectics of being as constituted through these relations. The economy, therefore, is present (to varying degrees) in every instance, while other social structures are present in the economic. Thus we can conceive of a social hierarchy of mutually determining and reinforcing structures, processes and relations (see Chapter 9 for how the conditions for economic reproduction need to be socially secured – thus giving a key role to hegemonic state strategies).

3 It is necessary to reject Althusser's later conception of Ideological State Apparatuses (the distinct institutions associated with education, religion, the family, legal system etc., which support the state ideologically). Such a position, particularly when developed by Poulantzas, moves from a structural to an institutional theory of ideology (instead of viewing ideology as secreted by social practices it sees ideology as propagated by institutional apparatuses) and leads politically to a Euro-communist strategy of 'capturing' civil society in order to control these ideological institutions. It leads back to the unsatisfactory reading of Gramsci which gives so much strategic primacy to a careful war of positions that the more offensive war of manoeuvre, and the intrinsically capitalist nature of the state, is forgotten. It is important instead to defend Althusser's materialist conception of ideology as grounded in social practices. This is at its best in the early Althusser:

> *So ideology is as such an organic part of every social totality.* It is as if human societies could not survive without these *specific formations*, these systems of representations (at various levels), their ideologies. Human societies secrete ideology as the very element and atmosphere indispensable to their historical respiration and life.
>
> (Althusser 1977a: 232)

The stress that we must make is therefore that ideology is the product of a number of material practices, but that it is not a single practice in its own right. A basic error of Laclau and Mouffe is to focus increasingly on ideology (and then discourse) as a single totalising practice *within* which hegemonic struggles occur. This is also a problem with Derrida and the all enveloping nature of the text. Once this sort of totalisation takes place, the Althusserian conception of ideology as a lived relation *to the world*, is replaced with ideology, discourse or text *as the world*. The result is the effective abandonment (even if not denial) of the intransitive dimension.

Notebooks from prison

Laclau and Mouffe's 'post-Marxism' is typical of a current trend which is to combine the worst elements of deconstruction with a relativist language-game theory. This attempts to deal a double blow to Marxism's main thrust. At a *theoretical* level, discourse is reduced to hegemony, while, inversely, at a *practical* level, hegemony is reduced to discourse.

Theoretically, such postmodernist theories attack the idea of truth or knowledge. In a Nietzschian–Foucauldian world of power struggles, meaningfulness is judged not in relation to the real objects of the world, but on the basis of theoretical ascendancy. Hegemonic struggles decide what counts as truth. This truth is established over competing discourses, rather than in relation to any object of enquiry. For postmodernists, truth becomes the 'will to truth'.

Then, just to hammer home the point, the postmodernists turn to language-game theory in order to further extend their relativism. Judgements are given meaning by criteria internal to the language game. Knowledge is relativised to whichever discourse is hegemonic. As Christopher Norris has argued, with this approach, the neo-Nazi ideologues who deny the existence of the gas chambers are simply held to be playing a different sort of game. Likewise, if 'reality' is considered a mere product of language games, then Baudrillard's absurd claim that the Gulf War was a media construction, goes unchecked (see Norris 1992).

Practically, such an approach ties the theory of hegemony to discursive articulation, denying any effective relation to non-discursive structures. As we saw, Laclau and Mouffe ignore Gramsci's conception of the historical bloc as unifying structure and superstructure and instead redefine it in contingent and atomistic terms:

> Every historical bloc – or hegemonic formation – is constructed through regularity in dispersion, and this dispersion includes a proliferation of very diverse elements: systems of differences which partially define relational identities ….
>
> (Laclau and Mouffe 1985: 142)

They may try to disguise the consequences of this under a cloak of fashionable radicality, but without a relation between hegemony and other social structures, there is no possibility of it playing any kind of transformatory role. To properly conceive of hegemony it is necessary to locate it within structural relations which make clear its limitations and its conditions of possibility. That hegemony is possible is due to the fact that human agents play an active and fundamental role in the reproduction of these social structures. Under conditions of structural tension and heightened human awareness, the transformation of these structures becomes a possibility. Such a process requires a hegemonic project which can unite agents around a programme or a set of interests and a collective, structurally located so that it is in a position to effect a transformation and to counter those forces hostile to such a project.

Post-Marxism, post-structuralism and deconstruction do not allow for such a project. While they may develop a concept of hegemony, they deny the necessary conditions for hegemony's meaningful operation, i.e. relatively enduring social structures, practices, interests, identities and relations. While some sort of structural analysis is maintained, this is invariably reduced to discourse or text. Rather than seeing hegemony as strategically located on the terrain of objective relations, it is instead held to be the articulating element of various discourses. Instead of changing the world, we can only change our descriptions of it. Of course, post-modernists would claim that these are one and the same thing. But then the problem arises, why should one description of the world be better, or more desirable that another? Indeed, what is the basis for a socialist strategy? The reduction of being to discourse means that hegemony is sustained by means of an epistemic fallacy.

Critical realism, by contrast, holds that the world is comprised of real structural relations independent of their discursive description. The meaningful nature of transitive discourse presupposes the intransitive structures and objects to which it refers. Hegemony is therefore not reducible to a role as articulator of discourse. The nature of such a project is defined by the relations between social structures, human practices and group interests. Otherwise hegemony is thrown to the winds of arbitrary signification with nothing to hold it down or define it.

Politics means a lot more than discursive or textual articulation and a serious socialist strategy requires much more than simply subverting accepted significations. The fact that neither Derrida nor Laclau and Mouffe can offer any sort of coherent strategy is testimony to their imprisonment in discourse as well as the antinomies of their own particular notebooks.

Part 2

Theoretical questions

6 Two types of hegemony
Structural hegemony and hegemonic projects

Introduction

We found that Gramsci's elaboration of hegemony refers not just to hegemonic projects, but to a deeper level of organisation. The historical bloc, he argues, connects the structure and the superstructure. For a group to become hegemonic it must have behind it the economic, political and cultural conditions which allow it to put itself forward as leading. These conditions form the basic material background out of which hegemonic projects emerge. Hegemony is concerned not just with the construction of a ruling bloc, but with the reproduction of the social structures that create the material conditions for such a bloc. Gramsci gives as an example the idea of the passive revolution. Here the ruling bloc maintains its hegemony by advancing a dynamic of social reorganisation and modernisation. Thus hegemony is linked not just to social alliances but also to structural processes. The success of a hegemonic project depends on how well it can relate to these objective developments. Class interests must be advanced in relation to the dominant trends in the capitalist economy.

We have seen, however, that classical Marxism has often developed an instrumentalist conception of society which sees it simply in terms of the interaction of different groups, rather than as the interrelation of groups, structures and mechanisms. Trotsky, for example, sometimes gives hegemony a more shallow, surface role related to the way classes organise, failing to give it a deeper, more material basis securing the cohesion of the social whole. Hegemony is seen in an instrumental rather than in a structural way. This often comes across in Trotsky's analysis of fascism. He argues that fascism is the means by which monopoly capital mobilises the petite bourgeoisie and the declassed layers against the organised working class and he compares it to a battering ram that can be picked up and used. However, the ruling class cannot simply wield fascism for its own purposes. It has its own dynamics which reflect a deeper level of structural crisis. It grows out of this material crisis and is manifested at the political and ideological level. The project around fascism is a response to a hegemonic crisis, not the cause of it.

Indeed, both Trotsky and Gramsci have analysed how particular hegemonic projects in Italy, Spain and, to a lesser extent, Germany are a product of the historical weakness of hegemony in general. This weakness of hegemony is deeply rooted in the nature of these societies – their economic structure, national and political development, ideological relations and so on. Italy, for example, had a historical crisis of bourgeois hegemony of which fascist hegemony was one manifestation. This clearly points to two levels of hegemonic crisis: a more general crisis of the Italian state and civil society and the specific crisis posed by the fascist project. The two are obviously interlinked in the sense that the hegemonic project represented by fascism presupposes a general crisis of social hegemony and a historical weakness of the Italian state and civil society, while this general hegemonic weakness finds expression in different hegemonic projects, not least, the fascist one.

We have argued that humanist accounts of history are unable to maintain this distinction since they end up reducing such processes to their expression. Humanism's rejection of a structural analysis means that the world is reduced to one level of appearance with no underlying causes. Hegemony is based on the relation between different human agents rather than on the relation between these agents and social structures, so that hegemonic projects end up defining their own conditions of expression. A humanist account would see hegemony purely in agential terms (blocs, projects and struggles) without addressing fundamental questions of social structure (the historical bloc as the unity of structure and superstructure, projects as possibilities within social contexts, struggles as representing attempts to conserve or transform structural conditions).

A critical realist theory of hegemony should counter this with the argument that hegemony can only operate under conditions of social and material causality. It is necessary to examine the social whole and its different structures and mechanisms, each of which has its own dynamics. It must study the nature of these various relations and the types of co-determination or conflict that are taking place. It must determine the dominant forces within each society so that, with an analysis of capitalism, an attempt is made to link the question of social hegemony to the dominant dynamic of capital accumulation.

It is the work of structuralists like Poulantzas that starts to get to grips with these underlying mechanisms. In Poulantzas's definition, hegemony performs a structural–functional role. It secures the cohesion of the social formation (thereby providing the basis for capital accumulation). However, we have also argued that Poulantzas goes too far. While humanist accounts reduce hegemony to its expression, structuralist accounts tend to reduce hegemony to its functional determination (i.e. the general requirement to secure the unity of the social formation). Instead, both aspects of hegemony – its function and its expression – should be examined. The fact that hegemony, as Poulantzas argues, must perform a basic social function in securing the unity of the social formation, means that groups are given the potential to develop projects that express their own particular interests. The functional aspect of hegemony is not automatically fulfilled (as a hyper-structuralist schema might claim). Rather, the functional requirement of hegemony must be performed by real, living agents with their own specific interests and projects.

Because of this, it is necessary to recognise that the particular hegemonic projects pursued by these groups are not always best suited to hegemony's more structural role in securing the cohesion of the social formation. We will deal in a later chapter with the contradictory character of Thatcherism – a hegemonic project usually associated with new economic strategies of monetarism and laissez-faire deregulation. While, in one way, Thatcherism was in line with – or indeed promoted – new economic trends, in another way, Thatcherism hindered such developments through its political contradictions and the way that its message for the aspiring petite bourgeoisie was mixed with the more traditional Conservative influences of Empire, militarism, the City and so on. The political constitution of Thatcherism was clearly not an ideal basis for facilitating effective capital accumulation.

Finally, we saw that post-structuralist and discourse-based theories of hegemony are unable to make this distinction between the levels at which hegemony operates. These accounts usually reduce hegemony to the role of articulating discrete elements. In the case of Laclau and Mouffe, hegemony is reduced to the articulation of subject positions within discourse. More generally, those deconstructors around Derrida reduce the hegemonic process to the capture of 'floating signifiers'. Hegemony becomes a textual matter, cut off from the extra-discursive world, and the material relation to the reproduction of social structures is lost. At best, post-structuralist accounts reduce hegemony's location to various human practices and the exercise of power, an ontologically flat description that fails to look at the underlying social structures and generative mechanisms. Such theories cannot say where hegemony comes from, or give any political specification. Indeed, post-structuralism makes any political project impossible by detotalising and de-collectivising any sort of representation. Identity is turned into fragmentation and political action is reduced to discussion.

As an alternative to these accounts, this chapter will argue that there are two distinct but inter-connected types (or aspects) of hegemony, concerned with (1) structural hegemony and (2) a surface hegemony of actual hegemonic projects. This second part of the book will develop the insights of the first section, taking up those theories that offer the best way of conceiving of the duality of hegemony in order to elaborate a conception of hegemony that does justice to both its agential role and its structural location. This chapter will concentrate on outlining such a distinction, necessarily schematic, but useful as a working guide. It will go on to look at how hegemony, in its two aspects, relates to issues of nation, civil society and ideology. Subsequent chapters will seek to relate this emerging conception to questions of space, time and history, objectivity and inter-subjectivity, and economics and state regulation.

Two aspects of hegemony

It is becoming clear that rather than talking about hegemony in a general sense, we have to distinguish between different aspects of the concept in accordance with the general stratification of the social formation and the distinction between social structure and human action. To start to tackle this we first need to make a distinction, necessarily crude in its nature, but apparent in the theoretical history outlined above, between a deeper hegemony that operates at a structural level and a surface hegemony which is embodied in conscious hegemonic projects.

As we started to explore in the first section, hegemony in its deeper sense has the role of securing the unity and cohesion of the social system and in ensuring the reproduction of basic structural processes and relations. In this sense, hegemony is fundamental to the unity of all human societies and is a basic material necessity concerned with the interrelation of the different parts of the social whole. We found that of particular importance is the relation between the state and the economic system, although a strong social hegemony will be backed up by the fortresses and earthworks of a developed civil society and cultural domain.

Hegemony in a more conscious, political and manifold sense concerns concrete hegemonic projects and practices. This is the sense in which hegemony is often understood, but it is necessary to maintain that such hegemonic projects and strategies are emergent out of the deeper hege-monic conditions (and function). How these conscious projects emerge, however, is not pre-given and the concept of emergence stresses that such projects have their own irreducible dynamics. To study hegemony in its manifold sense requires an examination of different social projects, the particular social groups and classes involved, the interests that they repre-sent, the various values and world-views that they hold and the political blocs and alliances that are constructed.

This distinction between different aspects of hegemony is not parti-cularly easy to make, for hegemony is not a thing or discrete social object but a series of mutually dependent social relations. To make sense of hegemony it is necessary to engage in what Bertell Olman calls a process of *dialectical abstraction* (Olman 1993) in order to separate out in theory two aspects of a continual process. While we may distinguish between a deeper, structural hegemony and a surface hegemony of actual projects, these two aspects are clearly linked and mutually dependent. The deeper, more structural form of hegemony is expressed through various hegemonic projects. In turn these projects are dependent on and determined by the underlying hegemonic conditions. And while the underlying hegemony is the pre-existing cause for such projects, these projects are an important manifestation of this cause. Thus the distinction is between hegemony's basic material necessity and various forms of its actualisation through concrete projects and intentional agency.

Hegemony is a societal concept as shown in Gramsci's extension of its applicability to the way in which a group rules *in general*. It has a complex character, stratified across a number of social layers and organising a number of different relations. It organises the relations between different social groups *within* a ruling bloc (e.g. the different strands of the bourgeoisie), and also the relation between the ruling bloc and wider layers in society. These wider layers are themselves stratified, with some groups being closely implicated in the bloc (e.g. different capitalist interests, sections of the military, bureaucracy, etc.), others lending a degree of support (e.g. sections of the petite bourgeoisie and peasantry), while others may require more direct coercion (e.g. sections of the working class, some different ethnic or national groups perhaps). Further, the dominant hegemonic process may itself be undercut by other hegemonic processes. These may be sub-hegemonies, or even counter-hegemonies. Some hegemonies may feed off the dominant hegemony, others may be in direct conflict. However, to adequately explain these processes we must go beyond them and look at the basic material conditions which give rise to them. Central to this conception is the reproduction or transformation of society.

The transformational model of social activity (TMSA)

Critical realism argues that society is both the condition and outcome of human agency. Social structures do not exist independently of the activities that they govern, and in a sense it is true that they are reproduced through intentional human activity. But it is also maintained that this activity has prior material causes and that although social activity is intentional, the understanding that agents have of the wider social processes is limited. So human activity, although intentional, usually has wider unintentional consequences owing to the powerful influence of pre-existing social structures. As Bhaskar writes, intentionality is limited in that:

> the TMSA requires that the present actions which serve to reproduce social structure only be intentional under *some* description, not under the description of reproducing the structure concerned (which would make all social reproduction or persistence the product of conscious acts).
>
> (Bhaskar 1994: 95)

As has been argued, hegemonic/counter-hegemonic struggles are necessarily a key part of the TMSA. These struggles represent a political moment in the process of reproduction whereby agents may act to preserve or transform the existing conditions. The TMSA presupposes various political interventions into the process of reproduction as represented by various hegemonic projects. But hegemony is equally present in a negative sense. The absence of a challenge to a certain social practice or structure is the mark of a stable hegemonic system. We must say that these structures are therefore relatively enduring in a deep hegemonic sense. The various structures are relatively smoothly reproduced through human praxis. In the distinction between a structural and a surface hegemony, structural hegemony has this largely unconscious or reproductive character.

Sometimes a ruling group may consciously mobilise hegemonic support for a set of social structures and practices. This is the case when projects of social reconstruction or modernisation take place. An example would be the restructuring that took place after the Second World War. Here the reorganisation of production methods corresponded to a reorganisation of state intervention and political practice. A new ruling bloc was created. This fits in with Gramsci's notion of the passive revolution, which may be taken to refer to an objective rather than merely subjective dynamic of hegemony. It is something that is not reducible to the actions of any one group, but is a state-led process of social, political or economic renewal.[1] In other (more common) circumstances, a ruling group is forced to mobilise to conserve a situation and to guarantee the reproduction of various structures. These specific hegemonic projects will be based on perceived interests, although the consequences involve structural reproduction. Whatever the case, these sorts of hegemonic projects necessarily involve intentional causality, although social structures are a necessary condition for this. Intentional agency is a necessary condition for the reproduction of these social structures (Bhaskar 1993: 154).

For normal reproduction, this intentional activity is relatively docile and non-political, reflecting the wider hegemony across society. Social structures and processes are taken for granted and their functioning is unchallenged. Agents' conception of their activity is confined within these structures, their consciousness is shaped by the ideologies associated with their practices, and the basic societal relations are unconsciously reproduced. The process of transformation is much more political and requires intentional activity that challenges the working of the system and poses an alternative. A hegemonic battle may challenge particular social and political practices and the activity of certain groups, but a real transformational struggle will go beyond hegemonic practices and challenge the deeper structural processes at the root of society. This is the moment where strike action goes beyond a struggle for wages and starts to challenge the whole basis of the capitalist production process, as might be seen, for example, with the British miners' strike of 1984–5. When such struggles truly move to the deeper hegemonic level, conflicts emerge between agents and the structures themselves.

The duality of hegemony and the process of emergence

The distinction made in this chapter between two aspects of hegemony is necessarily rough and abstracted. Table 6.1 tries to make this distinction between a structural hegemony and a surface hegemony a little clearer. However, the distinction, if it is an abstraction, is a *dialectical* abstraction (which attempts to redress the imbalance towards an agential or culturalist reading of hegemony) and it should be clear that each side of the hegemony distinction depends upon the other for its being. So, for example, conscious political expression depends upon underlying conditions, while these conditions, in turn, would be nothing without some kind of expression. And while structural hegemony has a certain causal primacy, the workings of surface hegemony have an emergent character; that is, they are not predetermined but have their own specific dynamics.

Structural hegemony and surface hegemony are two aspects of a continual process. Structural hegemony concerns the deep, underlying conditions within society and the unity of the social formation. Surface hegemony concerns the actual hegemonic projects that arise out of this situation it represents a manifestation of the underlying conditions, albeit, with its own character and dynamics. Structural hegemony performs the function of ensuring the reproduction of social structures and structural ensembles, while this functional requirement allows for the manifestation of various attempts at hegemonic projects that try and relate to this underlying requirement. In this sense, surface hegemony may be said to be the more active element representing, as it does, conscious political projects and interventions within the context of the underlying, more unconscious process of social cohesion and structural reproduction. If we make the necessary distinction, we can then give the political activity embodied in hegemonic projects, practices and struggles a real and active dynamic reflective of the open character of society. Although it is materially presupposed by and dependent upon the deeper, structural hegemonic

Table 6.1 The duality of hegemony

Structural hegemony	Surface hegemony
Deep	Actual
Functional	Manifest/realised
Structural	Agential
Secures unity of social formation	Hegemonic activity, projects and practices
Reproduction of social structures and structural ensembles	Emergent from underlying structures (but with their own powers and dynamics)
Underlying conditions	Conscious political expression
Reproduction	Struggle
Social cement	Coercion and consent
Largely unconscious structural reproduction	Conscious transformation, conservation or political advancement

conditions (securing the unity of the social formation), hegemonic projects and struggles represent processes with their own specific characteristics. Rather than simply representing the processes themselves, hegemonic practices and struggles necessarily entail some form of agential conception of these processes based on various forms of group or class understandings.

In this manifested state, hegemony represents conscious political activity linked to the defence, development or transformation of a given situation. The level of consciousness is variable. Indeed, owing to the stratification of the social formation, this conscious activity will have differing degrees of unintended consequences. Nevertheless, hegemony is a praxis which is, in turn, based on certain reasons and intentions which cause the course of action or, as Bhaskar writes: 'The intentionality of praxis is shown in the capacity to transform the world in a way which ... would not otherwise have occurred' (Bhaskar 1993: 278).

We have tried to show the duality of hegemony in relation to its structural and agential aspects, functioning to secure the unity of the social formation but also as expressed in conscious social projects. However, the first type of hegemony (structural hegemony) and the second type (hegemonic projects) presuppose one another. Hegemonic projects and struggles are *emergent* out of a deeper hegemony. This means that these projects and struggles are determined by the basic structure of society but they are not reducible to this. Although a great deal can be explained by examining the material cause (fundamental social structures and corresponding structural hegemony), this is not sufficient as an explanation. Hegemonic projects and struggles develop their own dynamics which need to be analysed in their specificity. Although they are dependent on the underlying structure of society (and structural hegemony), they are not reducible to it, but have their own irreducible set of mechanisms, properties and powers. Because they are emergent out of the underlying structural hegemonic conditions, these projects ultimately cannot escape these conditions, but they can at least develop in their own individual way and may come into conflict with these conditions in a dialectical overdetermination.

To give an example, the growth of fascism as a specific hegemonic project may be linked to a deeper hegemonic crisis in the basic structure of bourgeois society. This deep hegemonic crisis may be represented by a crisis of capital accumulation, a crisis of bourgeois political representation, and a crisis of cultural hegemony. However, while this greatly advances an explanation of fascism, it is not sufficient. It is also necessary to study the dynamics of the specific hegemonic project itself – its aims, its programme, its political representatives, its social base, how it has cultivated its relations to big business, its international context and so on. However, we have seen that specific hegemonic programmes like fascism are frustrated by the general underlying hegemonic conditions. The demands of the petite bourgeoisie are soon replaced by the needs of big business. This gives the structural determination of a deep hegemony a certain primacy over the political expression of hegemonic projects and practices. However, these projects and practices may develop these contradictions in a number of different ways.

Comparing the traditional structuralist analysis to the traditional humanist one reveals opposite errors. The structuralist interpretation concentrates on the structural or functional role of hegemony in securing the cohesion of the social formation, while humanists emphasise hegemony's expression or actualisation through human activity without looking at the underlying hegemonic conditions. Neither is therefore able to develop a conception of *emergence*, whereby the underlying requirement for social cohesion depends upon a structural hegemony, and this structural hegemony generates (or allows for) actual hegemonic projects which have their own specific dynamics and which are not simply reducible to their structural–functional origin but must be analysed in their own right. Emergent projects have their own powers and properties that are specific to them. Reference to underlying causes is important but does not provide a sufficient explanation.

For hegemonic projects to take place, objective social divisions and distinctions must already exist at a deeper level. This allows certain groups to become dominant and to construct their own hegemony out of these divisions. Indeed, a hegemonic project may consciously seek to develop these divisions, or alter them. In other words, these hegemonic projects are emergent out of the material conditions present in society and the more structural requirement of hegemony to reproduce the social formation.

The hegemonic processes represent the political moment in the reproduction of the structures of the social formation. Hegemony combines the structural aspect of reproduction with the political moment of agency. The fact that social structures need to be reproduced and that this is done through varying degrees of intentionality, gives hegemony its important social place. While the process of social reproduction has an automatic element to it (representing the dominance of the structure over the agent), society is an open system and some sort of hegemony or political intervention is required if the complex of social structures, generative mechanisms and human practices are to function together.

Under capitalism, the process of accumulation must be facilitated. This is done politically through state intervention in the economy. In other words, because the social is an open system, the conditions for capital accumulation are not given but have to be socially secured through various mechanisms – political and ideological as well as economic. Hegemony operates through the state to achieve this, with the state having a functional relation to the economy as represented by our conception of the deep hegemonic conditions. Out of this basic relation comes the more complex problems of the realisation of this function through particular hegemonic projects. Again, the realisation of this function is not given and hegemony is affected in its concrete realisation by the particular interests of the dominant groups and class fractions. The balance between capital accumulation and class interests is not always a stable one. Conflicts may emerge between hegemonic class interests and the broader process of capital accumulation and state intervention where structural hegemony is responsible for securing the conditions for social cohesion.

Bhaskar's hegemony

Bhaskar's later works – *Dialectic* (1993) and *Plato Etc.* (1994) – begin to outline a concept of hegemony, although it is largely underdeveloped. Correctly, hegemony is linked to the social stratification of power relations and given that 'a complex may be hierarchicised, this opens the way for concepts of hegemony and counter-hegemony, and *a fortiori* for counter-hegemonic hermeneutic struggles' (Bhaskar 1994: 94). Unfortunately, Bhaskar's work gives hegemony only a restricted role. He limits hegemony exclusively to hermeneutic struggles at a level of relations called power2 where power is exercised or manifest. Yet this power distinction itself provides a basis for a realist reworking of the hegemony concept.

Power1, Bhaskar argues, represents 'the transformative capacity intrinsic to the concept of agency as such'. He contrasts this with power2 relations as 'possessed, exercised, mobilised, manifest, covert, indirect, mediated' (Bhaskar 1993: 153). Power1 relations are seen as fundamentally enabling, as the power to do something, and they emerge through social structures as a basis for our activity. Power2 refers to a level of expression of power relations, usually as power exercised over something else. Unfortunately, it can be seen that if Bhaskar is restricting hegemony to what he calls power2 struggles, then he is limiting hegemony to its expression or exercise and cutting it off from its intrinsic materiality. It is clear why Bhaskar is doing this – in his later works he is keen to outline a theory of praxis and he believes that a theory of hegemonic struggles can contribute to this. But in his efforts to theorise a notion of praxis, Bhaskar strays too far from a structuralist analysis and commits some of the errors of the humanist tradition. Hegemony is reduced to the power relations between dominant and dominated groups (power2) and is not related to social structure at a more fundamental (power1) level.

Nevertheless, we can still use Bhaskar's distinction between power1 (as basic, intrinsic and enabling) and power2 (as exercised, manifest, mediated) and draw an analogy between the two types of hegemony described above. Hegemony1 might (roughly) be said to correspond to its basic materiality and its more intrinsic, functional role in relation to securing the reproduction of the social formation. It is hegemony in what we have called its deeper, structural sense. Hegemony2 would (roughly) correspond to the manifestation and expression of these hegemony1 conditions in actual hegemonic projects, practices and struggles; hegemony as the power of one dominant group exercised over another.

By contrast, Bhaskar's restriction of hegemony to the terrain of power2 results, in effect, in hegemony being seen as a conscious agential process, without the underlying structural aspect (hegemony2 but not hegemony1). Thus Bhaskar defines hegemony as a process of struggle or '*hermeneutic hegemonic/counter-hegemonic struggles* in the context of generalized master–slave power2 relations' (Bhaskar 1993: 62). Yet because of its structural aspect, hegemony may also be said to exist by virtue of an absence of counter-hegemonic struggles. We have argued that the most stable hegemonic systems lack concerted hegemonic struggles, and how, for Gramsci, the strong hegemony of the West is based on the strength of civil society. Social hegemony may be deeply woven into the very fabric of society, existing at the deeper level of hegemonic reproduction of the social formation. The main weakness of Bhaskar's account is this failure to link hegemonic practices to the crucial matter of the reproduction, conservation or transformation of social structures and to his own TMSA. His overly hermeneutic conception of hegemony has a tendency to reduce hegemonic struggles to discursive battles, where hegemony becomes a battle over description and re-description. Above all, Bhaskar's account tends to see hegemony as a relation existing between agents, albeit in a wider structured context, whereas we have argued that, by virtue of the process of repro-duction, hegemony also represents a relation between agents and the structures themselves. And hegemony operates not just within but also between various social structures and practices. A strong hegemony is therefore not simply a power2 hegemony but a deep structural and civil hegemony which operates across rather than simply over society.

Civil society

We can illustrate this in relation to the Russian revolution. As Lenin, Trotsky and Gramsci admit, the weakness of Russian civil society, as well as the economy, led to a situation in which state power could be seized, but where a strong civil hegemony was a more difficult and longer task. To a certain extent this was a product of the peculiarities of the Bolshevik project. A working-class revolution necessarily entails difficulties in trying to reconstruct society, given the weakness of the working class and its historical disenfranchisement. However, the problem can also be attributed to the general historical weakness of Russian civil society. This is admitted by Trotsky when he argues that revolution in the East is easier to make but harder to maintain, while in the West the process is longer, but ultimately more stable. Thus the task in Russia was not simply to make a revolution, but to create a firm civil society. Trotsky argues that a new working-class culture cannot just be imposed and that instead it is necessary to create the *conditions* for the development of a socialist culture. This recognises that hegemony is much more than simply the actions and decisions of the ruling group. Indeed, even the dictatorship of the proletariat is distinct from the question of wider social hegemony. The stability of the Russian revolution depends not only on the hegemony of the Bolshevik Party, nor even on the dictatorship of the proletariat, but on the hegemony of the whole working class over society. As Buci-Glucksmann has argued, hegemony *qualifies* the dictatorship of the proletariat and determines its expansive character (Buci-Glucksmann 1980: 182).

The deeper material basis of hegemony is reflected in civil society, but it is linked to a number of factors including the economy and also the basic relations between economy, civil society and state. Actual hegemonic projects may be more or less successful in drawing upon this deeper level of hegemony in order to sustain themselves. To achieve the power2 relations over other groups in society it is necessary to draw on the intrinsic capacities presented by more structural power1 relations. The experience of Russia shows that it is possible to take power and establish hegemony at one level (power2 relations of domination), but that maintaining a firm social basis means that it is necessary to create the conditions for the development of a more secure society at a deeper level of hegemony. A strong hegemony will draw on the intrinsic capacities presented by a stable and developed civil society.

When revolutions do occur it is not simply because one group achieves victory in a power2 struggle, but is because of a fundamental *structural* crisis in society. This means that there is a crisis of hegemony in its deeper sense – affecting the unity and cohesion of the social formation and undermining the stability of civil society. In a sense, the chance to take power is a consequence of the new opportunities offered by a power1 crisis. But this necessarily means that taking power is a difficult task, for power is seized precisely at a time when the basic unity of society is most undermined and where social hegemony is in a state of crisis and civil society is wobbly. The deep crisis of hegemony undermines not only the old order, but also the efforts of the new to grow. For classical Marxists like Lenin and Trotsky this necessitates the period of the dictatorship of the proletariat where emergency measures are taken to ensure the development of a socialist society. But it must be remembered that this form of hegemonic leadership is enacted through the state precisely because the more stable conditions of hegemony present in a strong civil society have yet to be achieved.

National distinctions

Since early modernity, hegemony has been connected to the national project. And while the nation is connected to the state (even if sometimes only in terms of an aspiration), it is also connected to a wider forging of identity around social, political, historical, cultural and economic factors. Nationalist ideologies must therefore be seen as attempts to mobilise support around a national project, although in reality this national project represents the hegemonic interests of the few. By constructing a social project around the nation-state, nationalism can act in passing off the interests of a certain group as the national interest, in constructing belief in a shared community that cuts across notions of class, and other forms of social stratification. The ideology of nationalism therefore acts to legitimate the political practice of a leading group, and its struggle either to maintain power or to achieve it. It may, however, take on contradictory forms according to its social base and the dynamics of struggle.

We have seen recently in former-Yugoslavia how in some cases nationalist movements would seem to create their own basis or even their own nation. Despite their demagogy, the collapse of Yugoslavia cannot simply be attributed to the actions of a few nationalist leaders. Rather, the actions of these sections of the ruling class can be attributed to the severe hegemonic crisis, itself a product of economic collapse. Consequently, those around Milosevic made a deliberate turn to Serb nationalist demagogy in order to mobilise the masses around a new social project. Tragically, some of Milosevic's strongest supporters were the former Marxist dissidents around the *Praxis* group – intellectuals like Markovic and Stojanovic, although this turn to national chauvinism is nothing new as the history of the communist movement shows.

What is quite clear is that whatever nationalist ideologies are espoused, these are only expressions of deeper social and historical features – the development of civil society, culture, economic standing, historical legacy and so on. Gramsci identifies this in his study of Italian history. He argues that society is characterised by a basic lack of unity, expressed, in particular, by the economic, political and cultural conflict between North and South. There is clearly a problem at the deeper level of hegemony, and politics is marked by uncertain leadership resulting in oscillations between despotism and constitutionalism. A social group needs to act as a locomotive to pull through basic structural change, but how is it possible, Gramsci asks, to build a train out of the Northern urban force, the Southern rurals, Sicily, Sardinia and so on? (Gramsci 1971: 87, 98). Where there was some more rooted hegemonic rule, it was of a traditional character, based on an already existing leadership so that:

> although the course of events in the Risorgimento revealed the enormous importance of the 'demagogic' mass movement, with its leaders thrown up by chance, impoverished, etc., it was nevertheless in actual fact taken over by the traditional organic forces – in other words, by the parties of long standing, with rationally-formed leaders, etc.
>
> (Gramsci 1971: 112)

In Italy, the Moderate Party was more organic in its relation to the ruling classes while the more radical Action Party lacked any concrete programme. The likes of Garibaldi were thus controlled by the influence of the Moderate national bloc. Starting with this example of Italy we can look more generally at the question of historical development and hegemony.

Early twentieth-century Italy and Spain

Here, picking up on the analysis provided by Gramsci and Trotsky, it can be said that the underlying (structural) hegemony of the social structure is noticeably weak. Their capitalist economies are in an underdeveloped state and are dependent on foreign capital. This is matched by a weak civil society, lacking a strong, unifying class leadership, or any kind of stable historical bloc. It is not so much that the historical bloc in these countries is unable to bridge the relation between 'structure' and 'superstructure', but rather that it represents, only too well, the weaknesses of both.

In both these societies national divisions are prominent – although the Spanish state has enjoyed relative stability. What is lacking, however, is a stable unifying force. Instead, more traditional forms of ideology – clerical and feudal – still predominate. Hegemonic projects are expressed through a dominance of coercion over consent, reflecting a deeper disjuncture between state, politics and economy. Political hegemony is weak and turbulent, with progress followed by reaction, as traditionalists vie with an emergent but weak intelligentsia.

The task of a conservative hegemonic leadership is to maintain power by trying to carry through a project of social modernisation as a passive revolution, keeping revolutionary sentiments within a moderate, national framework, forging a link between the 'national' and the 'popular'. These examples might be compared to the situation in Greece where politics was divided between those who emphasised nationalist territorial expansion and those who emphasised social expansion and modernisation. Hegemony must be developed at both levels one and two, matching 'structure' with 'superstructure'.

Germany, 1930s–1940s

Here the hegemonic basis of society is in acute crisis. Deep economic problems cause a structural disjunction. In turn, there is a crisis of political representation. A division opens up between the economically dominant class and those groups in a position of political leadership. There is also a cultural crisis and a lack of general lack of authority and legitimacy. In such a situation, there is dissatisfaction among the traditional supporting classes like the petite bourgeoisie. In these rare instances, such classes can be mobilised into action. Matching the bourgeois crisis is a crisis of the workers' movement and this political vacuum allows extreme petit-bourgeois movements like fascism to emerge. Thus at the level of hegemonic struggles, fascism and Bonapartism emerge as a result of deep class divisions which are unmediated by social hegemony.

Britain in the twentieth century

Britain, according to Gramsci, is traditionalist, conservative, and ossified in its social structure (Gramsci 1995: 263). Like Anderson, he argues that Britain's traditional intellectuals were drawn from the old land-owning class.[2] The underlying conditions contain a relatively stable social hegemony. An established parliamentary government contributes to the ideological self-legitimisation of the system. It has a strong bourgeois state, parties and a culture which have claimed a near-universal scope of legitimacy, and ethical and cultural cohesion (Boggs 1984: 359). An imperialist legacy has strongly shaped national culture.

The working class is relatively strong but is co-opted. Ideologically, the working class is dominated by labourist and corporatist conceptions which may allow it to be mobilised, but only from within the system. This explains the dominance within the workers' movement of the 'gradualist' variant of reformism. The workers' movement is ideologically weak and divided between different strata. Hegemonic practice is centred on consensus politics where even Labour governments effectively act as national governments. Sections of the labour leadership have been co-opted into rulership through the post-war project, a situation we shall examine in a later chapter.

Hegemony and ideology

The metaphor of social cement has been used to describe the role played by both hegemony and ideology, and it may seem, after our elaboration of a depth hegemony, that the terms are virtually synonymous. We will therefore begin to distinguish them. Most obviously, hegemony is broader than just ideology in that it encompasses not just ideological processes, but the material forces that generate these ideologies. This includes a wide range of social practices, the institutional ensemble of the state, its repressive apparatus, education, welfare, economic processes, national institutions and so on. Hegemony concerns the articulation not just of ideas, but of many practices – ideological, cultural, political and economic – as well as the various social groups and interests associated with them. We have already witnessed the consequences of ideological reductionism in the work of Laclau and Mouffe, who regard hegemony as an articulator of discourse, but not of objective or material interests. The consequence of their approach is an idealism which reduces hegemony to the process of description and re-description. Against this it is necessary to maintain that hegemony is not simply discursive or ideological, but concerns the articulation of a number of social and material elements.

There are two false conceptions of ideology. One is the reductionist view, sometimes found in neo-Gramscian accounts, which links it to world-views, the outlooks of social groups and to the effects of class rule and counter-hegemonic opposition. This position reduces ideology to its expression in hegemonic projects, while also believing ideology to straightforwardly reflect the 'ideas' or consciousness of the ruling class or opposing forces. Here, ideology is given a straightforward, instrumental nature, as a class tool that is wielded in struggle. Another false view tries to give ideology a more objective basis within the framework of society, but reduces it to a superstructural role, limited to the political or cultural spheres. Again this error is found in some neo-Gramscian accounts, but in its classical form, ideology comes to mechanically reflect the determination of the economic base.

It is Althusser who makes a forward leap in rejecting the base/superstructure and the class instrumental views. Leaving aside Althusser's later theory of ideological state apparatuses, his conception of ideology is based on the view that it is secreted by various material practices. As long as these social practices exist, then ideology will necessarily be produced. This breaks from the class instrumental view that sees ideology as *solely* a class construction and instead sees it as a basic material prerequisite for the functioning of all societies. It is related to basic human practices so that 'there is no practice except by and in an ideology' (Althusser 1971: 44). Thus ideology will never go away; it is a necessary feature of all societies. It is based on an essential need of all societies to express the way that people live their material conditions of existence.

Althusser also breaks from the view that there is one basic ideological form – as presented by the base/superstructure model. Ideologies are plural and overdetermined. They are part of the lived relations between people and their conditions of existence in the world and part of the processes by which we experience the world and reproduce it. It forms a somewhat imaginary relation to the real relations which individuals live (Althusser 1977a: 233–4). But ideology itself is very real. It is an active material force that is related to social practices. It is due to ideology's basic materiality that particular ideas have the force that they do. The fact that bourgeois ideas have a hold over the working class is not because of their superiority but because they are rooted in the material conditions of day-to-day life and the social conditions which in turn affect social consciousness.

Ideology is secreted by the various material practices which humans are engaged in and it functions to enable them to live their relations with these processes. Its nature, as Althusser puts it, is not so much of a conscious form, but in fact is more of a process that people unconsciously live. It is here that ideology may contain the element of concealment or even falseness (in Heideggerian terms we could call it the ground of inauthentic understanding). Ideology contains a picture of the world which may well be misleading, but it is a real picture nonetheless. As Bhaskar puts it: 'The relevant question is not whether ideas are real, but what kind of reality they have' (Bhaskar 1997: 142). However, if ideology is misleading, it is so in the sense of being inadequate or simplified, although given the complexity of the social world this may be necessary to the functioning of social life. In the sense that ideology is a simplification of social relations, it can be compared to a plan or a map which allows us to operate and to chart our way through the world. But drawing on Heidegger again we can say that we only really become aware of this process when we lose the map or fail to understand it. Ideology is a vital process which cannot be escaped or lived around, although Althusser's critics should note that he leaves plenty of room for intentional action in that deliberate action may be founded on this more basic function:

> So ideology is not an aberration or a contingent excrescence of History: it is a structure essential to the historical life of societies. Further, only the existence and the recognition of its necessity enable us to act upon ideology and transform ideology into an instrument of deliberate action on history.
>
> (Althusser 1977a: 232)

Likewise, we have argued that hegemony is essential to the historical life of society, and that, at another level, it can be developed into concrete political projects. Hegemony and ideology are very closely related and they intersect, both at the level of the reproduction of the social formation and as concrete projects are constructed and elaborated. However, hegemony, in its structural role, is specifically concerned with the unity of the social formation, or aspects of it, securing the conditions for reproduction, whereas ideology, by contrast, is more closely connected to specific human practices. Ideology is intrinsic to these processes, whereas hegemony has a broader, more extrinsic role. While hegemony helps secure the cohesion of the system by organising the relations *between* different structures and practices, ideology is the means by which subjects function *within* their social practices.

To take up Althusser's position, ideology exists in a general sense in all societies as a necessary part of the relation between social processes and human subjects. Ideologies are secreted by human practices. However, ideology does not exist in the general sense implied by the base/super-structure metaphor. Rather, the overdetermined and stratified nature of the social totality means that just as we have to recognise a multiplicity of social practices, so we have to recognise a plurality of ideologies. Ideology is intrinsic in the sense that it is secreted by human practices which in turn are governed by social structures. They are adhered to almost unconsciously as a way in which social agents operate in a given social environment. The limitations of practice produce the limitations of ideology. It is only when certain agents consciously intervene that ideologies may be said to be external constructs which have been put together in order to serve certain interests. But here ideology is again intersecting with hegemony and hegemonic struggles.

We have accepted a very structuralist and functionalist account of ideology which sees it as intrinsically related to social practices that are in turn determined by social structures and mechanisms. But we can do so only because the functioning of ideology in itself is insufficient. Therefore the social formation is not reproduced in an automatic way through the relations between structures, practices and ideology. Ideology does not automatically guarantee that we happily live our relations with the world. Rather, the reproduction of the social formation needs to be *secured*. Because of ideology's close proximity to human practices, and because of the plurality of ideologies that exist, it cannot play this wider role.

In the reproduction of social reality, hegemony deals with the *extrinsic* relations necessary for the reproductive process. It is insufficient to say that structures are reproduced because practices are ideologically regulated. A depth hegemony is necessary to secure the relations between different structures, and between structures, mechanisms and practices. An analysis of hegemony combines the functioning of structures with their over-determination, which in turn opens a space for the active intervention of a hegemonic process which adds a contingent and agential dimension. None of this is possible if our study is restricted to an examination of ideology 'producing subjects'. Therefore, while we might say that ideology, in its most fundamental sense, is intrinsically bound up with human practices, we may add that hegemony is necessary in order to preserve *ideological unity*. This distinction draws on the fact that ideology, *in general*, is an intrinsic product of human practices, but that, *in actuality*, it exists in a plurality of forms, and that hegemony therefore plays an extrinsic role in securing ideological unity across the social formation. Moreover, as has already been said, this extrinsic role requires the articulation of more than just ideologies. Even to talk of ideological unity requires us to look at how hegemony relates to numerous social practices and not just ideologies. However, hegemony is not just limited to the role of securing ideological unity but the unity of the social formation more generally. Hegemony relates to the wider range of social practices and to important social bodies and institutions.

We have stressed the extrinsic character of hegemony; however, hegemony may be intrinsic to a certain structure or practice. But, in this case, hegemony acts as the extrinsic articulator between different ideologies within that practice. For practices may not produce a single ideology, but a number of ideologies. Such a process needs organisation, and where ideologies clash a decision must be made. Thus in current production and management practices the idea of flexibilisation currently has hegemony over older corporatist methods. So we can say that hegemony has an extrinsic relation not just between mechanisms, structures and practices, but between the associated ideologies as well. Where hegemony is more or less confined to a particular ideological field, or to certain structures or practices, we can say that it has a more regional character. But in its wider role hegemony spans a range of such locations. We can say this because of the stratified nature of social reality and the way in which different forms of reproduction take place across the social spectrum.

Our conception of ideology has so far focused on its deeper social role as an intrinsic aspect of social practices. However, as we move towards the concrete it can be seen that ideologies can also be constructed into more elaborate theories, drawing on intrinsic ideologies, but developing them into more complex articulations. We may draw a distinction between a more intrinsic ideology – things like the wage form or the value form – and an elaborated theoretical ideology like classical economic theory. The latter is in part determined by its inability to get to grips with the former. But we can say that there are theoretical discourses, world-views, mentalities and ways of life which are not simply intrinsic or secreted, but have a more complex basis. At this point ideology becomes articulated, it is consciously taken up and developed.

This helps deal with the problems raised by Jorge Larrain in his analysis of ideology. He distinguishes between a negative conception of ideology in Marx which develops out of the material conditions (contradictions) of society, and a positive conception (e.g. in Lenin and Gramsci) which sees ideology as a class construction. As Larrain puts it: 'Whereas for Marx ideology originates *on* the terrain of contradictions, for the positive version ideology *is* the terrain of contradictions in theory' (Larrain 1983: 89). But as we have argued, it is here that ideology intersects with hegemonic practice, for such ideologies are *articulated ideologies*. They are constructed around certain nodal points – beliefs, positions, interests and so on. We may even go so far as to say that they have a certain logos.

However, having identified this intersection, it would be wrong to then reduce hegemony – even in its 'surface' role – to ideological articulation. Such a position is found in the works of Laclau and Mouffe, where subjects are interpellated outside of any real material structure. Both ideology and hegemony get submerged in the workings of the 'text'. Then, at the level of hegemonic activity, the reduction of hegemony to ideology effectively reduces it to world-views, or a kind of willed subjectivity. This is clearly wrong, but it is at this articulated level of hegemonic practices that the two coincide most closely. Here it is possible to say that ideologies are constructed around a world-view which reflects the interests of the dominant group. But again, in this relation, hegemony is the articulator while ideology does the representing. Thus Gramsci is correct to talk of 'historically organic ideologies' which are structurally determined in the sense that they are necessary to a given structure and that they organise human masses and create the terrain on which they move (Gramsci 1971: 376–7). Such ideologies are historically organic in the sense that they combine their social function with the active intervention of historical forces. And this active intervention of historical forces is part of the hegemonic project. Ideology then becomes the means by which hegemonic struggles are expressed and represented. Articulated ideologies assume a more explicit political character, serving certain interests. However, in the case of emancipatory projects, hegemony clearly goes beyond the limitations of ideology and exposes and transcends the limited and partial consciousness of ideological belief. Hegemony, in its more cognitive guise, may therefore even become an ideology critique, rejecting the limitations of an ideological viewpoint in order to articulate an alternative view of the way things can be.

Therefore, we may schematically conclude with the notion that both hegemony and ideology have a 'surface' articulation and a deeper structural basis. This latter aspect of ideology is based on the fact that its origins lie in its secretion through a plurality of material practices. Hegemony's structural origin is based on the general need to secure the unity of the social formation. Whereas ideology is an intrinsic product of human practices, hegemony is concerned with the extrinsic relations between these practices, as well as between other social structures, generative mechanisms and the various ideologies themselves. Ideologies, at least in their origin, may be said to be a set of beliefs internal to a particular social practice or group of agents, whereas hegemony is the external element capable of organising or uniting these various beliefs, or even, to a limited degree, going beyond them. In the second sense, ideologies may be said to become articulated, and it is here that the distinction between ideology and hegemony starts to become more blurred, although it is surely clear that the construction of a hegemonic project (associated with this surface definition) requires much more that just the articulation of ideas, and must also organise the relations between classes, groups, interests, social bodies, institutions, states and other concrete entities.

This chapter must conclude with a warning. For the concept of ideology has caused huge problems to Marxists. It must be remembered that Marxism is not analytical philosophy and that the Marxist understanding of the world makes it impossible to apply precise categories. Thus there should be no counterposition between different forms of ideology – either in its intrinsic sense or as an articulated discourse. The world is complexly structured out of a multitude of relations. For critical realism, the objects of knowledge are not things as such (for this would represent a form of atomism), but relations, processes, causes, mechanisms, contradictions and dialectical determinations. This means ideology cannot be defined in such a precise way – indeed, it would be ideological to try to do so. Just as ideology itself spans many social fields, so too must the concept.

But by noting the complexity of ideology we can also examine how it is closely related to hegemony. As it spans society, hegemony interacts with ideology in its different forms. In securing the conditions for the reproduction of the social formation hegemony must interact with the intrinsic ideologies secreted by human practices. But as dialectics teaches us, hegemony and ideology do not relate to one another in an exclusively extrinsic way; they are also intrinsically linked so that hegemony is also what it is by virtue of its relation to ideology. This is most apparent at the level of hegemonic practices where the concepts cannot be properly separated, although we must stress again that while ideology is the articulation of ideas, hegemony articulates other social features as well.

7　Objectivity and intersubjectivity

Introduction

So far, it has been argued that hegemony has different aspects: structural and agential, deep and surface, functional and manifest. This chapter will be concerned with establishing in what kind of way hegemony has an objective validity and on what basis this objectivity is to be understood. This involves questioning the concept of intersubjectivity, which is often opposed to a more objective approach. The intersubjective view of the social draws upon the phenomenological approach to human interaction and communication, so that the mutual actions and understandings of social actors constitute the fundamental basis of social life. It can be seen how such an emphasis on mutual understanding and interaction contrasts with a more objective approach based on a study of dominant social structures. This is evident in the understanding of hegemony, where the emphasis is shifted from structural conditions so that hegemony comes to represent the inter-subjective actions of social groups and the world-views that these groups possess. But what is at stake in this debate is not just the concept of hegemony, but the concept of the social within which hegemony is located. Does society have an objective basis in the way that the natural world does? Or can it only be understood as a set of intersubjective relations between people? Does the social world contain objective social structures, or should social science consist of a study of mutual understandings and interactions?

Our argument is a critical naturalist – or indeed a critical hermeneutic – one. Human society is distinct from the natural world in the sense that it contains intersubjective relations and is mediated through knowledge, language and other systems of understanding. The hermeneutic tradition is correct to stress this, but it errs in seeing such processes as the funda-mental basis upon which the social world is constituted. It is necessary to stress that the social world is not exhausted by its conceptual aspect and that, like the natural world, it is also comprised of important structures and generative mechanisms. Society, after all, is not opposed to the natural world, but is ultimately a part of it, albeit a part with its own distinctive emergent features. So if the natural world is structured in a certain way and contains basic material relations, then the social world should also be considered in this way. The distinction between intersubjective and objective accounts of society is therefore a distinction between those approaches (like the hermeneutic one) which give primacy to processes of mutual understanding, communicative behaviour, normative consensus and so on, and those (realist) approaches which give primacy to the material structure of society. Among the generative mechanisms the mode of production is of particular importance given that material production and reproduction is fundamental to the human species. By upholding the intransitivity of these processes and structures, critical realism maintains that meaningful scientific enquiry is possible, not only into the structures themselves, but also into the associated beliefs and meanings which hermeneutic historiography fails to structurally situate.

In terms of hegemony, we are distinguishing between intersubjective accounts which give primacy to the hegemonic processes of agential interaction, group interests, particular hegemonic projects and world-views, and a more objective account which also sees the need to examine the deeper hegemonic basis of the reproduction and cohesion of the social formation, and the relation between agent and structure. The argument presented below is that the intersubjective approach to hegemony focuses too much on agential interactions and hegemonic projects while the objective or realist view attempts to relate these to underlying social structures and the structural hegemony of the social formation. This chapter will explore these issues by examining the implications of an intersubjective approach to the social as outlined in the work of Wittgenstein and Habermas. Having examined these positions we will return to Gramsci to consider in what ways he can be considered to be a hermeneutic theorist.

The philosophical tradition

Intersubjective accounts of human activity tend to make two reductions which can be distinguished as:

1 An ontological reduction which reduces *society* to human forms of action, behaviour and meaning. Such an approach is anthropocentric, often embracing a praxis ontology which defines the social, and the limits of the social, on the basis of human practice alone. The social world is reduced to human activity. This approach looks at human practices while denying or minimising the effect of social structures. At best these social structures are reduced to the forms of human activity that they govern. Consequently, intersubjective accounts of society shift emphasis from an analysis of intransitive social structures to the transitive processes of human understanding and communication. This explains the emphasis on language and discourse as the basis for social consensus and mutual activity.

2 There is also the epistemological matter of the status and content of *social science*. This is linked to the fact that the social world is seen as distinct from the natural world. The effect, however, is a rigid separation of the methods of social and natural science based on this conception of radically different subject-matters. It is common for the intersubjective approach to view social science as mainly conceptual with its role reduced to the study of meaning, rationality, human behaviour and other forms of social interaction. It is true that these aspects do need serious examination, but social science is not exhausted by such an examination. Indeed, we can only properly understand the conceptual basis of social science if we can also explain the objective structure of the social world which forms, shapes and generates human action and knowledge. Yet many approaches to social science either deny that society has an objective or intransitive structure, or else they claim that it cannot be studied. Yet such views still require an onto-logical account of what the social world is like, so we get what Steve Fleetwood calls hermeneutic foundationalism (Fleetwood 1995: 18), whereby the social world is not merely concept-dependent but concept-exhausted.

   The adoption of a realist position allows for a conception of social science as an *explanatory critique* which in turn recognises the conceptual – or perhaps more to the point, ideological – character of social relations while also attempting to examine the processes that underlie these ideas. By seeking to explain the prior material basis, it is possible to analyse and debunk the various ideologies that are secreted by material practices. If these ideas are false, misleading or partial, then a correct explanation of society exposes not only the inadequacy or outright falsity of these ideas but also why they should be so by virtue of their relation to social practices and hence why they are necessary for the reproduction of society. The subversive nature of an explanatory critique rests with the fact that in challenging social ideas, it examines the relation between these ideas and social reality and hence challenges aspects of social reality itself. It thus moves from a critique of intersubjectively held beliefs to a critique of the objective relations that sustain them.

   The intersubjective view of the social world cannot do this since, in committing the epistemic fallacy, it reduces social being to social knowledge and abandons the intransitive dimension of social structures as either non-existent or unknowable. But the intersubjective activity which takes place is dependent on pre-existing social material causes. Activity is not simply founded upon the relation between groups of people, but is based on the relation between agent and structure. For example, we cannot simply speak of the relation between the proletariat and the bourgeoisie, but rather, we need to look at the relations between the proletariat and bourgeoisie and the capitalist mode of production. To deny this is to reduce the capitalist mode of production to the activities of the bourgeoisie creating an instrumentalist view of history – and the conspiracy theory that the bosses simply sit down and decide how the economy will work. In reality we know that it is the economy which largely determines the way the bosses work. The bosses and workers are both the products of a system.

Agents do have an important role in determining how social structures may develop, but this is through the sort of process characterised by Bhaskar as the transformational model of social activity. Unlike natural structures, these social structures are dependent on human practice and some human conception of this practice. But this, as we have explained, is of a limited nature, and has many unintended consequences. The social world has an ontological status, rather than being merely conceptual, subjective or intersubjective. This means that it is comprised of not just of human actions or even just practices, but underlying social structures and generative mechanisms which are relatively independent and enduring. Like the structures of the natural world, social structures, when we study them, have an intransitive status. While these structures are dependent on human activity for their reproduction, this is on the basis that 'people, in their conscious human activity, for the most part unconsciously reproduce (or occasionally, transform) the structures that govern their substantive activities of production' (Bhaskar 1989b: 80).

Thus we are also rejecting the humanist accounts which reduce society to the expression of groups and individuals, while ignoring structural determinations and constraints. And, likewise, such accounts reduce hegemony to its expression, rather than its conditions of being. Such a view is ontologically flat, reducing society to a surface level of operations without developing the kind of depth analysis which is necessary if we are really to develop any kind of meaningful explanation.

The hermeneutic turn

The hermeneutic tradition can be traced back to many sources, but it is Kant who stands out as the most significant influence. Kant's phenomenology means that the world is knowable insofar as it is knowable *for us*. The emphasis in Kant is on establishing the conditions for and limitations of human understanding based on the knowing and reasoning subject. The neo-Kantian and hermeneutic traditions move away from Kant's emphasis on the universal mental constructs of the transcendental consciousness, replacing it with a more intersubjective and interactive view that sees knowledge as developed through communities. Instead of meaning being derived from the universal categories of the mind, the world now becomes meaningful to us though our social interactions. The transcendental aspect of the Kantian approach remains, with emphasis still on the necessary conditions for knowledge and experience. The difference then is that Kant seeks to locate the conditions for knowledge in the human mind, whereas the hermeneuticists locate them in intersubjective communities, while transcendental realists like Bhaskar would seek to locate these necessary conditions in the wider structure of the world.

Hegel helps hermeneutics break from Kant's emphasis on the transcendental consciousness so that self-reflection is radicalised into a social and historical form. Heidegger also helps to historicize understanding, which is seen as the disclosure of meaningful experience, embedded in a practical context. Understanding is fundamental to *Dasein* (being-there), which is not simply cognitive, but is pre-structured and located in time. In this way, Heidegger 'ontologises' hermeneutics. Understanding is both the horizon and the structure of *Dasein*. For the hermeneutic philosopher Dilthey, human interaction and mutual understanding is mediated by the intersubjectivity of language and symbols (Dilthey 1988). This forms the basis of our actions and understandings which in turn is the basis upon which we objectify ourselves – a self-formative process. Dilthey's intersubjective understanding – *verstehen* – looks for the possibility of a universally valid interpretation. Still implicit in (particularly the early) Dilthey is the individualistic and psychologistic view that the social world is created by the mind.

Gadamer (1979) seeks to move beyond this through his use of Heidegger's *Dasein,* incorporating ontological questions of temporality, otherness, 'thrownness' and so on. In the process of understanding, there is a fusion of horizons which goes beyond our own private understanding and which embraces a historical horizon that is related to the past. The horizon forms our range of vision, but it is not fixed. It is something into which we move and which moves with us. This gives understanding a critical aspect. Thus Habermas would seem to side with Gadamer against Wittgenstein on the basis that language can reflect on its own conditions – rather than being a given set of games – so that more emphasis is given to the conditions for meaningful dialogue and the problems of interpretation (Habermas 1984: 133–6. However, the result is that objectivity is now intermeshed with intersubjectivity. The notion of a fused horizon means that we are always inside our situation. We have a hermeneutic circle whereby texts can only be understood as representative of a world-view, and world-views can only be understood as a synthesis of such texts. Understanding, rather than being related to gaining knowledge of an object, is tied instead to the processes by which we reach agreement. Objectivity is now inseparable from the intersubjective context. Philosophy's role is reduced from examining the world, to examining the necessary conditions of knowledge, and the problems and uses of language.

The hermeneutic method

Hermeneutics was initially confined to matters of interpretation in relation to a text. Gradually its field was extended, resulting in the position that interpretations effectively define the social world. The result is an emphasis on language and meaning and a distinction between the method of the natural and social sciences, which, it is claimed, have radically different subject-matters. The unfortunate consequence of such an approach is to leave the natural sciences in the grip of a positivist methodology. This effect is still visible even as late as Habermas (who has never adequately got to grips with the status of science and who describes the method of natural science as rational–instrumental).

In contrast to the empirical methods of natural science, hermeneutics poses the social scientific method as conceptual, concentrating on meaning and interpretation. The task of social science is to focus on conceptual connections – for example, between behaviour and human understanding – while the social world is seen as a system of rules and human practices. The emphasis on meaning can lead to human behaviour being connected to an intersubjective rationality, implying a transcendentally universal notion of reason, tied to a dialogical conception of human practice. Reason is linked to human practice, while human practice is linked to processes of mutual understanding and meaningful interaction. Society is seen as rule governed, its basis is one of consensual activity. The rationalism involved here is clearly a problem, for by reducing human interaction to its conceptual aspect, this form of hermeneutics implies that agents are fully aware of their reasons and motives. Yet critical realists have argued that intentions and meanings are often either not known, or only partially known to agents (and they cannot therefore constitute the primary element of social explanation). By giving primacy to questions of human interpretation, meaning, understanding and rationality, hermeneutics constructs a social ontology that is based on intersubjective human practices. This undermines the view that society is an intransitively structured entity, within which human activity plays a reproductive or transformatory role (and where meanings and intentions are associated with rather than constitutive of these structures). Andrew Sayer notes 'the tendency of hermeneuticists to assume that society is *only* like a text, requiring *nothing more* than interpretation of its meanings. Yet although this interpretive understanding is indispensable, it is not sufficient to explain material change: causal explanation is still required' (Sayer, A. 2000: 143).

This also affects how we conceive of hegemony. An intersubjective approach leads to the view that hegemony's basis lies in either (a) the universally valid conditions for rational human consensus, or (b) the distortion of an ideal situation (these positions would correspond to the notion of hegemony as both consensus and domination). But it is defined through the notion of intersubjective human rationality and consensus, rather than being given any material basis in the actual structures of the world. A realist conception of hegemony is incompatible with such intersubjective views of society that reduce it to forms of mutual understanding and behaviour. Instead, hegemony is concerned with the unity of the social formation and with the reproduction, conservation or transformation of social structures. It is only through this process that the particular projects (and intentions) of human agents can be understood.

Habermas begins a critique of the hermeneutic tradition by arguing that the problem of interpretation has been reduced to this consensual basis and that it fails to see that forms of social activity (and their conceptual basis) may be false or misleading. In particular, Habermas is keen to stress the distortion caused by political and economic factors. However, Habermas leaves us with a *critical* hermeneutics without really challenging its basic assumption of a conceptually defined social world based on intersubjectively valid, rational social activity. His conception of distorted communicative behaviour is only valid if we accept the transcendental premise of an ideal speech situation.

Wittgenstein's language games

If hermeneutic accounts reduce social reality to the conditions of its intelligibility, Wittgensteinian accounts go a stage further, questioning intelligibility itself. Thus, in the famous remark, we should not look for meaning but rather for use. If by this Wittgenstein means that something can only be understood in the context of its relations with other things and processes, then he is more or less correct. But the statement also implies the reduction of the real to the actual, switching attention from structures and powers to practices, meanings and the expression or exercising of powers. Hence, rather than enquiring into understanding, philosophy's concern should be with description. Thus, while Kantians and hermeneuticists reduce philosophy to the problem of knowledge, Wittgensteinians reduce philosophy to questions about language. Wittgenstein gives a prime example of the epistemic fallacy when he says in the *Tractatus: 'The limits of my language* mean the limits of my world' (Wittgenstein 1922: 5.6).

The early Wittgenstein assumes that only truth functional propositions are meaningful and that the world is made up of facts. Simple objects fit together to form states of affairs which in turn make up reality so that '[t]he world is everything that is the case' (Wittgenstein 1922: 1) and the 'world is the totality of facts, not of things' (Wittgenstein 1922: 1.1). As a consequence, reality is elucidated through the use of language: 'The object of philosophy is the logical clarification of thoughts' (Wittgenstein 1922: 4.112). This emphasis on thoughts indicates a solipsistic streak in the early Wittgenstein. The subject does not so much belong to the world as constitutes the limit of the world (Wittgenstein 1922: 5.632). He argues:

> In fact what solipsism *means*, is quite correct, only it cannot be *said*, but it shows itself.
>
> That the fact that the world is my world, shows itself in the fact that the limits of the language (the language which I understand) mean the limits of my world.
>
> (Wittgenstein 1922: 5.62)

The view in the *Tractatus* is that the world is my world and the way I live it determines its structure. This is important because Wittgenstein's break from this position is founded on a new concept of the intersubjectivity of the social world – most famously the private language argument. Obeying a rule becomes a practice that cannot be done privately. So Wittgenstein moves from a solipsistic theory of the subjective certainty of inner experience, where our reality is a picture made up of propositions (reflecting a state of affairs), to an external, intersubjectively valid knowledge shared by those involved in various social practices. Wittgenstein demonstrates how the sameness of meaning is based on our ability to follow a rule. This is intersubjectively valid, for how else would we know that we were following the rule correctly? Thus Wittgenstein's private language argument leads to the view that rules are social and that they provide the grounds for use and consistency. But while Wittgenstein makes an important shift from private meaning to social usage, he is consistent in that his philosophy remains trapped in the study of language, and for him, the main philosophical problems arise when language goes on holiday (Wittgenstein 1958: 19).

It is open to speculation whether or not Wittgenstein would allow for a social science that can study extra-linguistic practices and social structures. His own writings make no such reference, although we can see in the Wittgensteinian Peter Winch a reduction of the social to its conceptual basis (Winch 1958). Wittgenstein, however, is solely concerned with the task of philosophy. He argues that its role is to describe rather than to explain – hence the argument that we should look at use rather than meaning. He goes on to say that 'we must do away with all *explanation*, and description alone must take its place' (Wittgenstein 1958: 47).

It is clear that Wittgenstein is offering description as an alternative to explanation, but is it possible to adequately describe something without giving some sort of deeper explanation? Wittgenstein's refusal to do this leads to an ontological flatness which suggests that things can be known at their surface level. This brackets off what lies behind the language games and effectively denies that this reality has any bearing on the description of social objects. Hence:

> Philosophy simply puts everything before us, and neither explains nor deduces anything. Since everything lies open to view there is nothing to explain. For what is hidden, for example, is of no interest to us.
>
> (Wittgenstein 1958: 50)

And of course, 'whereof one cannot speak, thereof one must be silent' (Wittgenstein 1922: 7).

Combined with his notions of rule following and the private language argument, we can see that Wittgenstein's social ontology is founded upon intersubjective practices rather than on objective structures. Whether or not they do exist, since they have no bearing on philosophy's role, nor on our ability to give a description, external structures might as well not exist.

Intersubjective language games have replaced objective social structures. However, this is problematic to Wittgenstein's arguments, for without an adequate ontology, he cannot say why a particular language game might take place, nor what it might represent, nor how it is determined. Language games just are what they are, and we must ask no further than that. We are left with a surface description of human practices, with no ability to understand or criticise them.

There are also relativistic implications since, without any objective criteria, it is only possible to criticise a language game from within it. And without an account of any underlying structures, each language game becomes its own foundation.[1] The postmodernist philosopher Jean-François Lyotard uses this to his advantage to argue that each language game has its own separate and distinct narrative creating an '"atomisation" of the social into flexible networks of language games' (Lyotard 1984: 17), thereby making an overall or totalising view impossible.

Finally, Wittgenstein's remark that we should not look for meaning but rather for use can be taken in two directions: first, we can go in the direction of postmodernism and conclude that the search for a theory of meaning is a lost cause; second, we can follow Jurgen Habermas and focus instead on questions of usage, practice, action, pragmatics and communicative action. This we will now investigate.

Habermas and world-views

Continuing in the Kantian tradition, Habermas is concerned with knowledge, reason, enlightenment and modernity. These drive his social theory and his concern for such issues as social reification, the loss of meaning, the distortion of public life and the possibility of emancipation. Central to his work is the Kantian belief that we have a practical interest in reason: 'Self reflection is at once intuition and emancipation, comprehension and liberation from dogmatic dependence' (Habermas 1972: 208). By extending this, Habermas can argue that historical materialism is a theory of society with practical intent (Habermas 1974: 3) and Marxism is seen not so much as a science, but as a form of critique that expresses the fact that we have a practical interest in our freedom.

Habermas argues that Marx's advance over Kant is based on the emphasis that is given to social action. But Marx's conception is criticised by Habermas since he believes that Marx throws together interaction and work as praxis – whereas Habermas is insisting on the distinction between what he rather reductively calls 'instrumental action' (in particular economic activity) and communicative action (Habermas 1974: 62). It is argued that by bringing the two together, Marx reduces the study of society to a scientific practice – thus undermining epistemology and the basis for knowledge and understanding. Marx, according to Habermas, screens out reason and fails to grasp the normative content of modernity (Habermas

1987: 320). But Habermas's critique should be seen more as a reflection of the weaknesses of the hermeneutic tradition, for Habermas is unable to conceive of Marx's work except in a narrow positivistic way. Paradoxically, the more emphasis that hermeneutics places on the conceptual and intersubjective nature of social life, the more a positivistic view is embraced in conceiving of the non-social other. In most cases it is natural science that is left to positivism, but in Habermas's case this also extends to economic life, leading to a misreading of Marx's work. As Bhaskar has written:

> it may be argued that Marx understands labour not just as technical action, but as always occurring within and through a historically specific society and that it is Habermas, not Marx, who mistakenly and uncritically adopts a positivistic account both of labour, defining it as technical action, and of natural science, which he sees as adequately represented by the deductive-nomological model.
>
> (Bhaskar 1989b: 141)

Much has been made of Habermas's shift from a critique of ideology to a study of the lifeworld and how communicative action is reified and distorted. But Habermas is consistent in his project and in his errors. The early emphasis on ideology and knowledge-constitutive interests is now absorbed into his theory of communicative action. Marx is criticised for failing to realise that power and ideology stem from the distortion of communication, rather than from the process of production. Habermas later reformulates this in terms of Marx's conflation of the lifeworld and system.

The distinction between system and lifeworld refers to different spheres of social reproduction, the material and the symbolic, and their corresponding forms of human action – strategic and communicative. Habermas conceives of the system in a positivistic way, as a sphere of instrumental activity intimately related to the capitalist economy. The lifeworld, by contrast, is intersubjectively constituted and symbolically structured. It is a symbolic terrain that 'both forms a *context* and furnishes *resources* for the process of mutual understanding' (Habermas 1987: 298). It represents a set of background resources that make human interaction and communication meaningful. Again the influence of the neo-Kantians is evident – it is a transcendental feature of any society that we realise ourselves through our conditions of intersubjective communication. These communicative practices in turn draw upon and reproduce an intersubjectively shared lifeworld based on mutual understanding. This lifeworld, argues Habermas, 'is bounded by the totality of interpretations presupposed by the members as background knowledge' (Habermas 1984: 13). Communication fulfils the function of reaching understanding, co-ordinating actions and socialising individuals. It has become the medium through which cultural reproduction, social integration and socialisation take place (Habermas 1987: 86). This, as we shall later argue, can be seen as a new conception of a sort of underlying hegemony centred around achieving consensus. The problem, however, is that such things as human interests and actions are all constituted intersubjectively (Habermas 1974: 13). No connection to material structures is made since these belong to the system and do not form a part of the lifeworld. Instead, the lifeworld is seen as woven out of language games, rules and practices. So we lose a sense of objectivity in relation to interests and actions – they are related to the structure of communication and mutual understanding, but not to the real material structures of the system.

As is to be expected, Habermas attacks positivism for failing to establish the connection between knowledge and human interests. But like others in the hermeneutic tradition, Habermas leaves unchallenged positivism's assumptions about science, technology and the realm that Habermas calls the 'system'. Habermas therefore implicitly inherits a positivist ontology, and explicitly combines the lifeworld of communicative action with an instrumentalist conception of labour, power and money. Habermas's main interest in the system concerns how it comes to constitute a threat to the lifeworld, and the capitalist system is not seen in terms of how it helps constitute the lifeworld, but rather, in terms of how it distorts the lifeworld, encroaching upon it, and causing reification and cultural impoverishment. Social consensus, it must be remembered, is transcendentally given, so the role of the capitalist system is a secondary one in the sense that it distorts the lifeworld through the influence of power and money. Comparisons can be drawn with Weber's theory of rationalisation and bureaucratisation. The crisis of the lifeworld is shown through a loss of meaning and freedom as it is colonised through monetarisation and the spread of bureaucratic power. But, as with Weber, such an approach depends upon pure ideal types which never in reality existed. For Weber these ideal types act more as a methodological device to aid concrete analysis, but for Habermas, the ideal type is ontologised as a prior transcendental condition of social life. The problem with seeing the lifeworld as colonised by the system is that it begs the question, raised by Perry Anderson, of when was it not colonised, of when it existed in its ideal state (Anderson 1998: 45)?

Here the influence of the Kantians is at its most troublesome. Rejecting Wittgenstein's 'positivism' of language games, Harbermas argues that 'language games only work because they presuppose idealisations that transcend any particular language game; as a necessary condition of possibly reaching understanding' (Habermas 1987: 199). Habermas is arguing that there is a universally valid transcendental basis for communicative action and the lifeworld. The system, as a set of material processes closely related to economic life, intrudes upon the lifeworld and distorts it. But this implies a radical separation of the two realms, so that material structures have no bearing on how we initially understand communicative action. The equivalent of this in critical realist terms is to see the intransitive realm not as constitutive of the social world, but merely in terms of how it intervenes in and distorts some ideal or transcendent transitive behaviour. This generates a dualistic separation of discourse from other material processes. According to Habermas's ideal speech situation, validity is not context bound, it is not based on actual social relations, but is the 'transcendental moment of universal validity' (Habermas 1987: 322).

Habermas's argument extends to the welfare state. Displaying deep illusions, he argues that the goal of the welfare state system is to set free life forms structured in an egalitarian way allowing individual self-realisation and spontaneity. However, the power–functional system grows beyond the lifeworld and becomes independent (Habermas 1987: 362). This fails to see how the welfare system is, on the one hand, an aspect of state regulation and structural integration, and on the other, the product of concrete class struggles. It cannot be transcendentally separated from either the capitalist system or the class struggle and seen as some ideal form which somehow, in a secondary sort of way, becomes distorted by power and money. It is not the case that power and money act as a medium by which functional systems cut themselves off from the lifeworld and get integrated into the system. Welfare systems do not fall from the sky in a nice neutral sort of way. They are a concrete embodiment of the regulatory needs of the capitalist system and the effects of the actual struggles.

By holding the lifeworld position, Habermas generates a simplistic picture of the social as a series of world-views that 'function in the formation and stabilisation of identities, supplying individuals with a core of basic concepts and assumptions' (Habermas 1984: 64). This is clearly inspired by Weber's concern with the institutional embodiment of human conscious-ness and the rationalisation of world-views: 'These worldviews establish an analogical nexus between man, nature, and society which is represented as a totality in the basic concepts of mythical powers' (Habermas 1987: 56). World-views support a particular order, leaders and groups, and basic norms. They interrelate with consensus and institutional systems, generating the social order.

Habermas's views on the lifeworld have an important bearing on the concept of hegemony because of their emphasis on social cohesion and consensus. The issue of consensus is bound up with communicative ration-ality and the achievement of mutual understanding. However, because the normative foundations of mutual understanding are seen as transcendental and universal rather than historical and specific, Habermas's theory of social consensus lacks the kind of concrete social and political analysis to be found, for example, in Gramscian theories of hegemony. Habermas's search for general human conditions of rationality, consensus and mutuality is at the expense of an account of concrete interests and real social struggles. Hegemony becomes bound up with the inherent consensus present in our social interaction, it becomes something that is given rather than contested.

Moving from the question of social consensus to the matter of social cohesion it can be seen that Habermas's theory opens up new possibilities in that it problematises the relation between the lifeworld and system. The question of social cohesion is explored through the theory of legitimation crisis and through a study of government intervention into the economic and public spheres. Because the state intervenes in social life in order to try and support the economy, it allows economic problems to be transmitted back onto other social spheres causing a wider crisis of social cohesion. So the legitimation crisis can usefully be compared to the idea of a hegemonic crisis, but this still leaves the problem of social dualism along with the feeling that hegemony only comes into being as a crisis point caused by an undermining of an ideal lifeworld where social consensus is a transcendental feature. A crisis is represented by the disintegration of a unified world-view and the fragmentation of knowledge and culture. However, while for Habermas this occurs when the system encroaches on the lifeworld, we might argue precisely the opposite. A crisis of world-view occurs when it becomes detached from the system. Thus hegemonic unity is in accordance with the 'system' rather than fragmented by it. This is based on the notion of a depth hegemony as representative of the reproduction of the social formation as a whole. However, Habermas does not have such a notion and instead sees the material world as an obstacle to hegemony, which for him would be reduced to the consensus/domination dichotomy. The problem with Habermas, as Larrain argues, is that 'domination is no longer based on class differences or material inequality; domination is now an ideological problem which can be located at the level of those consensual structures where communication is systematically distorted' (Larrain 1983: 108).

It should be argued that consensus and understanding are not automatic or transcendental processes, and that they are much more than intersubjective notions. Since social consensus is not given, it needs to be constructed in accordance with the dominant trends in the 'system'. In the course of this process, class and group interests become prominent. Thus there is no division between lifeworld and system, but rather, as Gramsci puts it, hegemony is constitutive of the relation between structure and superstructure. And as David Held has argued, what matters is not so much the consensus of the majority, but of the dominant groups. Yet Habermas's notion of the lifeworld is a flat one which does not really allow for the stratification of consensus, interest or hegemony.

For Habermas, consensus has a transcendentally universal basis. Conflicts are a product of a failure of rationality. But we have argued that hegemony, although it is a general requirement, is not universally given, but rather, is a particular intervention, borne out of the impossibility of such things as universal action, consensus and agreement. Habermas reduces ideology and hegemony to questions of universal consensus and distorted communication. In fact they are connected to the reproduction of the 'system', as well as its occasional transformation.

The objectivity of hegemony

The reduction of society and social science to human action or interaction must be avoided. Such a focus fails to provide a sufficient objective basis for hegemony. However, Gramsci too is also often said to have an inter-subjective and hermeneutic approach. Indeed, Bhaskar brackets Gramsci with Lukács and Korsch in reducing Marxism to the expression of the subject (see Chapter 2). Certainly, in his efforts to escape mechanical materialism, Gramsci has talked of absolute humanism and universal intersubjectivity. Indeed, Bhaskar's charge of 'historicised anthropo-morphic monism' (Bhaskar 1989b: 140) is certainly affirmed by the statement:

> Objective always means 'humanly objective' which can be held to correspond exactly to 'historically subjective': in other words, objective would mean 'universal subjective'. Man knows objectively in so far as knowledge is real for the whole human race *historically* unified into a single unitary cultural system.
>
> (Gramsci 1971: 445)

At best, this statement means that objectivity can only be decided on the basis of 'that reality which is ascertained by all, which is independent of any merely particular or group standpoint' – although Gramsci goes on to say that this too constitutes an ideology (Gramsci 1995: 291). Certainly this is no guarantee of scientificity, especially if what is regarded as objective knowledge is a product of a long-established hegemonic viewpoint (such as the once universally accepted view, propagated by the hegemonic religious outlook, that the sun and stars go round the Earth). With this approach, as Gramsci admits, science becomes another form of ideology. Worse still, is the coupling of the above to the promotion of a single knowing subject – the Communist Party (or Modern Prince) – so that Marxism comes to represent the (best approximation to) scientific truth, approached asymp-totically through history and confirmed by the end-point of communism.

Bhaskar's critique rightly argues that such a position reduces the intran-sitive domain to the transitive processes of knowledge, and, as such, this is of no use to a critical realist theory. But we have also argued that there is a radical tension between Gramsci's philosophical arguments and his political analysis. By separating this out we can reject the intersubjective view of hegemony as based simply on the world-views of dominant historical subjects and instead examine the conditions for, and operation of, hegemony within the political sphere. Gramsci's formulation (archaic though it might sound) that the historical bloc represents the unity of 'structure' and 'superstructure' is important. This is a clear rejection of the intersubjective view that hegemony operates merely between groups and is reducible to world-views, praxis and hermeneutic struggles of interpretation and articulation. Under such a formulation history cannot be reduced to the actions of groups, but sets a context for such action within structural confines. Thus:

> it is not true that the philosophy of praxis 'detaches' the structure from the superstructures when, instead, it concerns their development as intimately bound together and necessarily interrelated and reciprocal.
>
> (Gramsci 1995: 414)

If we abandon traditional understandings which describe the base as economic and the superstructure as cultural and political we can see that Gramsci's statement is more meaningfully applicable to a structural base and superstructural forms of activity.

So Gramsci's writings can be interpreted as raising objective, rather than merely intersubjective or culturalist, aspects of hegemony. The stratification and interconnectedness of society makes hegemony a necessary part of the process of social reproduction in that it must attempt to hold the various structural processes together in a form of social cohesion. Hegemonic groups also reflect the stratification of society since they have their basis in the social divisions caused by material relations. But because the social whole is open and dynamic, objective location is not sufficient in itself to guarantee a group hegemony, but rather, provides the basis which hegemony must then activate. The fact that Gramsci emphasises the question of the tactics and strategy necessary for uniting diverse layers around a hegemonic project shows that Gramsci rejects the Lukácsian or humanist notion of a universal class subject in favour of the view that the working class is a product of complex social relations.

Analysis of hegemony which is limited to some conception of inter-subjective consensus cannot explain the basis on which this occurs. Without a conception of hegemony's material objectivity it is not possible to say why one group becomes more dominant and is able to lead. Even if inter-subjective theories of hegemony can hint at which hegemonic projects are successful, they are unable to answer why such a project should find success. Groups cannot just become hegemonic at the political/cultural level. They must have behind them the necessary material conditions and a favourable objective location (for the bourgeoisie, the ownership of capital and means of production, access to the state structures and so on for the working class the *potential* offered by their place in the production process).

We can refer again to the examples to be found in the work of Lenin and Trotsky. The question of hegemony in Russia is more fundamental than simply rulership, and concerns its sociality under the objective conditions of combined and uneven development. Only in this way can the weakness of the Russian bourgeoisie be explained as well as the difficulties faced by the Bolsheviks in establishing their rule. Likewise, the growth of the Stalinist bureaucracy cannot be explained simply in terms of its hegemony over other social groups. The hegemony of the bureaucratic strata can only be explained in relation to the general social conditions (the degeneration of the workers' state) and the weakness of social cohesion (and consequent social atomisation).

Similarly, Gramsci's notion of passive revolution is founded on the fact that a social group facilitates its hegemony through the development of economic factors (most dramatically, the new social hegemony and consensus created around the post-war boom). We might say that hegemony's viability is founded on its objective relationship to (and facilitation of) the dominant social structures and the most dynamic generative mechanisms. After the Second World War, this meant developing new state regulatory policies in line with changes in production methods and a growth in consumption (see Chapter 9).

So while hegemony might be said to represent a convergence of different social agents, it also marks out the sites of different spatial and temporal convergences involving different sets of relations, mechanisms, structures, practices and processes. Here we find hegemony in its most objective sense as securing the reproduction of social combinations such as relations between different aspects of the economic system or in relation to the various institutions of society. This then indicates the vital strategic importance of the state as an organiser of hegemony, not just in the interests of particular groups, but in order to secure the basic unity of the social formation. This is the objective basis for the distinction made between the structural hegemony that is fundamental to the unity and reproduction of society itself and the hegemony which concerns concrete hegemonic projects but which is rooted in the materiality of the underlying hegemonic conditions. In this way, the theory of hegemony combines the political moment of agency with the structural nature of social reproduction.

Therefore, those accounts that reduce society to its conceptual aspect, or an intersubjective approach that reduces society to the activities of different groups, cannot provide an adequate basis for a functioning concept of hegemony. Instead, society should be seen as an objective domain comprised of a variety of intransitive structures and causal mechanisms. Consequently, hegemony achieves an objective status as concerned with the reproduction and essential unity of these social structures and it becomes, as Bhaskar would say, the ever-present condition and the continually reproduced outcome of human agency. This outcome of human agency is an important emergent feature of the social sphere. But that this emergent human activity is possible is dependent on a pre-existing material cause which includes hegemony in its structural sense.

8 Hegemony through time and space

Introduction

This analysis of hegemony has argued that it has an objective basis in material conditions. It is more than just an intersubjective relation between groups and is based on the relations between groups and social structures. The next step is to enquire into hegemony's dimensions and its limitations. This chapter will deal with questions of hegemony's temporality and spatiality as well as enquiring further into its structure, stratification, location and function. It is argued that hegemony operates across space and through time, and like space and time it is structured and layered. Drawing on the idea of the duality of hegemony as both material cause and reproduced outcome, it is argued that hegemony is enabled, restrained and *ordered* by space and time but that it is also, itself, an *organiser*. The material conditions within which hegemony operates impose upon hegemony a spatiality and a temporality, just as it can be said that the concept of hegemony is inescapably historical and geographical. Yet at the same time it is necessary for hegemony to structure the social environment within which agents operate. This is part of the process whereby hegemony orders, articulates, describes, inscribes, locates, excludes and so on.

Although space and time do not exist independently of the elements and relations they contain, it will be argued that hegemony both structures and is structured by space and time. Hegemony is structured by the space it inhabits insofar as it operates within a given set of material conditions – within and between different structures, practices and mechanisms. In this sense, space and time are prior to hegemony in that they belong to society's dominant structures and generative mechanisms. But while hegemony is limited by this context, it can be seen that it also orders it. Indeed, through its operation it can be said to help bind together time and space. This is of course based on the idea that there are different spaces and times operating at different levels of the social totality.[1] This chapter will there-fore also be concerned with the methodology surrounding space, time and totality. Some of the most fruitful debates in this field have involved theorists of the Althusserian and Annales schools.

Braudel and the Annales School

In Fernand Braudel's famous analysis of the Mediterranean (1975), history is broken down into three timescales. Broadly speaking, these correspond to geographical time, social time and individual time. In turn there are different histories. First there is a history of people and their relation to their surroundings. This has a sociological and anthropological aspect comprising the study of material civilisations, traditions and mentalities, but it also requires that geographical, geological, biological, and even cosmological factors be studied. The second level concerns the social history of groups and groupings and involves the study of conjunctures, social cycles and economic mechanisms and structures. The third level is concerned with particular events and occurrences. Braudel's argument is that historical analysis often wrongly focuses on this level. These events comprise a very fast moving history, but analysis focused at this level is often misleading. Braudel disparagingly refers to this more traditional sort of history as 'surface disturbance'. His argument is that the historian needs to go deeper beneath this surface history and that such events are only really useful in providing signs and indicators. So the historian should be concerned with what lies beneath the waves – the history of structures, economic systems, societies, civilisations and states. Such histories move at a slower but more meaningful pace, a slow enduring pace that Braudel famously refers to as the *longue durée*. This emphasis on the *longue durée* means that social and material reproduction is given an almost natural aspect, yet it is still possible to insert a concept of hegemony into Braudel's structural division which would correspond to his three levels – the materiality of hegemony, a particular hegemonic process, and an individual hegemonic action.[2]

Hegemony, in a deeper Braudelian sense, is intransitive and enduring and might include such things as old-established methods and routines, inheritances, repeated actions and processes. It represents the very materiality of our human interaction, the most basic social relations and the relation to nature itself. As Braudel puts it:

> An order becomes established that it operates down to the very depths of material life. It is inevitably self-complicating, being influenced by the propensities, the unconscious pressures, and all that is implicit in economic societies and civilisations.

> (Braudel 1973: 243)

Such complications give rise to the functional necessity of hegemony in human societies – functional in the sense that it holds together and directs society at a material level, helping to ensure that the basic structures, or more crucially, the combinations of structures, are reproduced. This deeper, structural hegemony presupposes the various 'surface level' hegemonic practices in two senses. These are (a) *necessary*: the emergent sense – the actual realisation of the material conditions of hegemony in particular, but irreducible and dialectical, forms (this is the more functional aspect of hegemonic practices – they realise hegemony's material necessity, the fact that successful hegemonic projects have to maintain the basic hegemonic unity of the social formation); and (b) *possibility*: the deeper, structural hegemony also provides the necessary conditions for the possibility of hegemonic practices (the necessity of hegemony within human societies, stemming from its basic material role, allows for the elaboration of hegemonic projects by competing groups and classes). The distinction is therefore also one between hegemony (in an abstract sense) and concrete hegemonic projects.

This relates to the concerns of other Annales writers such as Ernst Labrousse, who writes on the history of resistances to change. The different levels of society are dictated by their material roots, an influence that moves upwards, from the simple to the more complex, from the lower to the upper, from material processes to intellectual articulation. He argues that there will be a certain delay in the response of these higher levels brought about by the 'dead-weight' pressure of the base (in Stoianovich 1976). Such pressure means that actually constructing hegemonic projects is a problematic business, leaving room open for counter-hegemonic projects. This is also taken up by Maurice Agulhon who is concerned to unveil popular cultures, traditions, attitudes and resistances – the forms of which depend on the various objective structures (Agulhon 1982: pp. ix–xi).

These conflicts are not simple struggles between the material 'base' and the more sophisticated ideological levels. Struggles exist between any number of conflicting rhythms and juxtaposed social practices. A whole range of intersubjective or 'community' feelings, attitudes and traditions may be contained or combined in institutionalised forms. But we must remember the connection that these hegemonic struggles have with the slower moving material base and the structural pressures that it exerts. This is not to say that the material base absolutely determines the success of hegemonic projects (inversely, however, hegemonic projects can influence this base). But, it is this material base (and the functional role accorded to hegemony) which provides the terrain for such projects. Hegemonic space must start from the raw materials of nature itself, before extending into its complicated strategic sphere.

Is a total history possible?

More generally, Annales history is important because it insists on the multiplicity of structures, their time and their history, and the way in which the different levels and layers overlap. It analyses their diversity, distinctions, dimensions, movements and speeds, but at the same time, history, through a notion of interconnectedness, is brought back to the totality or the whole so that everything is related. This is well expressed by Marc Bloch in his book *The Historian's Craft*:

> Each type of phenomenon has its own particular dimension of measurement and, so to speak, its own specific decimal. [But] when ... we consider the evolution of society as a whole ... [t]he problem is to find the dominant note ... We have come to note that within any society, whatever its nature, everything is mutually controlled and connected: the political and social structure, the economic, the beliefs.
>
> (Bloch 1992: 152–3, 155)

A fundamental problem concerning historical analysis is whether history should be viewed as plural and distinctive or unified and total. Certainly a rejection of the Hegelian idea of mono-linear development is desirable, but then how is it possible to maintain the idea of a social totality? The totality, by its very nature implies notions of total time, total space and total history.

An important aspect of Althusser's writing is his notion of a complex totality resulting from a process of overdetermination or multiple causality. Within the social formation are numerous distinct structures and practices which, rather than forming an expressive totality, are overdetermined and make up a differential totality marked by its stratification and non-contemporaneity. However, there is a tension in Althusser's work which tends to undermine this, as his notion of the relative autonomy of the different parts of the social whole has a tendency to become an absolute autonomy whereby different aspects of the social whole end up with their own time, space and history. The Annales historian Pierre Villar notes with concern how Althusser's theory of the social totality ends up by returning to a division of history into so many different histories (Villar 1994: 15). He claims that such an approach will end up producing misleading, partial or ideological theories of each special history unless they are in some way related to the social whole. While Althusser is correct to point out the existence of distinctive histories, each with its own peculiarity, he fails to sufficiently insist on the linking of these histories and their mutual overdetermination.

As Peter Osborne notes, Althusser's position requires us to 'think of the whole from the standpoint of a variety of different localised presents ... [W]hat it rules out in principle is any conception of the development of the whole as a whole, whether at the level of the social formation, mode of production or history itself' (Osborne 1995: 24–5). This makes it difficult to think of the various structures as part of an organic system that is reproduced and transformed through history. Althusser does invoke the notion of the structure of the whole, suggesting that we go about 'constructing *the Marxist concept of historical time* on the basis of the Marxist conception of the social totality' (Althusser and Balibar 1979: 97). This should be the way to draw out the notion of overdetermination. But to make sense of the overdetermination of the social whole surely implies that as well as the specific histories of different structures, it is also necessary to recognise the history and time of the totality itself. The Annales writers call this a 'total history' – a term that poses some serious problems. It could imply some sort of total time that imposes itself upon the various structures. If so, this could destroy Althusser's notion of overdetermination and return us to Hegel and the idea of an expressive totality. Villar's argument is that total history emphasises the dialectical matter of '*what the whole depends on,* and *what depends on the whole*' (Villar 1994: 40). To grasp the totality is not simply to see it as an aggregate of its parts, but as a dialectical relation. It is only possible to conceive of the whole through the articulation and expression of its parts. But, equally, the part can only be fully grasped by analysing the determining influence of the whole (or at least other parts) upon that part. How one part relates to another again depends upon the whole and to deny this would be to isolate the particular from its context.

A corresponding notion of 'total history' would not, therefore, refer to an inclusive mono-linear development by which all history can be judged, but to a *particular combination* of specific histories. 'Total time' would correspond to the overdetermination of particular times and its history can only be understood through its components. Total history could be said to correspond to the history of a particular social totality or ensemble. That is, not some general, universal history, but a history of a totality made up of particular social relations arranged in a certain set of combinations. The study of what is referred to as the social formation or the mode of production should be seen in this way – as a combination of a set of different social structures and relations.

Ultimately we are not studying individual 'parts' of the social whole because Marxism recognises that 'things' cannot be understood in their separateness but only through their interconnections. To study the part in relation to the whole means to understand each part as a relation and not as an individual, self-contained thing. The nature and meaning of a part is not fixed or given but is determined in relation to the totality. This carries over into an analysis of space and time, for we can say, following Lefebvre, that there is a 'total space' in the sense of it being a 'strategic space which seeks to impose itself as reality despite the fact that it is an abstraction (Lefebvre 1991: 94). Reworking this formulation, we can say that the 'total' has an abstractness about it so that it exists not so much in concrete entities themselves as in the mechanisms and structures that these presuppose. Thus, forms of ideology can be seen as fetishising the concrete entities in themselves without reference to underlying structures, generative mechanisms and social relations. In this way, ideology can be seen as the part imposing itself on the whole, or the reduction of the complex to the concrete. By contrast, historical analysis must seek to totalise its approach; hence the importance of abstraction. To examine space and time in the abstract is to address the underlying social relations and to pick out the influence of the dominant structures through their articulation and influence within the whole.

Historical method

Villar's idea of 'total history' only exists in any meaningful sort of way as a methodological guide and aspiration – to know each thing perfectly is to know everything and every connection, and can never be achieved. Realists should recognise that *the* totality is infinite and that knowledge can never hope to grasp this infinity in full, and hence a 'total history' of it is impossible. Nevertheless, the aspiration to a total history should drive a social scientific enquiry. 'Total history' is important insofar as it is desirable to attain a truer and greater understanding of the world and to achieve an investigative depth. As such, all scientific enquiry must aspire to total-isation. But this should not lead to the naïve belief that by developing a more total analysis, we asymptotically approach the truth. This is one of Gramsci's idealist errors noted by Bhaskar (in Chapter 2). Notions like totality, social formation and mode of production can only be grasped in the abstract. Concretely, the nature of the totality is disclosed by scientific and historical analysis. Thus, critical realism stresses the theory of onto-logical depth based on the idea that it is necessary to move from the knowledge of manifest phenomena to an examination of the underlying structures that generate them. It is the stratification of reality itself that imposes on science this necessary method of abstraction and totalisation.

However, because it is not possible to grasp the totality in its fullness, it is necessary to pick out its dominant features, its main dynamics and its hierarchy of causal processes, structures and generative mechanisms. Therefore, rather than talk of 'total history' – and in keeping with the Marxist categories of social formation and mode of production – it is more meaningful to talk about the analysis of stratified structural combinations or ensembles. The acquisition of a greater and truer understanding of a particular structure is through acquiring knowledge of its place and role in different structural combinations. Rather than remaining trapped within the autonomy of structures as followers of Althusser are prone to do, we can thus move to the structures of structures or combinatories.

We approach totality with a dialectical rather than an accumulative method. Bhaskar argues that 'totalising "outwards" from a particular feature is never just a matter of following up further connections; it is always potentially reciprocal, re-illuminating its point of origin' (Bhaskar 1986: 112). This method presupposes the fact that, in reality, different connections make up the whole, but that the whole helps make the connections as well as the elements that are connected. The structure of reality (like that of the mode of analysis Bhaskar describes) is also reciprocal. There are many different times and histories, but these have little meaning for us unless we can situate them in relation to a wider history. This does not mean 'relating the diversity of the different temporalities to a single ideological base time' or 'a single continuous reference time' (Althusser and Balibar 1979: 104–5). It is to recognise that Althusser's talk of the 'structure of the whole' implies a more 'total' history of this whole. If particular structures have their own history and time, then so too must the larger structures of structures. These structural combinations or ensembles must act, articulate and determine through their own properties and dynamics. This presupposes that they have some sort of history that acts upon and intervenes into the parts that make them up. Two aspects are noted by Bhaskar: (1) the form of combination causally codetermines the elements; (2) elements causally codetermine each other and so causally determine the form (Bhaskar 1986: 109).

So it is being argued that the social totality is indeed a complex construction, made up of parts each with their own specific time and history, but that these parts are not as autonomous as Althusser claims. They interact both with each other and with the broader combinatory, and they help determine the totality; but perhaps more significantly, they are also determined by it. This means that particular structures and practices cannot be understood in their own 'relatively autonomous' terms, but require reference to the wider totality, the social formation, the mode of production and other social combinations. Each structure is an integral part of a wider social system and its place, position, location and role within this combination is highly significant.

If we choose not to refer particular structures to a more 'total' history, then we simply end up with the particular history of that structure itself assuming a totalising function. Separated from a more 'total' history, particular histories become autonomous and inclusive, and hence themselves become total histories. It is also a process that becomes increasingly ideological since, if we do not have a broader, more abstract picture, then time and reality get broken down into smaller and smaller parts, each claiming to be inclusive. This becomes a destructive process since each inclusive structure contains other, smaller structures and times. Is each in turn to be granted an autonomy of its own? This is the road to post-structuralism and micro-structures. As Ellen Meiksins Wood writes:

> What better escape, in theory, from a confrontation with capitalism, the most totalising system the world has ever known, than a rejection of totalising knowledge?
>
> (Wood 1995: 2)[3]

Combinatories

Must we then say that these 'morals', 'attitudes', 'thoughts', etc. are 'advanced' or 'backward', are 'survivals', have an 'autonomous rhythm' and so on? Would it not be better to say: to what extent is this mode of production, taken to be in place, functioning, according to its own model? In what areas does it do so? Over what 'durational scale'? In which sectors is it an effective totality (already, if it is developing, and still, if it has begun to become destructured)?

(Villar 1994: 26)

As Villar illustrates, the parts cannot be understood if they are regarded as autonomous fields. It is necessary to study the part according to the determination of the whole. Instead of talking of the 'relative autonomy' of structures, we should refer to the *specificity* or *particularity* of structures. This is in keeping with a view of the totality as a complex product of over-determination. It contains an unevenness of developments, forward moving dynamics and various survivals and backwards persistencies. The structured parts are distinct from the whole, with their own time and history, but they are also determined by it. This allows for the kind of structuralism envisaged by the critical realists. It is a stratified totality, layered with overlapping and emergent times and spaces.

By contrast, the notion of social combinations present in the work of Althusser and Balibar is too static, passive and undialectical. These combinations are presented as simply a combination of their parts, as aggregates of different entities. As has been argued, this notion of com-binatories needs to be dialecticised so that not only do the parts make up the whole, but the whole must also be seen as making up the parts. The nature of the combination equally affects the nature of the parts, both in terms of the specific influence of the combination as a combination, and in terms of the place and function that the parts have within this larger totality. So if Althusser can say that 'the system of the hierarchy of concepts in their combination determines the definition of each concept, as a function of its place and function in the system' (Althusser and Balibar 1979: 68), then we can add that the system of the hierarchy of structures in their combination helps determine the nature of each structure and its function and place in the structural system. To understand a particular structure, we must also know its place in these broader formations (for example, the place of the legal system in relation to the state and the state in relation to the capitalist system and all this in relation to international relations). This is the structured and stratified whole that critical realism is at pains to promote and the question of structural emergence and interplay takes on a key importance. Returning to the question of method, it is therefore important to recognise that social and historical analysis must continually seek to totalise its analysis, examining the part in relation to the whole and aiming to reveal ontological depth. Analysis should look both at the parts which make up the structures and the structures which determine the parts. It must look at what each layer presupposes and how these combinations of structures develop and determine one another. It is important to stress that this is not just another structural matter, but is a historical matter as well. But here arises another thorny question, that of synchrony and diachrony.

Synchrony and diachrony

According to Saussure, the scientific study of the structure of language can be broken down into two aspects, the synchronic and the diachronic. Language as a system must be studied in its state of synchrony which represents structure or the place and determination of each of the elements within the system. If synchrony is structural then diachrony is more historical however, it is seen as of secondary importance, concerning the evolution of the system. This preference for the structural over the historical is reflected in Saussure's argument that if linguists take the diachronic perspective, they no longer observe language, but only a series of events that modify it (Saussure 1959: 90). Of course the label 'structuralist' has been denied by many of those accused of it, and for a *historical materialist* like Althusser such a label could be damaging. But this structuralist legacy is repeated in Althusser's comment that '[d]iachrony is then merely the false name for the *process*, or for what Marx called the *development of forms*' (Althusser and Balibar 1979: 108). It would seem that Althusser, like Saussure, sees the historical development of forms as secondary to the place of elements within the structure. Nonetheless, Althusser and Balibar claim that they never became structuralists and in *Reading Capital* they try to direct a few comments against Lévi-Strauss, and raise a few objections to the synchronic/diachronic distinction. In the chapter 'Elements of Self-Criticism' (Althusser 1976), for example, Althusser claims that he was in fact a Spinozist rather than a structuralist. But all the writings reinforce the structuralist emphasis on the primacy of the synchronic over the diachronic. This is most apparent in Balibar's contribution to *Reading Capital* where he writes that:

> the analysis of the relations which appertain to a determinate mode of production and constitute its structure must be thought as the constitution of a theoretical 'synchrony'... The concept of *diachrony* will therefore be reserved for the time of the *transition* from one mode of production to another.
>
> (Althusser and Balibar 1979: 297)

As a result, Balibar confuses himself in a notorious theoretical detour concerning the theory of historical transition. The argument is that 'all theory is synchronic insofar as it expounds a systematic set of conceptual determinations' (Althusser and Balibar 1979: 298). This leads Balibar to claim that the synchronic analysis of the mode of production leads to the realisation that there are several concepts of time. But as Peter Osborne puts it: 'Synchrony is not con-temporality, but a-temporality: a purely analytic space in which the temporality immanent to the objects of inquiry is repressed' (Osborne 1995: 27–8). Ted Benton points out (Benton 1984: 76–7) that to focus solely on synchronic relations is to study structures without regard to their persistence or transformation (since this is a temporal thing). It also undermines the notion of tendency since tendencies are what they are precisely because they operate historically and so contain a degree of contingency. As far as this study is concerned, it is essential to place the process of the persistence or transformation of structures at the forefront of our analysis since this is the context in which we understand human agency, and hence the concept of hegemony.

In structuralism the idea of a combinatory of structures lacks this historical element and is treated as a static thing defined in synchronic terms as the forms of combination. 'Marxism *is not a historicism*', writes Althusser, 'since the Marxist concept of history depends on the principle of the variation of the forms of this "combination"' (Althusser and Balibar 1979: 117). It is true that Althusser does have an account of the dominant effect that causes the whole to intervene – determination in the last instance. This conceives of the dominance of the main structure over the other structures and the hierarchy of effectivity so that 'only this "determination in the last instance" makes it possible to escape the arbitrary relativism of observable displacements by giving these displacements the necessity of a function' (Althusser and Balibar 1979: 99). Unfortunately we are left with the relativism and the autonomy of different structures because the last instance never comes. This is a direct product of structuralism's notion of synchronic unity, for without the diachronic the last instance never comes. Althusser privileges static structures over historical processes and the 'last instance' stands out like an essentialist leftover. Althusser claims that the pluralism of his theory depends upon his notion of the totality and that the degree of independence of each level lies within the articulation of the whole (Althusser and Balibar 1979: 100). But this, to use Martin Jay's terminology (Jay 1984: 409), is a latitudinal rather than a longitudinal conception and it denies historical developments a role in the constitution of these structures and relations.

The reproduction of structures may be of a 'synchronic' nature if looked at in terms of the unconscious reproduction of social forms by passive *träger* or bearers. But when looked at in terms of Bhaskar's transformational model of social activity, the process is immediately historicised. For as long as social agents are involved in the reproduction of social structures, then the possibility exists of transforming these structures. And against this threat, the ruling class may seek to secure the reproduction or preservation of these structures through their own historical, hegemonic projects. Previous chapters have argued that hegemony plays a deeper structural role concerned with securing the unity of these structural combinations. Hegemony is required because the unity of these combinations is not given but has to be secured. And the fact that hegemony must play this role immediately historicises these structural combinations because, first, these combinations occur within an open system and therefore the forms of combination are conjuncturally specific, and second, this function that hegemony has allows for the realisation of concrete hegemonic projects that are emergent from these structural combinations but also act back upon them.

So if the concepts of synchrony and diachrony are to be kept – and it is far from clear why they should (except perhaps as an analytical distinction) – then it is necessary to argue for the diachronic in terms of the 'longitudinal', which means the longer-term (enduring), overlapping, times of structures, and which entails relations of reproduction and possible transformation. Hegemony would be synchronic in the sense of its intrinsic relation to the structure of society and its determination by spatial location, and it is diachronic in the sense of being concerned with the reproduction, preservation or transformation of structures, allowing for the development of human practices articulated over a period of time. The interweaving of structure with hegemony leads us to conceive of the structuralisation and spatialisation of time as well as the temporalisation of structures and space, so that synchrony and diachrony mutually codetermine each other. Against 'historicism', history should be understood according to the synchronic logic of structures and against rigid 'structuralism', this synchronic structure should be seen in its diachronic context.

Hegemony and space

A realist theory of space is well outlined by writers like John Urry and Andrew Sayer (in Gregory and Urry 1985). Following them we can say that space and time are not substances in themselves but exist by virtue of the substances and relations that they contain. For critical realism, space and time are not reducible to the relations between simple objects or events, and it is necessary to analyse the structuration of space and time and the different underlying mechanisms, strata and other causal powers that constitute the materiality of the social and natural worlds. Space and time form the terrain for the endurance of these structures, powers and liabilities, something recognised in Sayer's argument that:

> *space makes a difference, but only in terms of the particular causal powers and liabilities constituting it.* Conversely, what kind of effects are produced by causal mechanisms depends *inter alia* on the *form* of the conditions in which they are situated.
>
> (Sayer, A. 1985: 52)

As has been argued, although space and time do not exist independently of the elements and relations they contain, they are in a sense prior to hegemony in providing the terrain on which it operates and which give it its particular powers and abilities. Hegemony is structured by the space it inhabits insofar as it operates under given set of material conditions – within and between different structures, practices and mechanisms. This space is constitutive of hegemony in the same way that structures are, given that this space is nothing more than the space of the pre-existing (but reproduced) structure of society. As Poulantzas puts it, at this fundamental level:

> transformations of the spatio-temporal matrices refer to the materiality of the social division of labour, of the structure of the state, and of the practices and techniques of capitalist economic, political and ideological power.
>
> (Poulantzas 1978: 98)

Hegemony is limited by this context, but through its deeper structural function it plays a fundamental role in securing the reproduction of society and hence the reproduction of the space of society. Hegemony works alongside spatial practices in the production and reproduction of particular locations, ensuring continuity and cohesion. It also works alongside ideology in developing representations of space which are tied to the dominant material practices. So an essential part of the operation and function of hegemony is to try and bind together space and time. And, since social reproduction and transformation is set within a spatio-temporal context, hegemony depends for its success on its integration into this matrix, but, as Lefebvre argues, the relation between space and hegemony is dialectical:

> Is not social space always, and simultaneously, both a *field of action* (offering its extension to the deployment of projects and practical intentions) and a *basis of action* (a set of places whence energies derive and whither energies are directed)? Is it not at once *actual* (given) and *potential* (locus of possibilities)?
>
> (Lefebvre 1991: 191)

Hegemony can therefore be seen in a strategic sense as well. The idea of hegemony as command over space and territory is graphically illustrated by Gramsci's talk of wars of position and manoeuvre, and fortresses and earthworks. It represents a process of colonisation by means of strategic interventions, confrontations and resolutions, either establishing a system of fortresses and earthworks, or attempting to capture them. But it would be wrong simply to see hegemony in these militaristic terms. For hegemony is not merely imposed but is a social necessity. The complex and open character of society and the nature of its dominant features means that the imposition of order and the creation and control of space are required impositions – or imposed requirements. Following Sayer, hegemony relates to what can be called 'social space' – that is, the space that is colonised, reproduced and transformed by human societies (Sayer, A. 2000: 110).

Although hegemony is a necessary social feature and its function is an essential social requirement, the carrying out of this function in an open context is not automatically given and therefore space is occupied by different projects and struggles related to reproduction, conservation, reinforcement or transformation. While the abstract space of dominant social relations is relatively enduring, concrete space can be radically restructured or rearranged. We can move, for example, from the endurance of capital–labour relations, to the more historically specific approach of something like Fordism, to the even more concrete issue of specific management techniques, and these relate hegemony to space-time co-ordination in different ways and at different paces. The development and deployment of management techniques occurs at a faster pace than the development of something like Fordism, not to mention capital–labour relations, and indeed in current society fast moving changes in space and time are integral to the maintenance of hegemony. In a modern society the pace of these changes is of the utmost importance to social stability – witness the social significance of changes in fashion, architecture, electronics and communications. These changes are not radical in the sense of fundamentally changing underlying structures, but they do make an important contribution to the reproduction of the underlying social hegemony and secrete the necessary ideologies to facilitate this process.

This indicates how space is literally filled with ideology. For what, asks Lefebvre, 'is an ideology without a space to which it refers, without a space which it describes, whose vocabulary and links it makes use of, and whose code it embodies?' (Lefebvre 1991: 44). In other words, space and ideology are inextricably bound in a basic material sense. Space acts as the site of ideological articulation and symbolic interaction. Space, in short, is representational, and, of course, the control of representation is crucial to the process of hegemonising. So from these material relations arise strategic relations, driven by hegemonising processes. The relation between space and ideology is both given and potential. Out of the necessary relation come different articulations and projects. Space is both necessary to the reproduction of ideology and the terrain for its application. As our earlier distinction between secreted and articulated ideologies indicates, the production of ideology is used strategically. Hegemonic projects and practices involve the articulation of ideology in conjunction with control over space. And when Harvey argues that those who command space have control over place (Harvey 1990: 234), he is recognising the correspondence of space and ideology so that place is not merely physical location but ideological location as identity. The place (in society) of workers, ethnic minorities and the poor is reinforced/articulated by their space (ghettos, slums, factories, dole queues, mental institutions, prisons etc.).

An aspect of the way in which space and place are controlled is disciplinary power. As Foucault's studies have shown, this is organised through techniques of regulation or self-regulation, whereby the individual consents to this power relation, or at least, follows procedures of self-discipline. One way of conceptualising this spatially is through the idea of surveillance as control over territory and therefore over the practices contained within it. Once subjects are aware of this surveillance they conform to the power relation through the regulation of their behaviour. Surveillance is an important *technique* related to the issue of social power; the problem with Foucault's analysis is that it tends to restrict itself to an analysis of these techniques without an accompanying analysis of underlying structures. Thus a Foucauldian analysis of space, time and hegemony tends to limit itself to relations of power, or how hegemony is exercised, without looking at how the regulation of society occurs at a more basic material level. It needs stating that there occurs through space and time a more general routinisation of social life into regulated practices and behavioural norms. Ideologically this can be passed off as the mundane condition of everyday life and social practices get presented as de-politicised or neutral relations. Of course, this is of clear advantage to the hegemonic group interests, but it is more fundamental than this as Marx's outline of commodity fetishism shows. The boredom of the shopping mall or the factory shift is typical of capitalism and the determination of its space and time by the commodified form. Marx goes beyond Foucault in showing that the regulation of social life and the ordering of space and time is not merely the result of hegemonic power relations or disciplinary techniques, but is more deeply inscribed into social relations through the dominant mode of production.

Structure, structuratum, strategy

Space and time might be said to belong to abstract sets of structured relations, while also existing in a more concrete form. This recalls the distinction made by Andrew Collier (1989: 85) between structure and structuratum. According to this argument, we, as agents do not act on the totality directly, nor do we act on the abstract structures that make up the totality, but rather, we act through more concrete and more specific entities. Abstract structures and abstract space and time tend to be reproduced unconsciously rather than intentionally. But we unconsciously reproduce them through intentional action directed through the concrete social entities and practices in which we are situated. When we act in this conscious or intentional way, we are relating more to the entities that Andrew Collier calls structurata, that is, concrete entities, as opposed the more abstract set of relations implied by the term structure. So a structuratum is that which is structured, rather than the structure itself; the term refers to concrete entities, like a social institution, which would themselves be structured in the more abstract sense of the term (made up of internally related elements). We act on the structuratum to change the structure. While the structuratum has a structure, it is also related to a wider set of structures (indeed its 'structure' includes 'external' relations). Thus we have a relation between structurata and the wider structures within which they are set. While we principally act upon structura, because of these relations we may also be changing the broader structures of which these structurata are a part.

As far as intentional human projects are concerned, we must pose the question of why we might attempt to change social structurata. Do we seek to actually transform the structures which lie behind them, or are we making changes to structuratum (like the National Health Service or the constitution) which are merely an amelioration of a state of affairs? Socially, we may change the structuratum to the point of either transcending or destroying it (revealing its contradictions) yet we may conceive of this as part of a broader project to transform a wider structure. Conscious hegemonic projects may seek to act upon or within the concrete structuratum (social institutions). But they are broader than this for two reasons. First, they may be part of a conscious, concrete totalisation. Such a hegemonic project might seek to transform a trade union structure as part of *wider project* to transform society. The former is part of the means for doing the latter. Second, hegemonic projects are always located within a *wider material context*. Actual hegemonic projects are dependent upon the material function of hegemony at a deeper level. Because of this, hegemonic projects often have broader (often unforeseen) consequences. Narrow political projects may have broader, unforeseen economic consequences. This relation between a hegemonic project and its broader context can be illustrated by the fight against the bureaucratic structures of Eastern Europe. The social agents, lacking a totalising hegemonic project, did not conceive that what they were doing had more far-reaching consequences in terms of the national and global economy. Many workers and students acted in good faith around a certain set of progressive political demands, without seeing that they were also being mobilised as part of a broader economic project of pro-capitalist elements of the bureaucracy, petite bourgeoisie and foreign capitalists.

This scenario could work the other way round. A more narrow economic project like a trade union struggle around pay and conditions or job losses may develop much wider political consequences – as was the case with the British miners' strike. As struggles develop, the more narrow consciousness may be transcended into a broader, more political conception. This makes a clear and coherent hegemonic strategy all the more necessary, basing itself on future possibilities or potentialities rather simply following the perceived limited consciousness of the time.

Structure and practice

The differentiation made between structure and structuratum can be complemented by a distinction between structures and practices. This is an important distinction to make if an objective conception of hegemony is to be upheld, and our argument is that approaches such as those of Habermas, Wittgenstein, Foucault, Lyotard and, to a lesser degree, Anthony Giddens, end up reducing social structures to human practices or a set of rules, conventions, techniques, behavioural norms or games. As against these positions, such practices should be seen as socially situated. A way of conceiving of such practices would be as the mediating factor that stands between social structures and human agents. It has been argued that agents do not act directly upon the abstract structures of the social formation but on the concrete structurata. This should be coupled with the view that the activities of agents are socially organised through established human practices. Social practices should not, therefore, be seen as things in themselves, but represent the mediation between structure and agent. However, the notion of human practices is important because, as this mediating factor, it introduces the element of collectivity, for practices represent the way in which social agents are collectively organised. Returning to critical realism's transformational model of social activity, we can say that the process by which social structures are both the necessary condition for and reproduced outcome of social activity is not based on a simple relation between social structure, on the one hand, and human agents, on the other, but is a mediated one. It is based, not on individual agents, but on (1) *collective* agential activity and (2) the fact that this collective activity is *organised* through established human practices, while (3) also, as we have said, it is *mediated* by concrete structurata. If the TMSA refers to the repro-ductive/transformational relationship between structure and agent, then we must stress that this is not a simple relation but a collective, organised and mediated one.

The important relation in critical realism's transformational model should not, therefore, be that between social structures and individual agents, but between structures and *collective* agents. The collective occur-rence of certain actions (like going to work, getting married or educating children) gives rise to our understanding of social practice as something distinct from individual agency but organising of it, and something distinct from social structures, but crucial to their reproduction. The survival of capitalism depends not on the individual intentions of certain people going to work but on the collective occurrence of this practice and other associated work practices, and the fact that these practices have an established organised form. The act of people going to work, organised into a collective practice, has the consequence of helping reproduce basic structural relations.

The relation we are outlining is an alternative to the traditional errors of the structure agency problem, namely either the intersubjective *agent–practice* model or an *agent–structure* model that is guilty of either (a) individualism (focusing on the power of the agent in relation to the structure) or (b) reificatory (focusing on the power of the structure over the individual agent). Instead, we are proposing a *mediatory* model more along the lines of *agent–practice–structure* but which recognises the complexity of social stratification so that mediating factors include not only (i) established human practices, but also (ii) concrete structurata, (iii) a structure's relation to other structures, (iv) a structure's relations to other agents, (v) a practice's relation to other structures and so on. This should qualify the TMSA and strengthen the idea of unconscious activity and unintentional consequences based on the fact that conscious or intentional activity is located within a wider nexus of social practices and structures, and that human activity is collectively organised into practices that are stratified across the social matrix. Hegemonic projects are located within this nexus of structures, agents and practices while Gramsci's notion of historical bloc as the unity of structure and superstructure can be theoretically recast in terms of the organised collective mediations of the agent–practice– structure relation.

Mentalities and modernity

Michel Vovelle is another Annales writer influenced by Althusser. In *Ideologies and Mentalities* he examines what he calls the co-existence of different forms of collective representations and the overlapping of different sensibilities. Vovelle's work also introduces the important concept of mentalities which provides a link between mental aspects of societies or communities and the array of material structures or what Vovelle calls 'the dialectical relationship between the objective conditions of human life and the ways in which people narrate it, and even live it' (Vovelle 1990: 12). For Vovelle, mentalities exist in the *longue durée* as ceaselessly reworked and distorted products, images, memories and traditions of the collective imagination. They are implanted in layers of slow history, cultural inertia and tradition:

> Moving from social structures to collective attitudes and representations involves the whole problem of the complex mediators between real human life and the images, or even the fantastic representations, which people construct and which are a basic part of the approach to the history of mentalities … [it] deals with the interlacing of historical time, to use Althusser's expression, meaning both inertia in the diffusion of key ideas and the co-existence, at various stratified levels, of models of behaviour inherited from different traditions.
>
> (Vovelle 1990: 12)

If these ideas are drawn together, a useful notion of mentality can be developed. This would include Bloch's notions of collective representations, attitudes, assumptions and unconscious beliefs. The importance of the concept lies in its linking of the collective, intersubjective, and even subjective modes of thought, with the objective structures of human society.

This link is not a momentary or conjunctural one, but a deep structural one linked to the very materiality of social being. With mentalities, the cultural aspect is prominent, starting from broad traditions and moving to particular sensibilities. It is an ideological viewpoint of sorts, but a more totalised one. If we recall our notion of ideologies as secreted by various human practices, then mentalities involve a broader, more articulated set of ideas ranged across a wider cultural sphere. Rather than belonging to a specific ideological process, these mentalities are perhaps best compared to Gramsci's notion of common sense, or to Lefebvre's 'everyday life'.

The fact that these mentalities or 'common senses in everyday life' have a strong cultural element highlights their deeper hegemonic aspect. Mentalities appear to have a kind of collective spontaneity but are in fact a series of quite predictable responses. They represent an ingrained back-drop or rolling landscape as seemingly natural as the hills themselves. For common sense depends for its functioning on its ability to 'naturalise' the space and time around it. And as these mentalities make their slow movement through history, they present themselves as tradition or the eternal future. Mentality may therefore represent a synthesis of tradition and common sense located in the *longue durée*. In this respect, mentalities may be said to be a part of the deeper, material hegemony of society based on a close unity between human practices and social outlooks. They also provide rich pickings for specific hegemonic projects as long as these projects can utilise those organic intellectuals who are in a position to articulate the project in relation to established viewpoints.

We may sense a partial breakdown of this, however, with the advent of modernity, or more particularly, with the development of capitalist society. The faster pace of capitalist production, its time as production time, labour time, commodity time or consumable time and its commodification, urban-isation and globalisation of space, has broken up the ways of the past. At a cultural level this is reflected in the arrival of 'modernity', a self-conscious breaking from the past and a tearing away from tradition. The result is a shift in the pattern of social hegemony from the *longue durée* of material life to the reproduction of the underlying hegemony (as part of the material conditions) through the application of various hegemonic practices and projects in the cultural and political sphere. Hence we can see what makes hegemony such a prominent feature of modern society. The acceleration (or even negation or 'emptying out') of time and the compression of space means that the basic unity of the social formation (underlying hegemony) has to be secured in a more prominent way, through political projects and state interventions.

As David Harvey argues, ideological and political hegemony within society requires the ability to control the material context of social and personal experience (Harvey 1990: 234). In the feudal period, this control was an accepted part of everyday life, legitimated by the cycle of the productive system itself. But with capitalism the political relations are not so intimately bound to the system and they do not have their own self-generating legitimacy. This has to be achieved through the conscious application of political projects at the 'surface' level of hegemony.

The explosive tri-unity of space-time

It is absolutely correct to reject the idea that there is some single objective time by which everything can be measured. But as David Harvey has written, this is more a case of recognising 'the multiplicity of the objective qualities which space and time can express, and the role of human practices in their construction' (Harvey 1990: 203). This implies that we examine space and time from the point of view of their relation to objective material processes and examine the social totality as a differentiated and stratified whole with emergent space and time (i.e. specific to each social strata and not reducible to some underlying level).

Hegemony is involved with processes of reproduction, conservation and transformation and is therefore located within this structured context. Given the complex stratified character of this material basis, hegemony must perform not just within social structures but between them. Its role is to secure a functioning unity among different levels, practices, structures and mechanisms. Hegemony encounters time and space within this material context as structured but plural and differentiated. They reflect the stratification, layering and overlapping of reality itself. However, hegemony, within structural limits, can rework this space and develop it – first, in accordance with the necessity of securing the unity and cohesion of the social totality or the reproduction of specific structures, and, second, according to the possibility of strategic intervention in relation to particular social projects. Such projects represent a different level of hegemony (a more concrete, actual or surface level) realised through a process of emergence and are reliant on the spatio-temporal possibilities of location.

Space and time are tied to the material structure of society and its dominant generative mechanisms, in particular the material basis of production. They affect the basis of civil society itself, rather than simply hegemonic projects within it. Under capitalism, time and space become 'emptied out' and technicised while social life becomes routinised and commodified. Social and political ideologies become abstracted and universalised. The ideology of 'modernity' launches its attack on the past and its severance from tradition – although in reality it is itself a tradition that portrays itself as starting from now-time and extending into an eternal future of progress (or, in its extreme form, a progress without history, or a postmodern messianic eschatology). At the deeper level of hegemony, time and space are presented as globalised into a single realm that is universal and dynamic. Meanwhile, counter-hegemonies are broken up and fragmented, confined to plural space and micro time. Therefore, if a counter-hegemonic project is to be truly successful, it must transcend 'surface' hegemonic battles with other projects, go beyond this terrain, and fundamentally alter the deeper hegemony of society. It has to challenge the relatively enduring space and time generated by the underlying social structures, the relatively unconscious character of these relations and engage in a process of transformation. Because of the relative weight that deeper, structural hegemony has over actual hegemonic practices, a transformative project is not easy and is really only achieved under conditions of structural crisis. Then the gaps and fractures that start to open up allow counter-hegemony more of a chance to squeeze out its own space. The structured context means hegemony must make what it can out of the limited space-time resources and work as best it can within what Giddens calls capability constraints.

The capturing of space is linked to the physical construction of a hegemonic bloc which can forge together a unity, while also maintaining a clear direction. Because of the complex spatial structure of society, such direction is only really secured when hegemony is able to operate through the aegis of state power. Through the centralisation of power it is then necessary to regulate and balance the different groups and the spaces that they occupy (including restricting certain groups and practices, enabling others, redirecting and reallocating resources, channelling communication, examining living conditions, planning production and enabling learning and leisure). Hegemony may be localised or regionalised and limited to particular hegemonic projects either in a geographical area or in a political, cultural or economic sphere. But hegemony, if it is ambitious, also seeks to move beyond these boundaries in line with its functional role in bringing things together. The strength of particular hegemonies (or counter-hegemonies) can be measured against the dominant hegemony and the degree of overlapping, co-operation or conflict between them. Just as hegemony seeks to construct a power bloc out of various groups and their interests, so the dominant hegemony must try to co-ordinate the more regional hegemonies. Indeed, the success of the dominant hegemony should be measured by its degree of success or failure in penetrating and co-opting, colonising or containing these various regional hegemonies. Hegemony's attempts to relate to the location of consciousness and its spatio-temporal unevenness might include post-war attempts to relate to groups of workers, women and ethnic minorities. Starting from the localised consciousness of a particular group, a hegemonic project must galvanise this consciousness (or in the event of real material developments facilitate and direct this consciousness) in order to transcend its location. While co-opting is an easier task for a project enjoying hegemonic ascendancy, this is the enormous task for a counter-hegemonic project. For while reproduction has a more unconscious character, transformative projects require the revolutionising of space and time. It must act against the inertia of the society expressed in its deep hegemonic form and attempt to mobilise the consciousness of agents.

Counter-hegemonic struggles express the radical nature of the concepts we have employed. Starting from a relatively limited location, they must seek to transform and transcend, utilising the capabilities of presence and overcoming or negating absences. They must squeeze out their own emergent space and time. A truly radical hegemonic project will seek to totalise its ambition. Its growth, if it is not contained, will express itself in the explosion of revolution, a radical expression of the tri-unity of space, time and causality. Periods of crisis, rupture and revolution witness new, emergent spatio-temporal totalities. This in itself will not be enough to guarantee radical hegemony's future. But hegemonic victories encourage spatial factors to fall into place. If hegemony can truly start to alter the basis of society, then capability constraints can be transferred to opponents, while structural enablements nourish hegemony's roots.

9 Economy and hegemony

Introduction

This chapter will attempt to bring together three modes of analysis that are mutually compatible and reinforcing. These are critical realism, a theorisation of hegemony and the debates around accumulation and regulation. Together, these offer an exciting potential, moving beyond traditional Marxist analysis of social and economic relations, and reacting against the more mechanical or schematic models. This means rejecting the model of base/superstructure determinism where the economic base is accorded an autonomy. This chapter will maintain that the economy is the main social driving force, but it will argue a position that sees it as dominant within a set of stratified and mutually co-determining structures. Replacing the base/superstructure model of mono-causal determination with a theory based on dialectically stratified multi-determination means that the economic 'base' can no longer be taken as given, and, since society is comprised of various interacting social structures, the conditions for economic reproduction have to be socially secured.

This is in contrast to the accepted wisdom of the 'classical Marxist' tradition. Even an economic theorist like Ernest Mandel, who is widely praised for his subtlety and originality, maintains a base/superstructure model that often gives the economic an almost autonomous status. Mandel's important book *Late Capitalism*, rather than looking at the effects of post-war hegemonic relations, sees history since 1945 in terms of a 'long-wave' economic cycle. This is based on a weakening of the working class by fascism and the Second World War leading to a rise in the rate of profit and technological developments (Mandel 1978a: 131). Mandel argues that after the Second World War there was a strong growth in material production and an expansion of the world market brought about by an increased rate of profit. Subsequently, there was an upsurge in capital accumulation (Mandel 1980: 81). However, Mandel's long-wave theory tends to encourage a view of history based less on social relations, human actions, class struggle and hegemonic projects, and more on the development of the productive forces. He makes a general law out of the idea that capitalism develops through long waves of some fifty years (decisive dates being the mid-nineteenth century, the 1890s and post-Second World War), and he argues that these long waves are based on revolutions in technology.

This chapter takes a different approach. In keeping with the thrust of critical realism and theories of hegemony, emphasis is shifted from the productive forces to social relations. The war facilitated new *methods of accumulation* and a more intensive form of *state regulation*. It is true to say that this post-war boom was dependent on the mass destruction of capital caused by the Second World War. But even if this laid the basis for the post-war boom, it could only have been developed by active state regulation of the type outlined below. Mandel does rightly argue that capitalist expansion floundered as a result of a slowing rate of profit and an upturn in working-class struggles in the 1970s. However, to understand this it is necessary to look at how the inherently crisis-ridden nature of capitalism requires certain socio-political interventions which are carried out though concrete projects. This means shifting attention from 'inherent laws of capital' to the *social conditions* necessary to try and overcome any inherent tendency towards crisis.

Although the state is clearly best placed to perform this central regulatory function, there is not a necessary link between forms of state regulation and the needs of capital. The state is a complex, heterogeneous combination of different institutions, apparatuses and social relations each with different political dynamics. Although it will be argued that the state should act to try and facilitate capital accumulation, the actual hegemonic strategies that are enacted through the state, because they reflect a variety of social interests, may actually act against the process of capital accumulation. Yet the state must try and act as a factor of social cohesion, and it is only really through the state and state strategies that the differences between particular capitalist interests can be reconciled or at least contained. In developing a historical analysis it is important, therefore, to combine a theory of structural tendencies with an analysis of the role of the state, with wider forms of social regulation, with deep lying hegemonic conditions and historical blocs and with specific hegemonic projects.

This chapter will look at theories of the state and state intervention. It will also examine how the period of 'Fordism', with its intensification of accumulation and regulation, presupposes certain forms of state intervention and the kind of political hegemony associated with the various post-war settlements. Gramsci, writing before the full emergence of this situation, was still quick to see the developing importance of three inter-related factors – Fordist-style production, the Americanisation of international relations (both political relations and relations of production), and the opening of a new period of state intervention. He recognises 'that *laissez-faire* too is a form of State "regulation", introduced and maintained by legislative and coercive means. It is a deliberate policy ... a political programme' (Gramsci 1971: 160). However, this is being superseded by

'Fordism as the ultimate stage in the process of progressive attempts by industry to overcome the tendency of the rate of profit to fall' (Gramsci 1971: 280).

Gramsci correctly sees the falling rate of profit as a *tendency* rather than an iron law, a theory of which is 'obtained by isolating a certain number of elements and thus by neglecting the counteracting forces' (Gramsci 1995: 429) but which, in the open context of capitalist society, meet with various counteracting forces, not least the development of Fordist methods of production. Thus economic developments cannot be understood according to the simple autonomous logic of the economic base (contradictions or not) but have to be examined in the wider socio-political context, including the wider relations of production, social organisation, production methods, state intervention and international relations.

Social relations

It is necessary to start by emphasising the importance of social relations as *social* relations. Along with the base/superstructure concept, classical Marxism has tended to go along with the distinction between forces of production and relations of production leading to the kind of mechanical determinism that views history according to the development of the productive forces. Such approaches are unable to explain actual historical developments except by resorting to timeless formulas of capitalist crisis which may have some formal correctness, but say nothing specific, and hence carry no real explanatory power. By emphasising social relations instead, analysis is shifted to the social context for the development of the so-called productive forces. These forces do not develop automatically or autonomously, they are embedded within social relations. 'Productive forces' are nothing outside of their socially organised form. It is necessary for them to be organised and directed, and how they develop is a social and historical matter. Economic processes do not stand alone, but operate within a complex totality where they interact with social structures, political strategies, class struggles and other features of the social world. Because economic factors do not have their own autonomous logic, but (a) are socially constituted and (b) interact with many other social factors, it is necessary to state that the conditions for economic reproduction are not given but are socially secured and politically advanced.[1]

It is necessary to reject arguments, such as that of Mandel, that the spheres of production and accumulation have become largely technicised and self-regulating (Mandel 1978a: 246).[2] There is a requirement to secure the conditions for capitalist development through different techniques of accumulation and associated forms of regulation. These forms of regulation relate to state strategies which in turn are based on particular historical blocs and hegemonic projects. These make economic reproduction a deeply political matter given that the state is also a political terrain and that the state must justify its intervention through embracing and espousing a whole number of social and political ideologies such as welfarism, populism and social democracy. These social, political and ideological structures are an integral part of the process of reproducing the mode of production. Economic reproduction occurs in an open social context and the accumulation process is politically and ideologically secured. Against theories that attempt to uphold the autonomy of certain branches of the social system, it is necessary to emphasise the *totality* of social relations and social functions. Hegemony has a fundamental structural role in securing the cohesion/ reproduction of an ensemble of social structures, while at the same time it is a site of political projects which may or may not provide the best conditions for the promotion of economic development.

The state

This talk of hegemonic projects and social interventions necessitates a discussion of the state which is the main means by which such strategies, projects and interventions are implemented. But the state is not easy to grasp. It is not surprising then that there is no agreed classical Marxist theory of the state, for the state is the outcome of several complex interactions and functions and any analysis of it must look at its specific form and nature. Nonetheless, there are perhaps two basic criteria for analysing the state form and its class nature.

1   The state operates in relation to the economy in what could be called a functional sense. The state acts in a functional way to help secure and reproduce the conditions for production and accumulation and to help extract and distribute surplus product. The state should be seen as a major player in maintaining what we have called the underlying structural hegemony of society.
2   The state is also a strategic terrain for the unfolding of political hegemonic projects. It is a major site of political struggles, where the interests of the ruling class are inscribed, and where an attempt is made to secure cohesion between different class fractions.

These two aspects of the state combine in a dialectical manner. The capitalist state, in a functional sense, must meet the general interests of capital. However, the state also acts as a terrain of struggle between different groups which may correspond to particular capitals. The situation is complicated further where more than one economic mode of production is present in any one social formation. Here, we must study which one is dominant and which one the state promotes and defends. It may promote other modes of production, for example nationalised property forms in Russia. But this is done in the context of the needs of the dominant (i.e. capitalist) mode of production. In Russia, to secure the necessary conditions for the expansion of the capitalist mode of production, it is necessary for the state to promote aspects of other modes of production in the interests of capital.

The idea of the state as a strategic terrain requires a cautious approach and must be balanced with the view that sees the state in relation to the capitalist economy. The principal error of Poulantzas and many Althusserians is to go too far when arguing for the autonomy of the political from the economic. As a result, their analysis of the state becomes more and more the analysis of the class struggle, although this takes a Euro-communist spin which argues for the capture of the state through civil society. This relational view of the state is intended to overcome the problems of an essentialist analysis, but while such a stance is necessary, it must also be maintained that the capitalist character of the state is inscribed into it from the very start. This derives, not simply from the role of the bourgeoisie or the leading group that holds state power, but from the *structural function* of the state in securing the conditions for economic reproduction and capital accumulation. If the state does have an autonomy, this is not the kind of political autonomy where the economy is determinant in the last instance, but is expressed in the fact that the economic determines every instance. Peter Burnham makes the important point that:

> Within the capitalist system there is no other basis for the formation of the general interest than the state. In this sense, the state has an autonomy which is not political but which rests on its role of expressing the general conditions of accumulation and determining overall economic strategy.
>
> (Burnham 1990: 182)

However, functional definitions of the state should not be used as an excuse for economic determinism or any other essentialist attribution of essence, purpose or telos. The capitalist state persists because it is best suited to the economic system. If it was no good, it would not persist and the problem would be a different one. Just as humans do not persist because of God, the capitalist state does not persist because of some essential cause. Both continue to exist because their functioning is suitable enough, in the circumstances, to allow the entity to be reproduced. In a Spinozist sense the state and its relations 'hang together'. It must be remembered though that although the state has a functional role, it is itself a complex combination of different apparatuses, each perhaps with different functions or roles, so the persistence of the state is a complicated and messy affair involving a large degree of interaction and contingency.

An understanding of the functioning of the state should be based on its relation to the dominant mode of production and the historical development of the organisation and distribution of surplus product/surplus labour.[3] In this most basic sense it is legitimate to say that the state has a functional role to play and that it should be assessed according to how it performs this function. Given that the dominant structures and mechanisms within the social formation are economic, the state must be measured by its 'functioning' in relation to the economy. It should be assessed on the basis of what property relations it promotes and defends and more specifically, the capitalist state must be assessed on how it helps secure the conditions for capital accumulation.

This description of the state's relation to the economy is 'functional' but not 'functionalist'. The important thing is how the main function is carried out. The capitalist state may have the function of helping to secure the conditions for capital accumulation, but how it does this, or what form of intervention and regulation it uses, is dependent on various state strategies and hegemonic projects. State strategies are intimately connected to the operation of hegemony through the state apparatus, and the role of hegemony in organising and directing society. However, it is important to see these state strategies in their structural context for it would be voluntarist to say that these state strategies are simply decided by different sections of the ruling class according to the particular situation. State strategies are longer-term affairs; they are modes of operation that are based on previous state strategies and underlying trends. They have a deep-rooted material basis concerned with the essential requirement to secure the reproduction of important social structures and ensembles. And, in an economic sense, state strategies cannot but reflect (in more or less adequate ways) the fundamental movements of capital. As the following sections will explore, the collapse of post-war state strategies has been, and will continue to be, a long and drawn out process. It is necessary to explain these factors by analysing underlying structural developments, the breakdown of Fordist methods of accumulation, the crisis of the national-welfare state form of economic regulation, changes in the international economy and the set of global political alliances and, finally, the shift in post-war hegemonic blocs and alliances. This clearly indicates the stratified nature of social reality and indeed the stratified character of the state itself. The state is not an 'object' or a 'thing' and an analysis of the state form cannot be based upon simple entities and occurrences. Our analysis must be based on a study of social relations, processes and generative mechanisms, bound up with the question of the social reproduction of the state form. The state is not a static entity, it is a dynamic set of social structures and relations, each carrying different functions.

The post-war settlement

Crisis may well be inherent to capitalism, but the fact of crisis says very little on its own. Inherent tendencies and generative mechanisms exist in an abstract sense, but it is necessary is to look at what these economic relations mean when manifested in an open social and political context. Economic processes pervade all aspects of social life and the reproduction of these economic structures is a social matter. Economic structures do not reproduce themselves automatically, rather, the conditions for economic development are socially secured, making it impossible to separate the economic from a wider social, and indeed historical context. This analysis will focus on the problems concerning the reproduction of the social conditions necessary for capital accumulation. It will concentrate mainly on the British social formation before moving to a discussion of the so called globalisation process, the re-shaping of world hegemony, and the question of a new historical period.

The post-war settlement has defined a whole historical period, and combines a development in forms of regulation with a new hegemonic bloc. Here lies the basis on which the state has legitimised its intervention into national and world economies. It is only by analysing the nature of this state regulation and intervention that we can assess the associated (and dependent) political alliances and projects. Therefore, the post-war era is inseparable from the phenomenon of Fordism, based on new more regulated work practices, conditions and management, new mass pro-duction, new wage structures, and mass consumption. The term itself is developed from Gramsci's writings and is very much connected to Americanisation and automatisation. The Fordian model's higher wages and work practices stem, argues Gramsci, 'from an objective necessity of modern industry when it has reached a certain stage of development' (Gramsci 1971: 341). Although this statement probably leans too much towards a productive forces determinism, we can still connect Fordism to the fact that mass production is part of the inherent capitalist tendency towards monopoly production. Gramsci rightly links the growth of Fordism to America's increasing international hegemony and big increases in world trade. However, it should be recognised that Fordism was not imposed uniformly, and its development takes various forms according to different state strategies and hegemonic projects.

The logic of monopoly production is not limited to the sphere of private corporations. Instead, there is an increasingly strong connection between Fordist accumulation and state strategies. Fordism has created the con-ditions for, and, vice versa, been facilitated by, state involvement and intervention. Mass production is the basis on which state interventionist Keynesian theories rest. The state injects large amounts of capital into the economy while growth is facilitated by large expenditure and use of credit which in turn provides the economic conditions for a consumer society. Through mass production and mass consumption a key factor in the maintenance of the post-war order is achieved. Also important was state ownership of industry. The nationalisation of ailing private monopolies was essential to the development of a healthily functioning economy. Around these state actions, new blocs and new political ideologies emerged. The accumulation–regulation model is strongly linked to a theory of hegemony, for the theory we are dealing with here concerns not just the organisation of the sphere of production, but the organisation of society as a whole, and the set of ideas and values appropriate to such projects. Thus the post-war economic project is inseparable from the post-war set of social alliances and to talk of economic development necessitates an examination of the social and political conditions through which this is expressed.

In the unstable period which followed the end of the war, when the working class was battered but potentially dangerous, and where expectations were high, it was necessary for the ruling class to grant greater concessions and to build a new social cohesion or structural hegemony. The guarantee of consumer growth is a key aspect of this order. Nationalisation plays the dual role of economic facilitation and social construction/concession. The other key part was the construction of the welfare state. Welfarism, consumerism and full employment provided the ideological cement for this new hegemonic order. In fact, the development of the welfare state and the rebuilding of social institutions after the Second World War is a fine example of what Gramsci called the 'passive revolution', so that, according to Gramsci:

> through the legislative intervention of the State, and by means of the corporative organisation – relatively far-reaching modifications are being introduced into the country's economic structure in order to accentuate the 'plan of production' element ... socialisation and co-operation in the sphere of production are being increased, without however touching (or at least not going beyond the regulation and control of) individual and group appropriation of profit.
>
> (Gramsci 1971:120)

After the war, when the trends of Fordism were generalised, the dominant classes were able to mobilise the masses around the construction of the welfare state, higher wages based on collective bargaining and full employment, thus gaining consent, but excluding the masses from having any real say in political affairs. Fordism is based on this compromise, which trades social benefits for political exclusion. Sections of the working class – in particular, the privileged, skilled workers of the labour aristocracy – were integrated into the capitalist order. These sections were won by limited concessions and the feeling of economic empowerment and partnership. A more exclusive power bloc – a constructed ruling alliance of different class fractions – integrated the labour bureaucracy, albeit as subordinates. The labour bureaucracy is caught between its power base in the organisations of the working class and its place in the historical bloc, determined by the structures of capitalist society and the state institutions themselves. But during the post-war golden period, the trade unions enjoyed a powerful social position and formed a crucial part of the historical bloc.

The current situation

It is particularly important to understand the nature of the post-war settlement because the current political period is marked by the ongoing collapse and replacement of that settlement and its historic alliances. This break-up is particularly advanced in Britain where by the 1960s the post-war economic recovery had been completed and offered little prospect of continued growth. Post-war reconstruction had been short-termist, failing to address economic modernisation and relying on Britain's legacy of Empire and the Atlantic alliance, concentrating on the markets of the Sterling Area rather than any specifically European orientation, and relying on London-based finance capital at the expense of the manufacturing base.

Internationally, the 1960s saw a fall in the rate of productivity growth and a devaluation of capital. As various states suffered internal difficulties, they turned more to the export of capital. This in turn challenged the market supremacy of the US and helped bring down the Bretton Woods system of fixed exchange rates. The abandonment of exchange controls was accompanied by other forms of market deregulation. This period also saw the crisis over oil prices, inflation, unemployment and a general crisis of profitability. The system of intensive accumulation and monopoly regulation began to break down, failing to counter the tendency of the rate of profit to fall, and to resolve the related problems of overproduction, stagnation and inflation. Accepted forms of state intervention were undermined by their failure to control the organic composition of capital (an inherent crisis tendency accentuated by Fordist production), increased labour unrest, the rising costs of bureaucracy, and a lack of confidence in production marked by a productivity crisis. The inflationary effect of the expansion of credit meant that capital moved from production to money and finance. Forms of state intervention shifted from the fiscal to the monetary, i.e. from large-scale state investment to control of the money supply and inflation. Fordism had facilitated the post-war recovery. However, its methods were now being exposed as inflexible and cumbersome. As internal markets became saturated, Fordism and its associated forms of state intervention proved unable to balance the departments of production and consumption.

This explains the unfolding conflict between the needs of capital accumulation and the associated hegemonic blocs of the post-war era. The hegemonic bloc may have succeeded in guaranteeing social and political cohesion and stability, but the associated state strategy of economic regulation began to fail. The readjustment of this strategy, principally for economic purposes, nonetheless required the reorganisation of the social conditions of production and the construction of a new historical bloc. This process is far from complete, and at a social level the effects of this restructuring are clear as the neo-liberal project continues to gain ascendancy. The role of the state has changed, and new forms and strategies of production are emerging. Many talk about the influence of the global market and transnational corporations which are gaining more influence over the national–economic structures. But equally important, at a national-state level, new cheap labour and flexible working methods are encouraged; new work practices and management techniques are being employed; many unions are either being removed from influence or forced into a social partnership role; the division between skilled and unskilled workers becomes starker; the segmentation of the workforce is occurring; and benefits and welfare provision are being minimised.

In Britain, capital asserted itself over labour by attacking the unions and weakening the power they enjoyed as a result of their place in the post-war historical bloc. The mass unemployment of the 1980s did not help the position of the unions as it affected membership and created a larger reserve army of labour. Changes in pay and conditions were forced through in a climate of job insecurity. To increase this effect, and following the defeat of the miners through a carefully prepared strategy, vicious anti-union laws were forced through, creating all kinds of legal barriers, effectively banning 'political' strikes, secondary action and the right to picket. It is important to stress that these laws not only strengthen the power of the bosses and the state over the workers, but also gives the labour and union bureaucrats more power to do nothing. The bureaucrats now use the anti-union laws as an excuse not to fight the bosses. New management techniques have brought in performance-related pay, individual contracts and no strike agreements, which all undermine the collective power of the unions.

This reflects a broad crisis of old-style social democracy, which has effectively been ousted from within by Blair's 'modernisation' project. The traditional ideas of labourism have been discredited by the failure of Keynesian policies, the collapse of Stalinism and the hegemony of the neo-liberal model. However, although the ideas of social democracy no longer have a place within the hegemonic bloc, this does not mean that social democracy is dead. Social democracy also exists as a set of institutional relations. While the role that old-style social democracy and labourism plays in relation to the capitalist state is in crisis, this is not its only definition as it is also determined from below and is based on a set of institutional ties including, crucially, the Labour/trade union link. It also includes a set of institutional gains that the ruling class was forced to make when it accepted social democracy in the post-war order. Although the ideology of social democracy is in crisis, these gains are still widely popular, most notably that of the welfare state, which is regarded by the public as being of paramount importance.

In the 2001 general election, the National Health Service remained the most important issue with the public, despite the efforts of the Tories to turn the election into a referendum on the EU and the Single Currency. But Europe remains the key issue as far as post-war hegemonic blocs are concerned. As former social democrats increasingly embrace the free market and neo-liberalism as an alternative ideology, it is logical that this should extend towards a pro-European position, for the single market is an extension of the neo-liberal project at a Europe-wide level. The support that Blair now receives from British capitalism is also reflected in the crisis of the Conservative Party. The traditional party of British business is divided over the key business question of the European Single Currency. The anti-Europe wing still sees Britain as an imperialist power although they are fawningly open about subservience to the US and trans-national capital, while more far-sighted sections have realised the need for a reorientation and consequently support the Single Currency. This division reveals the vulnerable nature of the Conservative Party as a hegemonic bloc based on a variety of groups and interests. Made up of Unionists, the military, layers of the petite bourgeoisie, finance capital, industrial capital and skilled workers, it has difficult interests to reconcile in a changing social context. Britain's unique historical bloc is founded on the Empire and its aftermath, contains strong imperialist and aristocratic influences, and is thus, by its nature, conservative in inclination. The British economy, and the dominance of the City, is peculiarly 'colonial' and the reorientation of the economy towards Europe has therefore brought chaos to the traditional party of British business.

The irony is that the European project, as a neo-liberal exercise, requires a strengthening of the power of capital over labour along the lines achieved by the British Conservatives under Thatcher. However, while the Conservatives led the way economically, they lagged behind politically. Giddens, in advocating a 'Third Way' alternative, notes the contradictory relationship between neo-liberal economics and Conservative politics. The Conservatives have traditionally held a cautious and pragmatic approach to social and economic change while the liberation of market forces undermines the traditional structures of authority on which Conservatism depends (Giddens 1998: 15). The radically traditional Tory policies of Thatcherism may one day be seen as the past's last stand. Capital, meanwhile, was already restructuring itself in line with European markets, leading first to the demise of Thatcher, then to the demise of the rest of her party. Still, the Thatcherites can claim that Tony Blair is really one of theirs, and perhaps a synthesis of pro-European and pro-US policies can be achieved through the 'Third Way' variant of neo-liberalism.

The expression of the national question has also undergone a shift in emphasis. Previously, national antagonisms within the British state were contained. Consent to English hegemony was achieved through a shared vision among capitalists of Britain's role in the world order. Britain's imperialist role was matched by the legitimating ideology of the national-welfare state. Now this is changing, national antagonisms are finding a new expression. Under Thatcher, the moves towards a hyper-liberalism in the economic sphere sought legitimacy in a populist appeal to traditional values – in particular, militarism, racism and national chauvinism. Economic policies resulted in the virtual collapse of many of the industries that were the traditional bedrock of the Scottish and Welsh economies, bringing mass unemployment, poverty, and the effective destruction of communities. Although this occurred in parts of England, there was of course a nationalist response in Scotland and Wales. The Tory vote in Scotland and Wales has collapsed, resulting in a questioning of the Tories' electoral mandate there. As a result of the break-up of the domestic consensus, Scottish and Welsh nationalist movements, having achieved a limited form of devolution, are looking to the dynamics of the unfolding international blocs and developing a misplaced trust in the European Union. Indeed, it can be noted that the European project encourages both macro and micro economic projects. Forms of nationalism have become tied up with economic regionalism, i.e. some sort of regional independence within the EU.

In this wider-European context, the demands for political hegemony flow naturally from the demands for economic union. The EU is different from the other two world blocs in precisely this sense. While the NAFTA and Pacific blocs are under the direct hegemony of certain powers – the USA and Japan – in Europe no one country dominates. The construction of the European Union will be a balancing job. However, the dominant axis centres around Germany and France, and the current project depends upon this alliance holding together. With monetary union now having taken place, the momentum will push the EU in the direction of something resembling a Europe-wide state The European project necessitates a shift from national-state regulation to 'harmonised' trans-national regulation. This unleashes the dynamic towards an undermining of national-state-based economic and political powers. The move towards Europe will inevitably reduce the ability of national bourgeoisies to maintain their own domestic hegemonic control, yet the national state will still be expected to implement the economic policies of the EU and contain any social unrest that follows from them. It seems likely that the EU project will continue to cause major political tensions and will weaken the national hegemony across each of the nation-states. It also seems likely that major class struggles lie ahead and that the future direction of the EU project depends upon the outcome of these battles.

Hegemony and international relations

The last section shows how quickly analysis of national issues slides into an international context and this section will look at the emergence and decline of the post-war settlement in this broader context. As we have seen, Gramsci was already linking the process of national-state regulation to a wider internationalisation of methods of production, linking the methods of Fordism to what he calls Americanisation. And this Americanisation refers not just to the spread of new techniques and methods of organising production, or to the rise of new technology, but also to the dominance of the United States in the political and military spheres.

Following the Second World War the USA was at a huge advantage. The war had caused no damage to US industry or infrastructure but factories had been working full tilt on military production, and this war economy led to closer ties between industry and the central apparatus. In this climate, Fordist techniques developed further. At home, economic might, cheap raw materials and a large internal market produced a consumer boom. Abroad it financed the Marshall Aid injections into the European economies. The different conditions in the US after the Second World War meant that there was no need for the US ruling class to buy off the working class in the same way as in Europe. In place of European social democracy and welfarism, America had the New Deal and the military–industrial complex.

The effect of US Marshall Aid on the post-war economies was significant, although it can be overestimated.[4] However, it did mark a new period of international intervention and regulation including, most importantly, the Bretton Woods system of exchange convertibility as well as other US-dominated bodies and mechanisms like the UN, IMF, World Bank and GATT. The world economy was dominated by US corporations taking advantage of trade liberalisation and a huge boom in world trade. The economic model for the West was based on variants of the corporate state.

Japan, by contrast, had only very recently emerged from a pre-capitalist state with an economy based on agriculture. Growth was facilitated by rapid developments in technology and a boom in capital goods, although a major shift occurred in the 1980s with the revolutions in electronics and communications. The post-war Japanese workforce was highly skilled but poorly organised at a class level. While there were some sharp outbreaks of militancy, the lack of an established labour movement meant it was possible to industrialise Japan through much greater oppression of the working class. The consequences of this situation can still be seen today in the role that the employer plays in the life of the worker. Trade union organisation is based on the individual companies, often encouraged by partnership and no-strike deals. Indeed, Japan is at the forefront of new management techniques and new flexible production methods, or what Makoto Itoh calls 'Toyotism' (Itoh 1992: 201). Politically, Japan has been dominated by conservative governments. However, forms of Japanese state intervention and regulation are not so far removed from those of Western Europe, based on social democratic style social and welfare reforms as well as Keynesian fiscal policy. And, as in Europe and America, these reforms are now being cut back, partly helped by the historic weakness of working-class organisation. On a world level, however, Japan has suffered from its defeat in the Second World War. Article nine in the Japanese constitution has prevented Japan from being a military, and hence, world hegemonic power. Despite a large share of the world market, Japan continues to have to rely on US military hegemony.

The consequence of this is that the crisis of US hegemony is in effect a crisis of the whole international system. In 1945, the US was the world's biggest creditor. Its balance of payments deficit became a major sponsor of international growth and global demand. Now the US is the world's biggest debtor. The fiscal crisis of the US state has led to massive budget cuts being passed and a period of mass poverty and class polarisation seems likely. It was the emergence of this economic instability, in particular US inflation, which caused the international monetary system to collapse. The breakdown of the Bretton Woods system, which tied currencies to the dollar, led to the abandonment of exchange controls and the liberalisation of financial markets. The US had attempted to play the role of central regulator of the world economy, something which is now weakened. However, as Hirst and Thompson argue (1996: 14), US hegemony is multi-dimensional. Militarily, the US is dominant and it can use this to ensure that no other state can politically attempt to restructure the international economy. The openness of the international markets depends on the US, while, despite its problems, the dollar remains the medium of world trade. The continuing dominance of the US, despite its financial problems, may well be a product of military might and foreign money, but it is hard to foresee any immediate alternatives. As Itoh says:

> From the perspective of the hegemony issue in a new world order, six scenarios are conceivable: (1) The second phase of Pax-Americana, (2) The age of Fortress Europe, (3) Pax-Nipponica, (4) Pax-Japamerica, (5) Trigemony led by the US, EC and Japan, (6) Pax-Consortis without any hegemonic country.
>
> (Itoh 1992: 199)

Itoh sees little chance for many of these projects and it is easy to concur with him that we will continue to see a system of co-operation and rivalry between the US, EU and Japan and that international affairs will be dominated by an uneasy political, economic and military balance between these main blocs.

The new world dis-order

In global terms, the existence of the USSR restricted the role that US imperialism could play. This gave space, for example, to nationalist–Bonapartist regimes in the Third World, to military dictatorships or client states who could play on the strategic space between the imperialist and Stalinist blocs. Now these states have no option. There is no longer any need for partitioning along superpower lines as occurred in Africa. Although the strength of the imperialist countries is in part an illusion, the collapse of the East European workers' states is a historic defeat for the working class and for those who advocate socialist projects. This has had an impact around the world, strengthening the ideology of the ruling class, weakening the role of the labour movement and social democracy, and hitting national liberation struggles in the Third World. Of course, more than anything else, it is a massive blow to the working class in those countries which have seen the progressive gains of collectivised property relations swept away. These events cannot but deal a heavy blow to all those counter-hegemonic struggles around the world.

The brutal attack on Iraq, followed by the Balkans intervention, were calculated attempts by the US to reassert its hegemony on the world stage. The Gulf War was not entirely a war about oil, although this played a role, as did US concerns over regional power and a fear of growing Iraqi supremacy. Above all, the invasion was designed to show the dependence of the other Western powers on US military and political hegemony. It was an important ideological victory for the US in that it persuaded Germany and Japan to contribute financially to the costs of the war. It was also important in highlighting the absolute dependency of the United Nations on the United States. The UN no longer even bothers to pretend that it is in control of military affairs. Its military operations in Bosnia were given over to NATO, while in the later actions against Serbia, the US by-passed the UN altogether.

Out of the Gulf War came George Bush's ideology of the New World Order and the attempt by the US to assert its cultural and moral leadership. There was an immediate contradiction between the idea of 'order' or world harmony, and the ideological offensive against the mighty new demons that were invented – the evil dictators, crazy populations, religious fundamentalists and so on. The US had to present these factors as a real threat to the world order, if only as a contrast to the West's own flagging cultural hegemony. This period of history is best illustrated by Fukuyama's 'end of history' thesis which enjoyed a fleeting moment of popular recognition. His message is simple:

> And if we are at a point where we cannot imagine a world substantially different from our own, in which there is no apparent or obvious way in which the future will represent a fundamental improvement over our current order, then we must also take into consideration the possibility that history itself might be at an end.
>
> (Fukuyama 1992: 51)

Unfortunately for the follows of Fukuyama, capitalism is not seen to be working very well anymore. Since the USSR fell apart, prospects for capital investment have hardly improved, while the vaunted East Asian economies have all suffered crises. The West held the belief that Eastern European economies would offer new possibilities, but most of these economies are still bad investments. Still, in line with the shifting patterns of world production, capital has sought cheaper labour markets. This process is part of the mobility of capital and the opening up of the labour market. More flexible systems of production may be centred in the metropolitan countries, but the manufacturing and assembling of components is conducted at the 'periphery'. An analysis of the developing countries should focus on the degree of industrialisation of these countries and the expansion of the working class in some regions of the world. Strong political movements have emerged in countries like Brazil and South Korea.

Yet, in contrast, struggles such as the Zapatista revolt in Chiapas, Mexico, have been held up as models of a new form of (postmodern) struggle in the new world order. Such an interpretation is very wrong. The Zapatista movement is not so different from more traditional peasant-based guerrilla strategists. However, Sub-commandant Marcos does talk a good postmodern game. His idea of the expansion of the democratic space is reminiscent of Derrida's talk of 'democracy to come'. Its goal is not to take power, but to operate within the system based on a democratic vision free from references to socialism. It would therefore be postmodern of us to blow this phenomenon up into a generalisable process. The struggle of the Zapatistas is a regional, peasant-based struggle. The dynamic of the Latin American economies, however, is one of industrialisation. State power, therefore, must be fought for through the organisation of the radicalising working classes. Those who promote the Zapatista model as an alternative strategy are turning an event of some regional significance into something with a universal, but largely symbolic appeal.

'Globalisation' as a hegemonic project

It is widely taken for granted that a process of globalisation is taking place. This is certainly true in the sense of market and currency deregulation, the massive growth in financial trade, a steady increase in trade flows, and a flexiblisation of production based on 'peripheral' development with a main centre based in the imperialist countries. There is also a kind of new inter-state consensus developing with new world bodies such as the World Trade Organisation and new trans-national trading blocs. But globalisation is a very slippery and ill-defined concept, and the use of the term is bound up with an array of different political positions. The view here is that these economic developments are not so much representative of 'globalisation' as of a change in the relation between nation-states and the global movement of capital (Holloway 1994: 41). The key question is whether 'globalisation', in itself, is what makes this a new and qualitatively different period of history. This is not necessarily to question the idea that this is a new period, but the idea that globalisation is the best way to describe this period should be questioned because:

1 Globalisation overemphasises economic factors and falsely claims that we are now living in one big global market.

2 Theories of globalisation usually downplay the role of the state and other political bodies, and ignore the role of class struggle.

3 The globalisation debate is in fact the class struggle in theory; it is an ideological façade used by the ruling class to legitimate their neo-liberal policies and the politics of TINA (there is no alternative). In effect, globalisation is itself a form of hegemonic project.

There remains a central contradiction between the logic of globalising forces and the socio-political conditions of existence within which these forces develop (Gill 1993: 120). Although it may seem like a matter of semantics, it is important to reject the connotations that the term 'globalisation' implies. It suggests that capital has entered a new 'global' epoch. Yet capital, by its very nature, has always been global. The dynamic of capital is ever-expanding and 'globalisation' is already inscribed into the nature of capitalism from the start. It is not so much the nature of capital that has changed, but the market–state relations within which it operates. If we look at globalisation claims in relation to trade figures it can be seen that world trade has reached an unprecedented volume. But if we look at the figures in Table 9.1, which show exports and imports as a percentage of Gross Domestic Product (GDP) in current market prices, then a different picture emerges.

The figures show that the world economy was as 'globalised' in 1913 as it is today. The big growth in international trade is in part due to the intervening period when, following depression and war, states turned to national regulation of their economies and Keynesian demand-management policies. Of the two biggest players, the United States' ratio has grown while Japan's has significantly declined! And neither figure is very large indicating that the majority of these countries' products are consumed domestically. What the figures do not show is who this trade is with, and this again undermines the view that the world market is truly globalised.

We can get a picture of who the trade might be with by looking at figures for Foreign Direct Investment (FDI)(see Table 9.2). In looking at volumes

Table 9.1 Exports and imports as a percentage of GDP

	1913	*1950*	*1973*	*1994*
France	30.9	21.4	29.2	34.2
Germany	36.1	20.1	35.2	39.3
United Kingdom	47.2	37.1	37.6	39.3
Netherlands	100.0	70.9	74.8	89.2
United States	11.2	6.9	10.8	17.8
Japan	30.1	16.4	18.2	14.6
Arithmetical average	42.6	28.8	34.3	39.5

Source: Went 2000: 11.

Table 9.2 Foreign Direct Investment (FDI) 1997

Inward FDI stock		
Developed countries	Developing countries	Central and Eastern Europe
68.0	30.2	1.8
Outward FDI stock		
Developed countries	Developing countries	Central and Eastern Europe
90.2	9.7	0.2

Source: Went 2000: 45.

of trade and FDI, Went (2000) rightly makes the point that globalisation is not at all an even or linear process and it is not leading to a truly harmonious unification of the world's economies. This point should be made against those positive globalists who argue that we are all benefiting from the creation of a single global market. Looked at in terms of FDI it can be seen that the great majority of the world's direct investment comes from and ends up in industrialised countries (the Triad).

If we bring all this data together, we can make a number of points that contradict the central ideas of globalisation. First, that despite their liberal and open attitude towards international trade, the economies of the USA, Japan and the EU are surprisingly 'closed' and a lot of their trade is domestic or regional, not global. We might therefore describe the current period as regionalisation rather than globalisation with three competing and often hostile markets, not one global economy. Finally, we should note these three spheres (the Triad) account for nearly three-quarters of all economic activity so that 85 per cent of the world's population is almost written out of this 'globalisation' process.

If the idea of a global economy is undermined by figures on trade and investment, it is clear than significant changes are occurring in certain areas. Most significant is the development of the financial sector, which is the most advanced of the global processes. Daily turnover on international currency exchanges has risen from $500 billion in 1990 to $1,200 billion in 1998 (Went 2000: 13). These developments clearly go hand-in-hand with the development of technology, which has revolutionised these markets allowing instant transactions and twenty-four-hour access. But the truth is that technology has only facilitated a globalisation process set in motion by conscious political decisions – policies that were pioneered by the right-wing governments of Britain and the US.

Others have claimed that the extent of globalisation is indicated by the growth of multinationals and the power that they now hold. Some, like General Motors, Wal-Mart, Ford and Daimler-Chrysler, have greater sales than the GDPs of Norway, Poland, Indonesia, Greece and South Africa. BP's turnover is greater than Ireland's. This has led some to take the view that multinationals are now more powerful than nation-states. But multi-nationals are still heavily dependent on their own domestic economy, and the resources, technology and facilities of their place of location. Of the world's top 100 multinationals, 38 have their headquarters in the EU, 29 in the US and 16 in Japan. Between 85 and 90 per cent of high-tech products are consumed in the Triad, most of the rest in the NICs (Went 2000: 45). Companies depend heavily on national or regional markets, on local education and training, the infrastructure, the enforcement of national (or EU) law, on relationships with governments, unions and other national institutions and organisations. So contrary to the popular view, multi-nationals are not really international. They nearly all have a home country on which they depend, and although they can certainly set up production in different parts of the world, they cannot just get up and go wherever they want, they are dependent on the facilities and resources of the host state.

All the above would indicate that states are not becoming powerless as many globalisers would have us believe it is more a case that the relation between state and economy has changed. But the relation between the two remains the crucial factor in global developments. There may be a movement towards a more international system of regulation, but these processes require nation-states to establish the legitimacy of decisions.

Globalisation theorists claim that national states are becoming – or making themselves – less effective. But are they really less effective at economic regulation, or are they practising a different type of (flexible) regulation? International bodies like the G7, WTO, IMF and EU have acquired new powers. But these bodies are not independent of states, they are in fact dominated by them. These bodies have allowed the dominant states like the US to present their own agenda as an international agenda. In this sense, the globalisation process represents that internationalisation of the neo-liberal agenda of the dominant states and their ruling classes. Policies like privatisation, changes in work practices, flexibilisation and the spread of inequalities are global developments that are the result of conscious state policies.

Maybe, then, the economic aspect of 'globalisation' is nothing particularly new, but is the continuation of the basic trends of capitalism (expansion and monopolisation), entirely in keeping with its intrinsic nature. But there is a new extrinsic aspect of this process and it is important to emphasise that this aspect is extrinsic or external – that it is not something inherent to capitalist development, but is the result of conscious interventions by states and political agents. For this reason it is preferable to label the process not globalisation, but neo-liberal flexibilisation. This does not represent an inevitable economic tendency as the globalists believe, but is a qualitatively new phase in the way that economic regulation is carried out. Those who see this process as external (albeit an external intervention into intrinsic tendencies) place their emphasis on the role of the state, political factors and class struggles. Those who see this process as intrinsic are forced to resort to economic and technological determinism and ideas about long waves of development and other hidden hands.

So, to call this period one of globalisation would be a mistake. If the notion is meant to attribute certain characteristics to capital movements, then the entire history of capitalism has been a history of globalisation and the term is virtually meaningless. If, however, 'globalisation' is meant to refer to a new and open period of international relations – political and hegemonic – then the concept of globalisation is clearly wrong. The major projects around, for example the EU, are attempts to *rebuild* and *reconstruct* hegemonic blocs and alliances in line with economic criteria. A true process of globalisation would indicate a *removal* of such blocs, or more appropriately, blocks. To restate: globalisation is not sweeping the world, rendering states and political blocs redundant. The nation-state is still the most important regulator of capital and labour relations, although clearly some of these functions are being transferred to new, wider bodies such as the EU or the World Trade Organisation. It is the *weakness* of hegemony, not its absence, which is shaping the international situation. Like the post-Fordists, the globalists have turned a crisis trend into an entirely new order.

Hirst and Thompson have made a fairly convincing case against globalisation theory. They correctly state that levels of integration, interdependence and openness of national economies are nothing new, while governance mechanisms for the international economy have been around for most of this century (Hirst and Thompson 1996: 49). In defence of the role of the nation-state they write:

> they are pivots between international agencies and sub-national activities … they provide legitimacy as the exclusive voice of a territorially bounded population. They can practice the art of government as a process of distributing power only if they can credibly present their decisions as having the legitimacy of popular support.
>
> (Hirst and Thompson 1996: 190)

However, it is necessary to balance this positive view of the state with an understanding of its current weakness. While the current period will not see the collapse of the state and the onward march of global capital, it will see the development of conflicting hegemonic projects and state strategies based on (a) the *hegemonic* weakness of the national state – the breakdown of old regulation strategies, the crisis and reorganisation of historical blocs, and the attempts to create a new hegemonic order; and (b) attempts to develop large trading blocs with the ultimate aim of developing political hegemony.

Why is it important to oppose the theory of globalisation as the globalists present it? Because it represents the ideological package used by neo-liberal politicians to justify their policies. They present their policies as the only possible response to a situation that is beyond their control. Thus jobs and welfare must be cut in order to fit in with a flexible world market. Yet it is this same flexible world market that the policies of these politicians have helped create. As Went says, 'politicians of various stripes are eager to point to the increasingly internationalised economy in order to justify harsh, unsaleable and unpopular policies' (2000: 3). Politicians across Europe now appeal to the Maastricht convergence criteria in order to justify cuts in spending. They claim that their hand is forced, yet these are the same hands that drafted and approved the criteria in the first place. The growing interpenetration of world's economies is the excuse used to justify turning over more and more power to international institutions like EU and WTO. But these institutions do not reflect the 'world economy', they are the tools of the dominant economic nations. The globalisation agenda is therefore an ideological façade which covers up for the actions of the ruling class and legitimates their neo-liberal policies. In this sense, globalisation is real, but what lies behind the globalisation discourse is in fact neo-liberalism.

Matthew Watson has argued that the globalisation thesis plays the role of an ideological façade or rhetorical device that is used to discipline expectations of what is feasible while the policies of neo-liberalism are implemented. What passes for an account of globalisation is often an account of state action. Understood in class terms, globalisation theory encompasses a range of ideas and normative assumptions that are used to legitimate certain forms of domination. Hence, what distinguishes the current period is not globalisation itself, but the institutionalised balance of class forces that have appropriated the discourse on globalisation to further their own interests (Watson 1999: 142–3). We can therefore relate globalisation to hegemony in two ways. First, as Watson argues, the globalisation thesis serves the interests of a hegemonic project. But, secondly, the thesis is contradicted by reality in that the world system, instead of simply becoming more globalised, develops unevenly through hegemonisation.

The current dominance of the neo-liberal model pioneered by the Anglo-Saxon countries is not based on the domination of the global economy over the nation-state, but on the deliberate 'deregulating' policy of dominant nation-states, most notably the US. In the world arena the US has attempted to force this neo-liberal model on the rest of the world through the use of its economic might and various subservient international bodies. However, the hegemonic status of the neo-liberal model is under threat following the economic turmoil in East Asia and already new attempts at regulation are beginning to emerge.

Post-Fordism?

Aspects of post-Fordist theory have been covered previously. The relationship to postmodernism and post-Marxism is particularly relevant as is shown in the case of the British *Marxism Today* current that linked post-Fordism to the ideas of 'new times' and 'farewell to the working class', which were as much philosophical and sociological inventions as economic ones. These theories derive from the idealist tendencies of the Althusserian school and from the culturalism of Gramsci. For although Gramsci did pay specific attention to aspects of Fordism, his writing as a whole overplays the cultural at the expense of the economic.

But does post-Fordism really exist as an economic system or mode of regulation? At best such theories might indicate the deficiencies of Fordism and it is certainly profitable to investigate the crisis of Fordism and the growth of flexibilisation or neo-Fordism. But the 'farewell to the working class' thesis is deficient in two major ways. First, this thesis defines the working class in the romantic mould of blue collar and cloth cap rather than that of Marx's more scientific description as those who are forced to sell their labour-power. Post-Fordism is therefore unable to grasp either the flexibilisation process or the incorporation of unskilled and cheap labour – often women and other oppressed groups – into the labour market. Second, this thesis is Euro-centric, concentrating only on the Western model, and ignoring the massive expansion of the working class around the world based on the increased mobility of capital.

The post-Fordism angle is linked to the work of the regulation theorists and, as I have argued in more detail elsewhere (Joseph 1998a: 91–4), there is a serious theoretical problem which underlies the work of theorists like Lipietz and Aglietta. In many ways the 'regulation school' develops an impressive analysis, but it is let down by its formalism. The regulation approach begins with the idea that there are such things as *regimes of accumulation*, which are based on the relation or balance between the departments that produce the means of production and consumption. It then proceeds to talk of *modes of regulation* which are responsible for ensuring the reproduction of the regimes of accumulation. They are represented by a combination of institutions and norms centred around state intervention and a complex set of social structures responsible for the reproduction of the capitalist mode of production, including the monetary system, corporate structures and a form of wage determination, all of which seek to establish behavioural routines. According to the regulation school, the post-war era is marked by a Fordist regime of accumulation and a monopoly form of state regulation.

Much of this has already been accepted in this analysis, but caution is needed. A model of accumulation and regulation can be accepted insofar as the conditions for economic reproduction need to be socially secured, and here the emphasis would seem to be on external or contingent factors that intervene into the production process. The danger is that for the regulation school these external and contingent factors have a tendency to become internal and necessary so that the conditions for capital accumulation are secured through the existence of inclusive, self-reproducing and self-regulating 'modes' or 'regimes'. The weaknesses of the regulation school are apparent in the attempts to analyse the crisis of Fordism. For the regulation school, Fordism represents an inclusive regime of accumulation with a corresponding mode of regulation. Instead of seeing Fordism as a dominant form of accumulation, regulation theorists tend to see it as *the* accumulation regime. All this produces a paradigmatic approach whereby the crisis of Fordism can only mean the replacement of one regime of accumulation with another, post-Fordist one. This idea that capitalism simply passes from one regime of accumulation to another concedes far too much to the view that capitalism is a relatively stable, self-regulating system with social forms that neatly correspond to the needs of accumulation. If Fordism is considered to be a regime of accumulation, then its crisis lies in precisely this fact. Fordist methods proved too regimented and inflexible, too committed to large-scale production, consumption and investment. So what is occurring now is not so much the development of a new regime but a flexibilisation processes.

Even here we have to be careful. As Andrew Sayer (1989) has persuasively argued, the term flexibilisation has become a catch-all category. In fact if we study Japanese capitalism – often seen as synonymous with concepts like flexibilisation and new management techniques – we can see that it has a highly organised and regimented character. To understand the success of Japanese capitalism we need to examine what Sayer calls the broader 'environmental' characteristics that cut across labour processes – culture and education, the social and institutional form of capital and so on (Sayer 1989: 667). We need to get away from a narrow focusing on production processes and examine the context in which these processes are reproduced, how the social totality is stratified and how its various structures and mechanisms are overdetermined.

In any case, the regulation theorist Bob Jessop has shown the way out of this problem himself, raising the necessity of state strategies and hegemonic projects as a complement to accumulation regimes. Accumulation cannot be seen as an insular regime but must depend on factors of a more external nature with contingent consequences. The accumulation process needs different state strategies to secure social cohesion, and these in turn require the construction of a historical bloc based on a set of social and political alliances. These bring in all kinds of other factors – different ideologies, different group interests, different class compromises. Jessop's analysis distinguishes between an economic cohesion that is derived from a general acceptance of an accumulation strategy, a political hegemony that requires the securing of an institutional unity of the capitalist state, and a class unity or compromise (Jessop 1990: 199).

So accumulation does not stand alone, nor does it stand within an exclusive regime. It is affected by a range of external, contingent, historical and political factors. Werner Bonefeld's analysis of the British state during the 1980s points to one such concrete case (Bonefeld 1993: 2, 9). While the regulation theorists were keen to argue that the British state was integrating a new post-Fordist regime of accumulation, many commentators later realised that Thatcherism was more of an aberration based on a radical approach to a traditional political agenda. Clearly there *was* a conflict between economic developments and the interests of capital, and political interests and motives. And as we have argued, the social and political basis of British Conservatism, as well as its particular hegemonic projects, are now at odds with the need for capital to orientate towards the European market.

Regulation theory places a great emphasis on regimes of accumulation, but capitalism's grand contradiction lies in the fact that it requires regulation even though it ultimately cannot be regulated. There are a number of regulating mechanisms which have a functional relationship to capital accumulation in a loose sense. But these are overdetermined by other factors – for instance, different forms of capital and economic factors as well as wider social and political factors like class projects and hegemonic strategies. Different forms of accumulation, regulation and hegemonic strategies are a permanent requirement. But they are never allowed to become permanent features.

Hegemony and regulation

Starting from the driving force of capital accumulation, regulation analysis attempts to show how this has to be organised and regulated, based on a series of social structures, institutions and state strategies. The notion of regulation should emphasise the fact that capital accumulation is not an automatic process and that society cannot be reduced to a base/ superstructure model. The conditions for capital accumulation are socially secured, which in turn requires the state and politics to play a leading role. Thus a study of forms of regulation leads to an analysis of state strategies, institutions and structures, and international bodies. These all represent forms of intervention in economic processes which in turn presupposes the centrality of a concept of hegemony.

The state must play a leading and directing role that is articulated through the projects of the leading or dominant social groups or class fractions. Through various state strategies, these groups must ensure both the conditions necessary for capital accumulation and the consent necessary for class rule. This relationship between class interests and the interests of capital is vital. Unfortunately, many analyses have lost this balance, becoming either 'capital theoretical' or 'class theoretical'. The key to this analysis is how a hegemonic project can reconcile the needs of capital with the needs of its own class leadership (Jessop 1990: 40). This problematic relation means that there is an inherent connection between forms of regulation and particular hegemonic orders. It means that a crisis – such as the crisis of the post-war order – must be analysed in relation to both forms of regulation and the hegemonic bloc. Recent developments have revealed a shifting of hegemony both at the state level and at the international level centring around the weakened role of US imperialism and the emergence of rival blocs. We thus have conflicts between hegemonic projects, structures of regulation, and economic generative mechanisms.

Again, this analysis reinforces the necessary distinction between different aspects of hegemony. Since the necessary conditions for economic reproduction are socially secured, hegemony plays a basic material role in securing the conditions for social cohesion. This in turn allows for the most fundamental of processes, that of capital accumulation. Therefore, in a complexly structured or overdetermined society, hegemony plays a basic role in ensuring the reproduction of economic relations. And again, in relation to the state, hegemony plays a key role in the state's functional relation to the economy. The state acts in a structural–functional way to secure and reproduce the conditions for economic reproduction. So hegemony operates at a very basic level, securing the cohesion of the different levels of the social formation and hence promoting the accumulation of capital. But out of this basic relation come the more complex problems of the realisation of this function through particular modes of regulation and so particular hegemonic strategies. Hegemony is necessary to the basic reproduction of the social formation. This necessity is emergent through specific modes of regulation and state strategies. The necessity of hegemony at the level of social reproduction also provides the necessary conditions for the possibility of hegemony at the level of agential actions. This is reflected in the complex projects of different class fractions and hegemony's attempts, through the state, to unify those interests. But that hegemonic projects are possible at all, and that different groups and classes can realise their own particular social projects, is due to the basic fact that the conditions for economic reproduction need to be socially secured and that this is an open-ended process. This therefore reinforces the fact that the state is the strategic terrain for the unfolding of political hegemonic projects, where different political struggles occur and where it is attempted to resolve them through hegemonic strategies. A central point of contradiction occurs where hegemony's functional role in securing the conditions for capital accumulation coincides with hegemonic strategies based on particular class interests. The compatibility of the two roles is certainly not guaranteed.

This in turn highlights the need for a critical realist method which is capable of analysing a complex and contradictory social whole and its different structures and mechanisms. The dominance of the economic within this whole, highlights the driving force of capital accumulation. But this cannot stand apart from the whole and therefore must be mediated through a multifarious set of social relations. Starting from a notion of social ensembles, it is possible to analyse the associated relationships between generative mechanisms, social structures, state strategies and hegemonic projects, each of which has its own dynamics. The interests of a hegemonic group cannot therefore be reduced to the needs of capital. However, the interests of that group, if they are to be maintained through the social order, must to an extent take up the needs of capital. Therefore these different layers are dependent, to a greater or lesser extent, on each other as well as presupposing and codetermining each other.

A particular generative mechanism may support a number of structures. A particular structure may relate to a number of mechanisms. A hegemonic project may be based on some of these dynamics but not on others. These stratified relations and the conflicts between them are of central importance. Beyond this, there are also the complex relations between national and international structures and strategies.

By basing itself on a set of transcendental arguments, critical realism can establish that the world is structured in a certain way such that the economic has a certain primacy. The mode of production is clearly a central driving force behind any society that aspires to reproduce itself, and from the centrality of production it is possible to say that the working class, insofar as it is the class of producers, is shown to be the main agent of social change. But it can also be seen that the social whole is heteronomously complex and that the economic is reproduced through a multitude of different social structures and mechanisms. Likewise, social classes are multiply determined and have heteronomous interests. Given that this is the case, it is the state which becomes the most important factor for leading and directing social change.

Critical realism, basing itself on the transformational model of social activity, points to the possibility of agents acting upon and changing social structures. But given the connectedness of these structures, and the difficulty faced in changing the whole set of relations, the capture of state power becomes the most important task. Rather than developing a heterogeneous model of transformation, the logic of the critical realist position points to the centrality of the working class as key agent (on the basis of its fundamental relationship to the processes of production) capturing state power and using this hegemonic position to lead and direct the transformation of society through its many different spheres. Given the nature of society, it is only through the leading role of the state that the transformation of society as a whole can occur.

10 Conclusion

It is possible to write much more on each of the specific areas covered in this book. Hegemony is present in many fields and it is only possible to get a feel for the concept by building up a picture of it in its totality. This study has tried to develop a theoretical perspective, employing critical realism as an underlabourer to examine and clarify and to build up a working framework. But although critical realism has been used mainly as an underlabourer, directed more at theories about society rather than at the nature of the social world itself, it is evident that an analysis of such theories soon leads to an analysis of the world itself. While critical realism may be a philosophy rather than a social science, it clearly operates through social science and gets caught up with the claims that social science makes. This book has found it impossible to apply critical realism to hegemony without operating through a broadly Marxist framework, although where necessary it has sought to clarify and correct this framework.

It has generally been through this Marxist framework that the study of hegemony has been developed. As far as the concept of hegemony is concerned, the arguments of this book have principally been directed against the various intersubjective approaches that present it merely in terms of the actions and interactions of different groups without proper reference to the social conditions within which this takes place. By employing critical realism an attempt has been made to outline a structural conception of hegemony, intimately linked to the reproduction, preservation and reproduction of intransitive, stratified social structures. We have therefore distinguished between this kind of underlying structural hegemony and the hegemony of actualised hegemonic projects.

This study has concentrated on drawing out this distinction and how this relates to social reproduction and transformation. It has looked at how hegemony relates to social structures, the state, social practices, political projects, alliances and strategies. It has looked at the concept of hegemony from the point of view of social structure, political strategy and practice, space and time, theories of history, notions of discourse, objectivity and intersubjectivity, state strategy and economic reproduction. But a lot more needs to be done. A further volume will continue the analysis of discourse theory, elaborate on Bhaskar's conception of hegemony as hermeneutic power2 struggles, and explore the concept of hegemony in the work of Foucault, in particular relating to his ideas on governmentality and techniques of power. The question of power is another important issue that requires further elaboration, as do theories of culture, modernity and rationalisation. But in particular, there needs to be more analysis of the relationship between hegemony, civil society and the state. The common claim in classical Marxism is that with a socialist transformation of society the state begins to wither away. This theory is highly dubious, but it leaves hegemony in an awkward position. For this theory of hegemony has argued that it is closely associated with the state. Yet it might be argued that hegemony gets stronger at the same time as the state starts to get weaker. Where does hegemony stand in this longer-term picture? Is a strengthened social hegemony an alternative to the power of the state or a complement? Or, as society becomes less uneven and fractious, does hegemony too begin to wither away? These are big questions requiring further analysis. But for now we will conclude with a briefer discussion of the state, social structure and hegemonic strategy.

Structure

Society is comprised of intransitive social structures and generative mechanisms which are related in a stratified and overdetermined manner. Within this structural hierarchy, economic relations have a certain primacy. This theory can be justified on the basis of the centrality of production and distribution within every society. The generation of surplus labour/product is fundamental to any developed society. Under capitalism this takes the form of the extraction of surplus value. However, this process is not independent of social and political factors. Although capital accumulation is the driving force of modern societies, the conditions for it have to be socially secured. This factor leaves a space for the concept of hegemony. For society *as a whole* is both the ever-present condition and the continually reproduced outcome of human agency. Hegemony intersects with the process by which social structures are reproduced or transformed. In some senses this process *is* automatic. Agential production or reproduction is largely unconscious. But the world is complex and different structures coincide and conflict. This means that hegemony will always play an important role in securing the reproduction of social structures and their combinations. By virtue of the world being an open system, hegemony is necessary to secure social cohesion. Because of this role, hegemony is clearly set within a structural location which is irreducible to the actions and conceptions of social agents. Hegemonic projects offer real possibilities of transformatory activity, but these should be understood in their structured context, rather than merely as the products of social agents.

Hegemony has a functional role in relation to the unity of the social formation. However, this role should not be interpreted in an essentialist or teleological manner. Hegemony does not have a unique privileged status as such but exists in its conditions of possibility. If hegemony holds things together it succeeds, if it fails, a hegemonic crisis emerges which has to be resolved. Structural hegemony refers to the need to secure the unity of the social formation and the reproduction of the complex and contradictory combinations of social structures, practices and generative mechanisms. The world is an open system and the success of hegemony is not guaranteed. In relation to its function, hegemony can be good or bad, strong or weak, stable or volatile, dynamic or stagnant. But weak or strong, dynamic or useless, hegemony is always with us.

What we are analysing here is not a particular form of hegemonic project, but the conditions of its being. The possibility of particular hegemonic projects is based on the necessity of a hegemonising process stemming from the requirements of a deeper level of organisation. Culturalist and humanist accounts that reduce society to the activities of groups and individuals likewise reduce hegemony to its expression, instead of looking at its conditions of being. Such a view is ontologically flat, reducing society to a surface level of events and interactions, without developing the kind of depth analysis of underlying structures and processes that is necessary if we are really to develop any kind of meaningful explanation.

By emphasising meaning, hermeneutics tends to reduce its study of human behaviour to an appeal to an intersubjective rationality. This implies a transcendentally universal notion of reason, tied to a dialogical conception of human practice, with society seen as based on rule-governed consensual activity. While in some senses this is true, hermeneutics often takes this as the only meaningful aspect of society, and limits its social analysis by refusing to ground such activity within a structured context.

In opposition to this view, critical realism argues that, like the natural world, the social world is comprised of stratified structures and relations – social, economic, political, communicative, etc. These relations are relatively enduring, but they are dependent on the activity of social agents for their reproduction. This structural context allows for the possibility of trans-formative practice and hegemonic activity. The problem for hermeneutics is that by ignoring the structural context within which social activity takes place, it deprives social activity not just of its reproductive role, but also, by implication, its transformative capacity.

So a structured and stratified conception of society is necessary if we are to conceive of the possibilities of human agency. However, we must guard against a hyper-structuralism where agents are reduced to mere *träger* and where hegemony is reduced to a static expression of synchronic structural determination. This would undermine all the emphasis that Marxist theory places on history, social practice and social consciousness. The theory of hegemony requires that classes and social groups become conscious of their interests and powers and seek to act upon them. The hegemonic process reflects in some way, agent, group and class conceptions of the processes in which they are involved. Hegemony involves a conscious attempt to act upon a situation. This is based on the desire or need to conserve, defend or transform social interests, embodied in material social structures.

On the basis of this we have made a distinction between a deeper, structural hegemony which is fundamental to the unity and reproduction of society itself, and the hegemony of the specific hegemonic projects of agents. They presuppose one another in that hegemony combines the political moment of agency with the structural nature of social reproduction. Hegemony in its deeper, structural sense is concerned with the cohesion of the social system. It secures the reproduction of the mode of production and other basic structural processes. It is fundamental to the unity of all human societies and the interrelation of the different parts of the social whole.

We then need to examine how concrete hegemonic projects are emergent out of these conditions, and how they give them a particular expression. Hegemony in this sense centres around different social groups and classes, the interests that they represent, and the political blocs and alliances that are constructed. Hegemony finds its clear expression at this level, but its successful or unsuccessful application is dependent on how it realises its deeper hegemonic function. An example might be the post-war period where, it can be argued, there was a fundamental underlying need for a kind of corporatist project that could guarantee the basic reproduction of social structures by co-opting sections of the working class and granting certain concessions in return for consent. However, this kind of structural hegemony needs to be guaranteed by actual political parties, trade unions and other bodies. Such a hegemonic function then allows for the possibility of different projects which may develop according to their own dynamics as represented, for example, by the specific aims of social democratic governments or according to the actual balance of class forces and the various competing political ideologies. The necessity of cohering the social formation allows for the actualisation of hegemonic projects which may or may not perform such roles.

So while hegemony represents a convergence of different social agents and political projects, it also marks the sites of different spatial and temporal convergences involving various relations, mechanisms, structures, practices and processes. Hegemony is vital to the reproduction of social combinations. It acts as the bridge between social structure and political strategy. And of all the sites of hegemonic power, it is the state which expresses this relation most clearly.

Structuratum, stratification

The overall nature of hegemony and its class character is determined by the functions it performs in society. What gives it its particular form is how that function is reproduced. In this way a space opens up for conscious hegemonic projects. Hegemony represents the political moment in the reproduction of the structures of the social formation. It combines the structural aspect of reproduction with the political moment of agency. The structural–functional role played by hegemony in its deeper sense emerges through the concrete, historical interactions of intentioned social agents. Hegemony is realised through, rather than simply created by social agents. But the actual projects of these social agents take on their own characteristics.

For hegemonic projects to take place, objective social divisions and distinctions must already exist at a deeper level. This allows certain groups to become dominant and to construct their own hegemony out of these divisions. Indeed, a hegemonic project may consciously seek to develop these divisions, or alter them. In other words, these hegemonic projects are emergent out of the material conditions present in society and the structural requirements of hegemony to reproduce the social formation. Hegemony operates with a given set of material conditions – within and between different structures, practices and mechanisms, across space and through time. The concept of hegemony is inescapably historical and geographical. The totality is stratified into different times and spaces. We are describing not a static structuralist scene, but a historicised, repro-duced, interlocking, overlapping set of histories, structures and forms.

The necessity of hegemony and the possibility of hegemonic projects is founded on the stratified and differentiated, non-contemporaneous nature of the totality and the agents which reproduce it. Social fractions corre-spond to different interests, powers and relations within classes. They can only be understood in terms of their objective basis – the stratification of the world itself – the intersection and overlapping of social structures, social practices and generative mechanisms and the specific determination of social groups in terms of their objective location in these stratified relations. Hegemony is a layered process which organises the relations between different social groups within a ruling bloc and between the ruling bloc and wider layers in society. Some groups are closely implicated in the bloc, others lend a degree of support, others may require more direct coercion. The dominant hegemonic process may itself be undercut by other hegemonic processes. There will exist sub-hegemonies, or even counter-hegemonies with some hegemonies feeding off the dominant hegemony, while others come into direct conflict with it.

Social structures have a deep, abstract character. As agents we do not relate directly to the totality or even to the general structures within the totality. These are reproduced in a largely unconscious manner by virtue of the situatedness of social practices. Our more conscious or intentional decisions are in relation to structurata – the concrete entities which are structured. Agents transform structures through acting upon structurata. Again, we should describe this in terms of stratification. Various structures may underlie a structuratum and a number of structurata may express a structure's functioning. Hence action may have unforeseen or totalising consequences. Likewise, unforeseen consequences emerge from the fact that the various hegemonic projects depend upon hegemony's wider material function in cohering the social formation.

Hegemony may be localised or regionalised and limited to particular hegemonic projects, either in a geographical area or in a political, cultural or economic sphere. But hegemony, if it is ambitious, also seeks to move beyond these boundaries in line with its functional role in bringing things together. The strength of particular hegemonies (or counter-hegemonies) can be measured against the dominant hegemony and the degree of overlapping, co-operation or conflict between them. Just as we say that hegemony seeks to construct a power bloc out of various groups and their interests, so the dominant hegemony must try to co-ordinate the more regional hegemonies. Indeed, we must measure the dominant hegemony by its degree of success or failure in penetrating and co-opting, colonising or containing these various regional hegemonies.

Hegemony must also relate to the location of consciousness and its spatio-temporal unevenness if it is to construct anything intentional. Starting from the localised consciousness of a particular group, a hegemonic project must galvanise this consciousness (or in the event of real material developments facilitate and direct this consciousness) in order to transcend its location. This is the enormous task facing a counter-hegemonic project. For while reproduction has a more unconscious character, transformative projects require the revolutionisation of space and time. Hegemonic projects must act against the inertia of society expressed in its deeper hegemonic form and the corresponding ideologies, mentalities and consciousness of agents.

Strategy

Critical realism talks of a transformational model of social activity, but the problem here is that most activity can be seen as transformatory – this is the nature of any practice which starts with certain raw materials and develops them. How then do we distinguish between activity that is genuinely transformatory and activity which simply alters a certain state of affairs? Combined with the theory must be some notion of a leading and directing role which seeks to transform not just anything, but the most important social structures and relations. Hence the transformational model of social activity must be linked to some kind of hegemonic project. It requires a strategic element that gives it purpose and direction.

As Gramsci stated, a group must have behind it the economic, political and cultural conditions which allow it to put itself forward as leading. Hegemony concerns not just the construction of a ruling bloc, but the reproduction of the underlying social structures that create the material conditions for such a bloc. But while it allows groups to develop projects that express their particular interests, there is not a direct correspondence between hegemony's function and its expression. A politically dominant group may not necessarily act in the best interests of capital (as the British Tories' stance over Europe shows). There is therefore no essential relation between class strategies and the process of capital accumulation which guarantees the success of the latter. Likewise, there are no homogenous classes or interests whose logic of development can simply be read from the objective situation. But ruling hegemonies do need to be assessed in relation to the underlying hegemonic conditions and the structure of society. Thus we need to examine the extent to which they facilitate structural growth, development and reproduction, as well as how they preserve existing social forms and fend off power struggles.

The state is key to the organisation of a ruling hegemony – organising both the ruling bloc itself, and the wider society. In rejecting an instrumentalist conception of the state we have argued (a) that the state is determined in relation to the economy both nationally and internationally and, more generally, that the capitalist state must act in a functional way to secure the conditions for capital accumulation and economic reproduction; and (b) that the state also provides the strategic terrain for securing and developing political hegemony (involving the unity of the ruling class, the support of various other groups and the consent of the masses). As we argued earlier (e.g. in relation to the Thatcherite project), these two aspects may not function in harmony. Indeed, friction between them provides the basis for a hegemonic crisis.

The state's functional relation to the economy is an important aspect of hegemony in its deeper, structural sense. It helps secure and reproduce the conditions for economic reproduction and promotes the cohesion of the different levels of the social formation. While this may sound like a functionalist argument, it is precisely because of the need for this function (and the fact that it is not automatically given) that actual hegemonic practices are possible at all and that different groups and classes can realise their own particular social projects. The state's function in securing the conditions for capital accumulation and hegemony's function in securing the cohesion of the social formation are realised through the complex projects of different class fractions and the development of different forms of state strategy and regulative mechanisms.

While we have argued that hegemony, like ideology, plays a basic functional role within all societies, the success of this role is not guaranteed. It cannot be stressed enough that capitalism is not a coherent system and that hegemonies are often wracked with contradictions. In contrast to hyperstructuralist accounts where every aspect of the social formation has a proper place and function, critical realism emphasises the open and dialectical character of society. Although it is materially presupposed by and dependent upon hegemony in its deeper, functional role, the realisation of hegemonic practices, in line with our understanding of emergence, is a process with its own characteristics that cannot be reduced to more basic levels.

Rather than simply representing the processes themselves, hegemonic practice necessarily entails some form of agential conception of these processes based on various forms of group or class understandings. Hegemony in its realisation represents conscious political activity linked to the strategic defence or transformation of a given situation. Levels of consciousness are variable with conscious activity having differing degrees of unintended consequences. Nevertheless, hegemony as a praxis depends on certain reasons and intentions which help to cause action to occur. Particular groups or classes articulate their interests through a hegemonising project or historical bloc. These interests represent a relation with the world. In opposing post-structuralist accounts it has been argued that a hegemonic project, in order to articulate certain interests, presupposes that these interests have an objective grounding. These interests are then developed as they are mediated by the hegemonic projects. Conservative hegemonies defend existing social relations by drawing upon the cloudy effects of popular ideology and the 'common sense' rules of everyday life, while promoting the interests of a privileged group as the common interest. Progressive projects enlighten agents as to their interests and their potentials. This gives the project a transformatory character. They encourage agents to transcend their localised environment and to realise their wider interests through common participation and struggle.

So although we have not been able to go into detail about aspects of hegemony as a strategy, we have begun the crucial (theoretical, under-labouring) task of establishing the objective basis on which hegemonic strategies operate, the conditions of its possibility. The functional role that hegemony has within society guarantees hegemony as a strategy. Different strategies may succeed or fail. But hegemonic strategy is a permanent feature of society.

Because there is a certain flabbiness about critical realism's conception of social strategy we will end this section with a reappraisal of Bhaskar's TMSA. In general the TMSA is not sufficiently clear on how it fits strategically into critical realism's argument about the stratified nature of the world. The question of the reproduction and/or transformation of social structures is posed at a very general level, leaving the question of stratification unanswered. If some structures, practices and generative mechanisms carry more weight and influence than others, then clearly there will be different degrees of transformative action. A revolutionary strategy is required to select the key structures within society, as well as the key transformative agents in relation to those structures. It would be easy to give a straightforward Marxist answer and point to economic structures with working-class agents. But the theory of stratification also points out the connectedness of these social structures.

This theory again raises the question of hegemony – in terms of a strategy which draws together and unites different agents and practices. But it also indicates that the question of direction and leadership is indispensable if a true transformation is to take place. And it ultimately points not to abstract structures, but the state as the main focus of social change. Hegemony and the state are raised to this importance because transformation, like the structures themselves, is stratified and multiple, and requires co-ordination. Because of the connectedness of social structures, a transformatory project must take into account the dominant dynamics within the social hierarchy and direct itself at the wider totality of social relations. The idea of significantly transforming structures in isolation is a dangerous illusion.

To move to conscious transformation requires a knowledge of the different layers, structurata, practices, institutions and so on. Without sufficient knowledge, transformative activity could have devastating unforeseen consequences (as with the democracy movements in Eastern Europe and the ex-USSR). So the link between the TMSA and hegemonic strategies is another way of expressing Marxism's traditional insistence on the relation between theory and practice.

Theory and practice

Rather than embracing blind spontaneity, Marxism insists that socialist strategy is aware of its conditions of possibility. The uniqueness about the revolution under capitalism is its need to draw on theory in order to construct a project and practice. The socialist revolution, unlike previous revolutions, is carried through by a class that is not already a leading class within existing society, but is instead disenfranchised from power, even if its intimacy with the production process makes it strategically well placed. Given that the working class does not already enjoy a 'leading position', it is essential that a prospective hegemonic project has a sufficiently developed understanding of the society it is attempting to transform.

Unfortunately, Marxism has often failed to adequately connect theory and practice, usually substituting one for the other. For example, forms of vulgar Marxism presuppose either that society passes through a series of predetermined phases, culminating in the communist paradise (for example, those influenced by Stalin, Plekhanov or by a particular reading of Engels) or, in opposition to this, that there is some essential class consciousness which will lead the workers to socialist revolution (for example, those influenced by Hegel, such as Lukács or Korsch). Views such as these draw upon a teleological view of history that sees purpose already inscribed into history, and ignores such things as actual hegemonic strategies and concrete practice.

It has been argued that Lenin's Marxism represents a real break from the mechanical viewpoint in that it makes the subjective factor essential to the revolution. Therefore it stresses organisational questions and particularly the role of the revolutionary party as an active, organic unit. The question of hegemony is raised by the struggle for leadership. But in order to fulfil the practical requirements of leadership, it is necessary to theoretically assess the question, which class and what section of that class is able to lead, and to carry through that leadership?

Marxist theory should see things in their totality. The masses are diverse rather than homogeneous. The world is as a complex set of relations into which the party must intervene. This complexity requires that the party is unified in its activity and that it seeks to unify the most politically advanced layers (the vanguard) around it. Given the complexity of the world, the key political struggle is therefore to capture state power in order to direct the necessary changes. Consequently, Leninist practice rejects adaptation to spontaneous consciousness, stressing instead the need for direction and leadership. Lenin argues that although the party is involved in the day-to-day struggles of the workers, it stands above them. Revolutionary class consciousness needs organisation and leadership.

Lenin's argument for the dictatorship of the proletariat is based not on an authoritarian urge, but on a proper study of social reality and the potentialities and possibilities (and lack of potentialities and possibilities) present within it. It reflects the extension of the leadership function to the whole of society. This transitional period reflects the weakness of the proletariat's material base and the need to begin laying the necessary conditions for a future communist society. These arguments reinforce the idea that there are different levels of hegemony. While political power may be won, the weak social position of the working class, as well as the dangers of the international situation, means that a deeper hegemony still needs to be established. The possibility of a socialist revolution depends upon a structural crisis in society, a fact that causes real problems for subsequent practice. The enormity of the task of socialism is expressed in the fact that the new hegemonic group is left with the job, not just of leading society, but of creating a new one.

In Bhaskar's terminology this can be an expression of the tri-unity of space, time and causality. Radical hegemonic practice does not confine itself to the existing spatio-temporal framework but attempts to transform it. Periods of crisis, rupture and revolution witness new, emergent spatio-temporal totalities. Radical hegemonies both facilitate this emergence and respond to it. Counter-hegemonies must take advantage of the social fractures and divisions which open up and generate their own space. The theory of hegemony argues that space is captured through the construction of a bloc which can be strategically directed. The different groups that comprise this bloc occupy different social and political locations. Hegemony must draw these together, preferably through the aegis of state power. A hegemonic bloc therefore entails not only a relation to different social agents, but also to the wider social and historical locations which they occupy.

Another aspect of hegemony's relation to stratified social space-time is its intersection with ideology. Because hegemony is bound up with social structures and human practices, it coincides with the secreted ideologies of these practices. Hegemony and ideology correspond, at a deeper level, to the processes of unconscious reproduction but as things become more conscious, hegemony and ideology may be said to become articulated in relation to particular groups and their interests. At the deeper structural level, hegemony must relate to these secreted ideologies in its efforts to secure the unity of the social formation while concrete hegemonic projects must attempt to articulate ideology around certain political positions, giving it a concrete shape and projection.

However, at whatever level, it is necessary to insist on the separation of hegemony and ideology. A materialist theory of hegemony depends upon the fact that it refers, not just to the articulation of ideological factors, but also to the material forms which generate these ideologies and to the social agents who may be attracted to them. Hegemony acts as an extrinsic articulator, not just of ideas, but of many practices – ideological, cultural, political and economic, and the specific institutions of the state, civil society and the economy. A hegemonic project uses ideas to make its case, but to make advances, it needs to organise people and relate to social and economic developments.

The meaningfulness of the ideas that hegemony articulates presupposes the intransitive structures and objects to which these ideas refer. The nature of a hegemonic project is defined by the relations between social structures, human practices and group interests. These are real, material relations, not the arbitrary, discursive constructions referred to by today's postmodern ideologues. It is of course true that things are discursively articulated. This is a basic fact of our social existence and is a central aspect of hegemony's function. But postmodernism reduces the intransitive structures of the world to their transitive aspect and relativises this knowledge by judging different discourses or language games to be incommensurable. The reactionary character of postmodernism is revealed by the fact that if social reality is reduced to a particular interpretation of it, then we are no longer left with any basis for criticising such an articulation. It might seem that under postmodernism, with the process of articulation becoming more important than that which is articulated, hegemony becomes all-powerful. But while we may have some sort of 'hegemony' we are denied the possibility of a meaningful *counter*-hegemony.

Here again is the connection between theory and practice. If we have a theory which lacks any ontological depth by denying, in various ways, structured, stratified, dialectical, intrinsic or necessary relations, then hegemony is not only rendered hollow as a concept, it is also rendered useless as a strategy.

Vice versa, the consequence of failing to develop a theory of hegemony is an ontologically flat, undifferentiated, unstratified, ahistorical, non-social or reified world with no grounds for meaningful interests, identities, ideas, practices or projects.

Those who do not understand society are doomed merely to reproduce it.

Notes

2 Gramsci's realist hegemony

1 Hegel's understanding of the concrete universal is taken from Rousseau's analysis of the general will which develops through the historical community and is embodied in the laws of the state.

2 Gramsci is also forced into a realist position when discussing the natural sciences – which conflicts with his conception of the physical sciences as being a part of human history. Morera produces some other notable quotes some of which are dubious in their implications, e.g. 'scientific theories reflect an unchanging reality' (Gramsci 1975, vol. 2: 1445), knowledge must fit reality not the other way round (Gramsci 1975, vol. 1: 332), Marxism is 'the theory of history most fitting to reality and truth' (Gramsci 1975, vol. 2: 1467), and on the importance of French realism (Gramsci 1975, vol. 2: 1250).

3 This is best translated by Buttigieg in Gramsci 1992: 136–7. See also Gramsci 1971: 59.

3 Classical Marxism: Lenin and Trotsky

1 The anticipation of revolutions across Europe in 1848 and, in particular, in Germany, led Marx and Engels to formulate a conception of 'permanent revolution' so that: 'While the democratic petty bourgeois want to bring the revolution to an end as quickly as possible, achieving at most the aims already mentioned, it is our interest and our task to make the revolution permanent ...' (Marx and Engels, 'Address of the Central Committee (March 1850)', in Marx 1973b: 323). Also, the workers 'themselves must contribute to their final victory, by informing themselves of their own class interests, by taking up their independent political position ... [not] doubting for one minute the necessity of an independently organised party of the proletariat. Their battle-cry must be: The Permanent Revolution' (Marx 1973b: 330).

2 E.g. Trotsky 1974d, vol. 1: 26–7, vol. 2: 27; 1973a: 19, 20.

4 English debates and the structuralism of Poulantzas

1 Most of these themes can be found in Anderson's book, although it is striking that Anderson seems to commit most of the 'crimes' that he condemns and adheres to whole areas of Western Marxist thinking.

2 Anderson argues that Thompson's notion of class must pass through the

criterion of consciousness and that 'Class consciousness here becomes the very hallmark of class formation' (Anderson 1980: 40).

3 For more on this, see Joseph and Kennedy 2000.

5 Posts and structures

1 An interesting book on this subject is Antony Easthope's *British Post-Structuralism Since 1968* (1988). In contrast to American schools of deconstruction, British theorists often passed through Marxism, and in particular, Althusser. The result is that these theorists are forced to maintain at least some semblance of 'left' radicalism.

2 See also the passage 'the mode of production, the relations in which productive forces are developed, are anything but eternal laws ...' (Marx 1963: 122). Althusser makes much of these passages (in Althusser and Balibar 1979: 97–8).

3 For Marx: 'Nature is man's *inorganic body* ... Man *lives* from nature, i.e. nature is his *body*, and he must contain a continuing dialogue with it ...' (Marx 1975c: 328). This dialogue with nature may be interpreted as concern or, as Heidegger puts it, '"Being-in-the-world" has the stamp of "care", which accords with its Being' (Heidegger 1962: 243).

6 Two types of hegemony: structural hegemony and hegemonic projects

1 For an elaboration of the passive revolution (particularly in relation to Piedmont and the Italian national question), see Gramsci 1971: 105–20.

2 Much favoured by the cultural theorists around Perry Anderson, this view appears in Gramsci 1971: 18.

7 Objectivity and intersubjectivity

1 Some followers of Wittgenstein, as is their inclination, would deny this relativism. Thus language games might be seen not as exclusive, but as overlapping and interrelated. But while this is a partial advance, it still fails to deal with the question of objectivity in relation to what underlies this matrix of language games, on what structures and mechanisms they depend, and on what basis we can theoretically distinguish and prioritise different games.

8 Hegemony through time and space

1 Although Althusser is commonly associated with this position, John Urry makes the interesting point that he ignores the question of geographical space and 'that there is no reason to suppose that there is any less relative autonomy spatially than temporally'. He also goes on to make the point which we will stress in this chapter that 'it is necessary to investigate both the temporal and spatial interdependence *between* different levels or structures, not only those relations within each' (Gregory and Urry 1985: 28).

2 The three levels might also be related in a different way to Giddens' notion of three timescales – the *longue durée* of historical time, the *durée* of activity and the *Dasein* of individual-time (Giddens 1981: 19).

3 Hay (1995) also argues that Foucault rejects metanarratives only to formulate equally totalising narratives in localised contexts.

9 Economy and hegemony

1   For a critical realist alternative to the forces/relations and base/superstructure distinctions, see Joseph and Kennedy 2000.

2   At its worst, Mandel embraces an strong version of productive forces determinism, arguing that the 'long period' since 1940 is 'characterised by the generalised control of machines by means of electronic apparatuses' (Mandel 1978a: 120–1). However, Mandel's work has a contradictory character, sometimes embracing productive forces determinism and at other times taking a more social and political viewpoint.

3   It might be argued that the distribution of social surplus is an intrinsic aspect of the capitalist mode of production. While this has a certain formal correctness, in reality this distributive mechanism is dependent on the active intervention of the state and hegemonic action in order to facilitate and mediate these processes across society.

4   The idea that the Marshall Plan was responsible for the regeneration of the European economies is countered in Peter Burnham's book *The Political Economy of Postwar Reconstruction* (1990).

Bibliography

Adamson, W. (1980) *Hegemony and Revolution*, Berkeley: University of California Press.

Aglietta, M. (1979) *A Theory of Capitalist Regulation*, London: New Left Books.

Agulhon, M. (1982) *The Republic in the Village*, Cambridge: Cambridge University Press.

Ahmad, A. (1994) 'Reconciling Derrida: *Spectres of Marx* and Deconstructive Politics', *New Left Review* 208: 88–107.

Alder, A. (ed.) (1983) *Theses, Resolutions and Manifestos of the First Four Congresses of the Third International*, London: Pluto.

Althusser, L. (1971) *Lenin and Philosophy*, London: New Left Books.

—— (1976) *Essays in Self Criticism*, London: New Left Books.

—— (1977a) *For Marx*, London: Verso.

—— (1977b) *Politics and History*, London: New Left Books.

—— (1984) *Essays on Ideology*, London: Verso.

—— (1990) *Philosophy and the Spontaneous Philosophy of the Scientists*, London: Verso.

—— (1993) *The Future Lasts a Long Time*, London: Chatto and Windus.

Althusser, L. and Balibar, E. (1979) *Reading Capital*, London: Verso.

Amin, A. (ed.) (1994) *Post-Fordism a Reader*, Oxford: Blackwell.

Anderson, P. (1965) 'The Left in the Fifties', *New Left Review* 29: 3–15.

—— (1966a) 'Socialism and Pseudo-Empiricism', *New Left Review* 35: 2–42.

—— (1966b) 'Problems of Socialist Strategy', in P. Anderson (ed.) *Towards Socialism*, Glasgow: Collins.

—— (1974a) *Passages form Antiquity to Feudalism*, London: New Left Books.

—— (1974b) *Lineages of the Absolutist State*, London: New Left Books.

—— (1976) 'The Antinomies of Antonio Gramsci', *New Left Review* 100: 5–81.

—— (1979) *Considerations on Western Marxism*, London: Verso.

—— (1980) *Arguments Within English Marxism*, London: Verso.

—— (1983) *In the Tracks of Historical Materialism*, London: Verso.

—— (1992a) *English Questions*, London: Verso

—— (1992b) *A Zone of Engagement*, London: Verso.

—— (1993) 'Origins of the Present Crisis', in P. Anderson, *English Questions*, London: Verso.

—— (1998) *The Origins of Postmodernity*, London: Verso.

Aronowitz, S. (1992) *The Politics of Identity*, London: Routledge.

Balibar, E. (1977) *On the Dictatorship of the Proletariat*, London: New Left Books.

Benton, T. (1977) *Philosophical Foundations of the Three Sociologies*, London: Routledge and Kegan Paul.

—— (1984) *The Rise and Fall of Structural Marxism*, London: Macmillan.

Bhaskar, R. (1978) *A Realist Theory of Science*, Hassocks and New Jersey: Harvester.

—— (1986) *Scientific Realism and Human Emancipation*, London: Verso.

—— (1989a) *The Possibility of Naturalism*, 2nd edn, Hemel Hempstead: Harvester Wheatsheaf.

—— (1989b) *Reclaiming Reality*, London: Verso.

—— (1991) *Philosophy and the Idea of Freedom*, Oxford: Blackwell.

—— (1993) *Dialectic*, London: Verso.

—— (1994) *Plato Etc.*, London: Verso.

—— (1997) 'On the Ontological Status of Ideas', *Journal for the Theory of Social Behaviour* 27, 2/3: 135–47.

Bloch, M. (1992) *The Historians Craft*, Manchester: Manchester University Press.

Bocock, R. (1986) *Hegemony*, Milton Keynes: Open University Press.

Boggs, C. (1978) *Gramsci's Marxism*, London: Pluto.

—— (1984) *The Two Revolutions: Gramsci and the Dilemmas of Western Marxism*, Boston, MA: South End Press.

Bonefeld, W. (1993) *The Recomposition of the British State During the 1980s*, Aldershot: Dartmouth.

Bonefeld, W., Brown, A. and Burnham, P. (1995) *A Major Crisis? The Politics of Economic Policy in Britain in the 1990s*, Aldershot: Dartmouth.

Bonefeld, W. and Holloway, J. (eds) (1991) *Post-Fordism and Social Form: A Marxist Debate on the Post-Fordist State*, London: Macmillan.

Bottomore, T. (1991) *A Dictionary of Marxist Thought*, 2nd edn , Oxford: Blackwell.

Braudel, F. (1969) *On History,* London: Weidenfeld and Nicholson.

—— (1973) *Capitalism and Material Life*, London: Weidenfeld and Nicholson.

—— (1975) *The Mediterranean and the Mediterranean World in the Age of Philip II*, 2 vols, Glasgow: Fontana.

Bridges, G. and Brunt, R. (eds) (1981) *Silver Linings: Some Strategies for the Eighties*, London: Lawrence and Wishart.

Brown, A., Fleetwood, S. and Roberts, J.M. (eds) (2002) *Critical Realism and Marxism*, London and New York: Routledge.

Buci-Glucksmann, C. (1980) *Gramsci and the State*, London: Lawrence and Wishart.

Burke, P. (1990) *The French Historical Revolution*, Cambridge: Polity.

Burnham, P. (1990) *The Political Economy of Postwar Reconstruction*, London: Macmillan.

—— (1991) 'Neo-Gramscian Hegemony and the International Order', *Capital & Class* 45: 73–95.

Callinicos, A. (1976) *Althusser's Marxism*, London: Pluto.

—— (1982) *Is There a Future for Marxism?*, London: Macmillan.

—— (1989) *Making History*, Cambridge: Polity.

—— (1995) *Theories and Narratives*, Cambridge: Polity.

Chalmers, A. (1982) *What is this Thing Called Science?*, Milton Keynes: Open University Press.

Chun, L. (1993) *The British New Left*, Cambridge: Cambridge University Press.

Cohen, G. (1978) *Karl Marx's Theory of History*, Oxford: Clarendon Press.

Collier, A. (1977) *R.D.Laing: The Philosophy and Politics of Psychotherapy*, Hassocks: Harvester.

—— (1988) 'Retrieving Structural Marxism', *Economy and Society* 17, 4: 543–52.

—— (1989) *Scientific Realism and Socialist Thought*, Hemel Hempstead: Harvester Wheatsheaf.

—— (1990) *Socialist Reasoning*, London: Pluto.

—— (1991) 'The Inorganic Body and the Ambiguity of Freedom', *Radical Philosophy* 57: 3–9.

—(1994) *Critical Realism*, Verso: London.

—— (1999) *Being and Worth*, London and New York: Routledge.

Cox, R. (1987) *Production, Power and the World Order*, New York: Columbia University Press.

Croce, B. (1915) *What is Living and What is Dead in Hegel*, London: Macmillan.

—— (1929) *A History of Italy*, Oxford: Clarendon Press.

—— (1941) *History as the Story of Liberty*, London: George Allen and Unwin.

—— (1949) *My Philosophy*, London: George Allen and Unwin.

Davis, J. (ed.) (1979) *Gramsci and Italy's Passive Revolution*, London: Croom Helm.

Davidson, A. (1977) *Antonio Gramsci: Towards an Intellectual Biography*, London: Merlin.

Derrida, J. (1973) *Speech and Phenomena*, Evanston: North Eastern University Press.

—— (1976) *Of Grammatology*, Baltimore: Johns Hopkins University Press.

—— (1979) 'Living On/Borderlines', in H. Bloom *et al.* (eds) *Deconstruction and Criticism*, London: Routledge and Kegan Paul.

—— (1981a) *Writing and Difference*, London: Routledge and Kegan Paul.

—— (1981b) *Positions*, London and Chicago: Athlone Press.

—— (1987) *The Post Card*, Chicago: University of Chicago Press.

—— (1994) *Specters of Marx*, New York: Routledge.

Deutscher, I. (1965a) *The Prophet Armed, Trotsky: 1879–1921*, New York: Vintage Books.

—— (1965b) *The Prophet Unarmed, Trotsky: 1921–1929*, New York: Vintage Books.

—— (1965c) *The Prophet Outcast, Trotsky: 1929–1940*, New York: Vintage Books.

Dews, P. (1982) *Logics of Disintegration*, London: Verso.

Dilthey, W. (1988) *Introduction to the Human Sciences*, London: Harvester Wheatsheaf.

Duby, G. (1980) *The Chivalrous Society*, Berkeley: University of California Press.

Dunford, M. and Perrons, D. (1993) *The Arena of Capital*, London: Macmillan.

Eagleton, T. (1976) *Criticism and Ideology*, London: New Left Books.

—— (1991) *Ideology: An Introduction*, London: Verso.

Easthope, A. (1988) *British Post-Structuralism Since 1968*, London and New York: Routledge.

Elliott, G. (1987) *Althusser: The Detour of Theory*, London: Verso.

—— (1994) (ed.) *Althusser: A Critical Reader*, Oxford: Blackwell.

—— (1993) *Labourism and the English Genius*, London: Verso.

Engels, F. (1962) 'On Certain Peculiarities of the Economic and Political Development of England', in K. Marx. and F. Engels, *On Britain*, Moscow: Progress Publishers.

—— (1976a) *Ludwig Feuerbach and the End of Classical German Philosophy*, Peking: Foreign Languages Press.

—— (1976b) *Anti-Dühring*, Peking: Foreign Languages Press.

—— (1978) *The Origin of the Family, Private Property and the State*, Peking: Foreign Languages Press.

Febvre, L. (1973) *A New Kind of History*, ed. P. Burke, London: Routledge and Kegan Paul.

Femia, J. (1981) *Gramsci's Political Thought*, Oxford: Clarendon Press.

Fiori, G. (1965) *Antonio Gramsci: Life of a Revolutionary*, London: New Left Books.

Fleetwood, S. (1995) *Hayek's Political Economy: The Socio-Economics of Order*, London and New York: Routledge.

Forgacs, David (1989) 'Gramsci and the British Left', *New Left Review* 176: 70–88.

Foucault, M. (1970) *The Order of Things*, London: Routledge.

—— (1972) *The Archaeology of Knowledge*, London: Routledge.

—— (1977) *Discipline and Punish*, London: Allen Lane.

—— (1981) *The History of Sexuality Volume 1: An Introduction*, Harmondsworth: Penguin.

Fukuyama, F. (1992) *The End of History and the Last Man*, New York: Avon.

Gadamer, G. (1979) *Truth and Method*, London: Sheed and Ward.

Genaro, A. (1966) *The Philosophy of Benedetto Croce*, New York: Citadel Press.

Genovese, E. (1972) *Roll Jordan Roll: The World the Slaves Made*, New York: Pantheon Books.

Geras, N. (1990) 'Post-Marxism?' in N. Geras, *Discourses of Extremity*, London: Verso.

Giddens, A. (1979) *Central Problems in Social Theory*, London: Macmillan.

—— (1981) *A Contemporary Critique of Historical Materialism*, vol. 1, London: Macmillan.

—— (1998) *The Third Way: The Renewal of Social Democracy*, Cambridge: Polity Press.

Gill, S. (ed.) (1993) *Gramsci, Historical Materialism and International Relations*, Cambridge: Cambridge University Press.

Le Goff, J. and Norva, P. (eds) (1985) *Constructing the Past: Essays in Historical Methodology*, Cambridge: Cambridge University Press.

Gramsci, A. (1971) *Selections from the Prison Notebooks*, ed. Q. Hoare and G. Nowell Smith, London: Lawrence and Wishart.

—— (1975) *History, Philosophy and Culture in the Young Gramsci*, ed. P. Cavalcanti and P. Piccone, St Louis: Telos Press.

—— (1975) *Quaderni del Carcere*, 4 vols, Turin: Einaudi.

—— (1977) *Selections from Political Writings 1910–20*, London: Lawrence and Wishart.

—— (1978) *Selections from Political Writings 1921–26*, London: Lawrence and Wishart.

—— (1985) *Selections from Cultural Writings*, London: Lawrence and Wishart.

—— (1989) *Letters form Prison*, New York: Noonday Press.

—— (1992) *Prison Notebooks*, vol.1, ed. J. Buttigieg, New York: Columbia University Press.

—— (1995) *Further Selections from the Prison Notebooks*, ed. D. Boothman, London: Lawrence and Wishart.

Gregory, D. and Urry, J. (eds) (1985) *Social Relations and Spatial Structures*, London: Macmillan.

Habermas, J. (1972) *Knowledge and Human Interests*, London: Heinemann.

—— (1974) *Theory and Practice*, London: Heinemann.

—— (1984) *The Theory of Communicative Action, Volume 1*, Cambridge: Polity.

—— (1987) *The Theory of Communicative Action, Volume 2*, Cambridge: Polity.

—— (1987) *The Philosophical Discourse of Modernity*, Cambridge, MA: MIT Press.

—— (1988) *Legitimation Crisis*, Cambridge: Polity.

Harding, N. (1977) *Lenin's Political Thought*, London: Macmillan.

Harré, R. (1972) *The Philosophies of Science*, Oxford: Oxford University Press.

—— (1986) *Varieties of Realism*, Oxford: Blackwell.

Harris, D. (1992) *From Class Struggle to the Politics of Pleasure: The Effects of Gramscianism on Cultural Studies*, London: Routledge.

Harvey, D. (1990) *The Condition of Postmodernity*, Oxford: Blackwell.

Hay, C. (1994) 'The Structural and Ideological Contradictions of Britain's Post-War Reconstruction', *Capital & Class* 54: 25–59.

—— (1995) 'Narrative as Metanarrative', in M. Zavarzedeh, T. Ebert and D. Morton (eds) *Transformations 1: Post-Ality, Marxism and Postmodernism*, Washington: Maisonneuve Press.

Hegel, G.W.F. (1977) *Phenomenology of Spirit*, trans. A.V. Miller, Oxford: Oxford University Press.

Heidegger, M. (1962) *Being and Time*, Oxford: Blackwell.

Held, D. (1980) *Introduction to Critical Theory*, Cambridge: Polity.

Hindess, B. and Hirst, P. (1975) *Pre-Capitalist Modes of Production*, London: Routledge and Kegan Paul.

Hirst, P. and Thompson, G. (1996) *Globalisation in Question*, Cambridge: Polity.

Hirst, P. and Zeitlin, J. (1991) 'Flexible Specialisation Versus Post-Fordism', *Economy and Society* 20,1:1–56.

Hoffman, J. (1984) *The Gramscian Challenge: Coercion and Consent in Marxist Political Theory*, Oxford: Blackwell.

Holloway, J. (1994) 'Global Capital and the Nation State', *Capital & Class* 52: 23–49.

Holloway, J. and Picciotto, S. (eds) (1978) *State and Capital: A Marxist Debate*, London: Edward Arnold.

Ingram, D. (1987) *Habermas and the Dialectic of Reason*, Newhaven: Yale University Press.

Isaac, J. (1988) *Power and Marxist Theory: A Realist View*, New York: Cornell University Press.

Itoh, M. (1992) 'Japan in a New World Order', in R. Miliband and L. Panitch (eds) *Socialist Register: New World Order?*, London: Merlin.

Jameson, F. (1981) *Postmodernism or the Cultural Logic of Late Capitalism*, London: Verso.

—— (1995) 'Marx's Purloined Letter', *New Left Review* 209: 131–45.

Jay, M. (1984) *Marxism and Totality*, Cambridge: Polity.

Jessop, B. (1982) *The Capitalist State*, Oxford: Martin Robertson.

—— (1985) *Nicos Poulantzas*, London: Macmillan.

—— (1990) *State Theory: Putting the Capitalist State in its Place*, Cambridge: Polity.

Johnson, R. (1978) 'Edward Thompson, Eugene Genovese and Socialist-Humanist History', *History Workshop* 6: 79–100.

—— (1980) 'Barrington Moore, Perry Anderson and English Social Development' in *Culture, Media, Language*, Centre for Contemporary Cultural Studies, London: Hutchinson.

Johnson, R., McLennan, G. and Schwarz, B. (undated) *Economy, Culture and Concept*, History Series Stencilled Occassional Paper, Birmingham: Centre for Contemporary Cultural Studies.

Joll, J. (1977) *Gramsci*, Glasgow: Fontana.

Jonnson, I. (1993) 'Regimes of Accumulation and Hegemonic Politics', *Capital & Class* 50: 49–97.

Joseph, J. (1997) 'Memory Versus Legacy: Derrida on the Ramparts', *Diatribe* 7: 33–41.

—— (1998a) 'In Defence of Critical Realism', *Capital & Class* 65: 73–106.

—— (1998b) 'Realistic Organisation?', *Historical Materialism* 3: 85–94.

—— (2000a) 'A Realist Theory of Hegemony', *Journal for the Theory of Social Behaviour* 30, 2: 179–202.

—— (2000b) 'Learning to Live (With Derrida)', *Historical Materialism* 6: 265–85.

—— (2001a) 'Derrida's Spectres of Ideology', *Journal of Political Ideologies* 6,1: 95–115.

—— (2001b) 'Hegemony in the Fourth Dimension', *Journal For the Theory of Social Behaviour* 31, 3: 261–77.

—— (2002) 'Five Ways in Which Critical Realism Can Help Marxism', in A. Brown, S. Fleetwood and J. Roberts (eds) *Critical Realism and Marxism*, London: Routledge.

Joseph, J. and Kennedy, S. (2000) 'The Determination of the Social', *Philosophy of the Social Sciences* 30, 4: 508–27.

—— (2001) 'The Erosion of Party Politics in Britain', *New Political Science* 23, 3: 267–83.

Kant, I. (1993) *Critique of Pure Reason*, London: Everyman.

Kaplan, E. and Sprinker, M. (eds) (1993) *The Althusserian Legacy*, London: Verso.

Kaye, H. (1984) *The British Marxist Historians*, Cambridge: Polity.

Keat, R. and Urry, J. (1975) *Social Theory as Science*, London: Routledge and Kegan Paul.

Kilminster, R. (1979) *Praxis and Method*, London: Routledge and Kegan Paul.

Kitching, G. (1988) *Karl Marx and the Philosophy of Praxis*, London: Routledge.

Knei-Paz, B. (1978) *The Social and Political Thought of Leon Trotsky*, Oxford: Oxford University Press.

Korsch, K.(1970) *Marxism and Philosophy*, London: New Left Books.

Labriola, A. (1966) *Essays on the Materialist Conception of History*, New York: Monthly Review Press.

Laclau, E. (1977) *Politics and Ideology in Marxist Theory*, London: New Left Books.

—— (1990) *New Reflections on the Revolution of our Time*, London: Verso.

Laclau, E. and Mouffe, C. (1985) *Hegemony and Socialist Strategy*, London: Verso.

—— (1990) 'Post-Marxism Without Apologies', in E. Laclau, *New Reflections on the Revolution of our Time*, London: Verso.

Larrain, J. (1983) *Marxism and Ideology*, London: Macmillan.

Lash, S. and Urry, J. (1994) *Economies of Signs and Space*, London: Sage.

Lefebvre, H. (1991) *The Production of Space*, Oxford: Blackwell.

Lenin, V.I. (1947) *What is to be Done?* Moscow: Progress Publishers.

—— (1950) *'Left-Wing' Communism, an Infantile Disorder*, Moscow: Progress Publishers.

—— (1959) *The Three Sources and Three Component Parts of Marxism*, Moscow: Progress Publishers.

—— (1961) *Philosophical Notebooks*, London and Moscow: Lawrence and Wishart.

—— (1962a) 'Working Class and Bourgeois Democracy', in V.I. Lenin, *Collected Works*, vol. 8, London and Moscow: Lawrence and Wishart.

—— (1962b) *Collected Works*, vol. 10, London and Moscow: Lawrence and Wishart.

—— (1964) 'The Collapse of the Second International', in V.I. Lenin, *Collected Works*, vol. 21, London and Moscow: Lawrence and Wishart.

—— (1965a) *Collected Works*, vol. 27, London and Moscow: Lawrence and Wishart.

—— (1965b) *Collected Works*, vol. 28, London and Moscow: Lawrence and Wishart.

—— (1965c) *Collected Works*, vol. 30, London and Moscow: Lawrence and Wishart.

—— (1970) *The Proletarian Revolution and the Renegade Kautsky*, Peking: Foreign Languages Press.

—— (1971) *Between the Two Revolutions*, Moscow: Progress Publishers.

—— (1975a) *The Two Tactics of Social-Democracy in the Democratic Revolution*, Peking: Foreign Languages Press.

—— (1975b) *Imperialism, the Highest Stage of Capitalism*, Peking: Foreign Languages Press.

—— (1975c) *On Marx and Engels*, Peking: Foreign Languages Press.

—— (1976a) *One Step Forward, Two Steps Back*, Peking: Foreign Languages Press.

—— (1976b) *Materialism and Empirio-Criticism*, Peking: Foreign Languages Press.

—— (1976c) *The State and Revolution*, Peking: Foreign Languages Press.

—— (1978) *What the 'Friends of the People' Are and How They Fight the Social Democrats*, Peking: Foreign Languages Press.

Lipietz, A. (1984) 'Imperialism or the Beast of the Apocalypse', *Capital & Class* 22: 84–111.

Lock, G. (1988) 'Louis Althusser and G.A. Cohen: A Confrontation', *Economy and Society* 17, 4: 499–517.

Lovering, J. (1991) 'Neither Fundamentalism nor "New Realism": A Critical Realist Perspective on Current Divisions in Socialist Theory', *Capital & Class* 42: 30–54.

Lukács, G. (1968) *History and Class Consciousness*, London: Merlin.

—— (1971) *Lenin*, Cambridge, MA: MIT Press.

Lyotard, J.-F. (1984) *The Postmodern Condition: A Report on Knowledge*, Manchester: Manchester University Press.

Machiavelli, N. (1965) 'The Art of War', in *The Chief Works and Others*, vol. 2, Durham, NC: Duke University Press.

—— (1988) *The Prince*, Cambridge: Cambridge University Press.

McLennan, G. (1981) *Marxism and the Methodologies of History*, London: Verso.

Mandel, E. (1978a) *Late Capitalism*, London: Verso.

—— (1978b) *The Second Slump*, London: New Left Books.

—— (1978c) *From Stalinism to Eurocommunism*, London: New Left Books.

—— (1980) *Long Waves of Capitalist Development*, Cambridge: Cambridge University Press.

Mandrou, R. (1979) *From Humanism to Science*, Hassocks: Harvester.

Manicas, P. (1987) *A History and Philosophy of the Social Sciences*, Oxford: Blackwell.

Marsh, D. Buller, J., Hay, C., Johnson, J., Kerr. P., McAnulla, S. and Watson, M. (1999) *Postwar British Politics in Perspective*, Cambridge: Polity.

Martin, J. (1998) *Gramsci's Political Analysis: A Critical Introduction*, London: Macmillan.

Marx, K. (1963) *The Poverty of Philosophy*, New York: International Publishers.

—— (1973a) *Grundrisse*, Harmondsworth: Penguin.

—— (1973b) *The Revolutions of 1848: Political Writings, Volume 1*, Harmondsworth: Penguin.

—— (1973c) *Surveys from Exile: Political Writings, Volume 2*, Harmondsworth: Penguin.

—— (1973d) 'The Eighteenth Brumaire of Louis Bonaparte', in K. Marx, *Surveys from Exile: Political Writings Volume 2*, Harmondsworth: Penguin.

—— (1974) *The First International and After: Political Writings, Volume 3*, Harmondsworth: Penguin.

—— (1975a) *Early Writings*, Harmondsworth: Penguin.

—— (1975b) 'Sixth Thesis on Feuerbach', in K. Marx *Early Writings*, Harmondsworth: Penguin.

—— (1975c) 'Economic and Philosophical Manuscripts', in K. Marx, *Early Writings*, Harmondsworth: Penguin.

—— (1976) *Capital Volume 1*, Harmondsworth: Penguin.

—— (1978) *Capital Volume 2*, Harmondsworth: Penguin.

—— (1981) *Capital Volume 3*, Harmondsworth: Penguin.

Marx, K. and Engels, F. (1962) *On Britain*, Moscow: Progress Publishers.
—— (1965) *The German Ideology*, London and Moscow: Lawrence and Wishart.
—— (1973) 'The Communist Manifesto', in K. Marx, *Political Writings, Volume 1*, Harmondsworth: Penguin.
Mepham, J. and Ruben, D.-H. (eds) (1979) *Issues in Marxist Philosophy*, vols 1–3, Hassocks: Harvester.
—— (1981) *Issues in Marxist Philosophy*, vol. 4, Hassocks: Harvester.
Mészaros, I. (1989) *The Power of Ideology*, Hemel Hempstead: Harvester Wheatsheaf.
Miliband, R. (1970) 'The Capitalist State: Reply to Nicos Poulantzas', *New Left Review* 59: 53–60.
—— (1973) 'Poulantzas and the Capitalist State', *New Left Review* 82: 83–92.
Morera, E. (1989) 'Gramsci's Realism', *Science and Society* 53, 4: 458–69.
—— (1990) *Gramsci's Historicism*, London: Routledge.
Mouffe, C. (ed.) (1979) *Gramsci and Marxist Theory*, London: Routledge and Kegan Paul.
—— (1981) 'Hegemony and the Integral State in Gramsci', in G. Bridges and R. Brunt (eds) *Silver Linings: Some Strategies for the Eighties*, London: Lawrence and Wishart.
Mouzellis, N. (1990) *Post-Marxist Alternatives*, London: Macmillan.
Nairn, T. (1964a) 'The English Working Class', *New Left Review* 24: 43–57.
—— (1964b)'The British Political Elite', *New Left Review* 23: 19–25.
—— (1970) 'The Fateful Meridian', *New Left Review* 60: 3–35.
—— (1981) *The Break-Up of Britain: Crisis and Neo-Nationalism*, London: New Left Books.
Nemeth, T. (1980) *Gramsci's Philosophy*, Brighton: Harvester.
Norris, C. (1987) *Derrida*, Cambridge, MA: Harvard University Press.
—— (1990) *What's Wrong With Postmodernism*, Baltimore: Johns Hopkins University Press.
—— (1992) *Uncritical Theory: Postmodernism, Intellectuals and the Gulf War*, London: Lawrence and Wishart.
—— (1993) *The Truth About Postmodernism*, Oxford: Blackwell.
—— (1996) *Reclaiming Truth*, London: Lawrence and Wishart.
Offe, C. (1984) *Contradictions of the Welfare State*, London: Hutchinson.
Olman, B. (1993) *Dialectical Investigations*, New York: Routledge.
Osborne, P. (1995) *The Politics of Time: Modernity and Avant-Garde*, London: Verso.
—— (1994) 'The Politics of Time', *Radical Philosophy* 68: 3–9.
Outhwaite, W. (1975) *Understanding Social Life*, London: George Allen and Unwin.
—— (1983) *Concept Formation in Social Science*, London: Routledge and Kegan Paul.
—— (1987) *New Philosophies of Social Science: Realism, Hermeneutics and Critical Theory*, London: Macmillan.
—— (1994) *Habermas: A Critical Introduction*, Cambridge: Polity.
—— (1996) (ed.) *The Habermas Reader*, Cambridge: Polity.
Paggi, L. (1979) 'Gramsci's General Theory of Marxism', in C. Mouffe (ed.) *Gramsci and Marxist Theory*, London: Routledge and Kegan Paul.
Palmer, B. (1981) *The Making of E.P. Thompson*, Toronto: New Houghton Press.
—— (1990) *Descent into Discourse*, Philadelphia: Temple University Press.
Picciotto, S. (1991) 'The Internationalisation of the State', *Capital & Class* 43: 43–63.
Plekhonov, G. (1920) *Fundamental Problems of Marxism*, Moscow: Foreign Languages Press.

—— (1947) *In Defence of Materialism: The Development of the Monist View of History*, London: Lawrence and Wishart.

Poulantzas, N. (1967) 'Marxist Political Theory in Great Britain', *New Left Review* 43: 57–74.

—— (1969) 'The Problem of the Capitalist State', *New Left Review* 58: 67–78.

—— (1973a) 'On Social Classes', *New Left Review* 78: 27–54.

—— (1973b) *Political Power and Social Classes*, London: New Left Books and Sheed and Ward.

—— (1974) *Fascism and Dictatorship*, London: New Left Books.

—— (1975) *Classes and Contemporary Capitalism*, London: New Left Books.

—— (1976a) 'The Capitalist State: A Reply to Miliband and Laclau', *New Left Review* 95: 63–83.

—— (1976b) *The Crisis of the Dictatorships*, London: New Left Books.

—— (1978) *State, Power, Socialism*, London: New Left Books.

Ransome, P. (1992) *Antonio Gramsci: A New Introduction*, Hemel Hempstead: Harvester Wheatsheaf.

Rockmore, T. (1989) *Habermas on Historical Materialism*, Bloomington: Indiana University Press.

Ruben, D.-H. (1977) *Marxism and Materialism*, Hassocks: Harvester/Humanities Press.

Rubinstein, D. (1981) *Marx and Wittgenstein: Social Praxis and Social Explanations*, London: Routledge and Kegan Paul.

Ryan, M. (1982) *Marxism and Deconstruction*, Baltimore: Johns Hopkins University Press.

Sassoon, A. (1982) *Gramsci's Politics*, London: Hutchinson.

Salamini, L. (1981) *The Sociology of Political Praxis: An Introduction to Gramsci's Political Theory*, London: Routledge and Kegan Paul.

Salvadori, M. (1990) *Karl Kautsky and the Socialist Revolution 1880–1938*, London: Verso.

Saussure, F. de (1959) *Course in General Linguistics*, London: Peter Owen.

Sayer, A. (1985) 'The Difference that Space Makes', in D. Gregory, and J. Urry. (eds) *Social Relations and Spatial Structures*, London: Macmillan.

(1989) 'Postfordism in Question', *International Journal of Urban and Regional Research* 13, 4: 666–97.

—— (1992) *Method in Social Science: A Realist Approach*, London: Routledge.

—— (2000) *Realism and Social Science*, London: Sage.

Sayer, D. (1979) *Marx's Method*, Hassocks: Harvester.

—— (1987) *The Violence of Abstraction*, Oxford: Blackwell.

Sayers, S. (1985) *Reality and Reason*, Oxford: Blackwell.

Smart, B. (1983) *Foucault, Marxism and Critique*, London: Routledge.

Soper, K. (1986) *Humanism and Anti-Humanism*, London: Hutchinson.

Sorel, G. (1975) *Reflections on Violence*, New York: Ams Press.

Spinoza, B. (1993) *Ethics*, London: Everyman.

Stockman N. (1983) *Antipositivist Theories of Science*, Dordrecht: D. Reidel.

Stoianovich, T. (1976) *French Historical Method: The Annales Paradigm*, Ithaca: Cornell University Press.

Therborn, G. (1978) *What Does the Ruling Class Do When it Rules?*, London: New Left Books.

Thompson, E.P. (1955) *William Morris Romantic to Revolutionary*, London: Lawrence and Wishart.

—— (1961) 'The Long Revolution', *New Left Review* 9: 24–33 (Part I); 10: 34–49 (Part II).

—— (1968) *The Making of the English Working Class*, Harmondsworth: Penguin.

—— (1975) *Whigs and Hunters*, London: Allen Lane.

—— (1978a) *The Poverty of Theory*, London: Merlin.

—— (1978b) 'Eighteenth Century English Society: Class struggle Without Class', *Social History* 3, 2: 133–65.

—— (1993) *Customs in Common*, Harmondsworth: Penguin.

Thompson, K. (1986) *Beliefs and Ideology*, London: Ellis Horwood and Tavistock Publications.

Ticktin, H. (1992) *Origins of the Crisis in the USSR*, New York: M.E. Sharpe.

Trotsky, L. (1969a) *The Permanent Revolution and Results and Prospects*, New York: Pathfinder.

—— (1969b) *Problems of the Chinese Revolution*, London: New Park.

—— (1971) *The Struggle Against Fascism in Germany*, New York: Pathfinder.

—— (1972a) *The Revolution Betrayed*, New York: Pathfinder.

—— (1972b) *The New Course*, London: New Park.

—— (1973a) *Problems of Everyday Life*, New York: Monad.

—— (1973b) *The Spanish Revolution (1931–39)*, New York: Pathfinder.

—— (1973c) *The First Five Years of the Communist International, Volume 1*, London: New Park.

—— (1974a) *The First Five Years of the Communist International, Volume 2*, London: New Park.

—— (1974b) *The Third International After Lenin*, London: New Park.

—— (1974c) *Whither France?*, London: New Park.

—— (1974d) *Writings on Britain*, 2 vols, London: New Park.

—— (1975) *My Life*, Harmondsworth: Penguin.

—— (1977a) *The History of the Russian Revolution*, London: Pluto.

—— (1977b) *The Crisis of the French Section*, New York: Pathfinder.

—— (1982) *In Defence of Marxism*, London: New Park.

—— (1991) *Literature and Revolution*, London: Redwords.

Vali, A. (1993) *Pre-Capitalist Iran: A Theoretical History*, New York: New York University Press.

Villar, P. (1994) 'Marxist History, a History in the Making: Towards a Dialogue with Althusser', in G. Elliott (ed.) *Althusser: A Critical Reader*, Oxford: Blackwell.

Vovelle, M. (1990) *Ideologies and Mentalities*, Cambridge: Polity.

Watson, M. (1999) 'Globalisation and the Development of the British Political Economy', in D. Marsh, J. Buller, C. Hay, J. Johnson, P. Kerr, S. McAnulla and M. Watson, *Postwar British Politics in Perspective*, Cambridge: Polity.

Went, R. (2000) *Globalisation: Neoliberal Challenge, Radical Responses*, London: Pluto.

Williams, R. (1963) *Culture and Society 1780–1950*, Harmondsworth: Penguin.

—— (1965) *The Long Revolution*, Harmondsworth: Penguin.

—— (1976) *Keywords*, Glasgow: Fontana.

—— (1977) *Marxism and Literature*, Oxford: Oxford University Press.

—— (1981) *Culture*, Glasgow: Fontana.

—— (1982) 'Base and Superstructure in Marxist Cultural Theory', *New Left Review* 82: 3–13.

Winch, P. (1958) *The Idea of a Social Science and its Relation to Philosophy*, London: Routledge and Kegan Paul.

Wittgenstein, L. (1922) *Tractatus Logico-Philosophicus*, London: Routledge and Kegan Paul.
—— (1958) *Philosophical Investigations*, Oxford: Blackwell.
Wood, E.M. (1982) 'The Politics of Theory and the Concept of Class: E.P. Thompson and His Critics', *Studies in Political Economy* 9: 45–75.
—— (1986) *The Retreat From Class: A New 'True' Socialism*, London: Verso.
—— (1995) *Democracy Against Capitalism*, Cambridge: Cambridge University Press.

Index

absence 12, 13, 182
abstraction 73, 76; dialectical 128, 131;
    space and time as 166, 167, 168,
    175
accumulation regimes 204–6
actualism 5–6, 12, 117
agency: critical realist 1–2, 9–10, 14,
    15, 38; and hegemony 129, 133,
    147, 212; intersubjective 149; Lenin
    on 49, 72, 85, 88; post-Marxist 115,
    120; and power 134; and
    reproduction 207; and structure
    161, 177–8, 210; Thompson on
    73–4;
Aglietta, M. 204
Agulhon, M. 164
Althusser, L. 83, 105, 108, 114, 118–19,
    222; combinations 169; Derrida on
    103; on Gramsci 34, 36–8;
    ideological state apparatuses 30; on
    ideology 140–1; interpellation 109;
    on space and time 178; on
    synchronic 170–2; Thompson on
    75–6; on totality 165–8
Anderson, P. 75, 79, 86; on English
    Revolution 80–5; on Gramsci 29, 40;
    on Habermas 156; on Western
    Marxism 69–70, 211
articulation 100; Derrida 103, 104;
    discourse theory 108, 113–14, 115,
    117, 120–1, 127; and ideology
    142–5, 174, 219
atomism 11, 12, 113, 117

Balibar, E. 48, 70
base-superstructure 7, 58, 70–1, 78,
    83–4, 85; and ideology 140; and
    social complexity 183, 185, 206
Benton, T. 171

Bhaskar, R. 74, 140, 150, 218;
    actualism 5; agency 161; dialectical
    critical realism; 13–4; freedom 36;
    on Gramsci 19–20, 26, 40, 159, 167;
    on Habermas 155; hegemony
    134–5, 210; on philosophy 12; and
    praxis 132; on social and natural
    7–8; TMSA 9–10, 38, 40, 129–30,
    149, 216–17; totality 167, 168;
    transitive/intransitive 4–5
biology 3, 6–7, 163
Blair, T. 192–3
Bloch, M. 165, 178
Bonefeld, W. 205
Braudel, F. 163
Buci-Glucksmann, C. 49, 136
bureaucracy 63–64, 91, 93; labour 46,
    57, 60, 95, 190, 192; Stalinist 160–1,
    176; Weber on 156
Burnham, P. 187, 222

capital accumulation 91, 126, 133,
    215; and state regulation 184,
    187–8, 189, 191, 204, 206–7
capitalism 46–7, 77–8, 80, 91, 92, 97;
    dynamics 184, 201, 205; and
    lifeworld 156–7; new times 111;
    space and time 175, 179, 180; and
    state 32, 88–9; weakness 138, 188,
    197, 206
catharsis 36
causality 5–6, 9, 34, 151, 184; space
    and time 172, 218
civil society 29–31, 84; crisis 126;
    Lenin on 48; Poulantzas on 90–1;
    Russian 135–6; and strategy 40–1,
    69; Trotsky on 53, 57
classical Marxism 43, 67, 125, 184,
    185, 210